READY TO
SERVE

A Texas Cookbook
by The National Guard
Auxiliary of Austin

Additional copies of **READY TO SERVE** may be obtained by sending $12.95 per book plus $2.00 for postage and handling. (Texas residents add $.05 per book for state tax). Make checks payable to READY TO SERVE.

READY TO SERVE
P.O. BOX 5733
AUSTIN, TEXAS 78763

First Printing   March 1984   10,000 copies

Library of Congress Catalogue Card #83-081468
ISBN 0-9612502-0-8

Printed in the United States by
Hart Graphics, Inc.
8000 Shoal Creek Blvd.
Austin, Texas 78758

Foreword

Flags—those "pieces of gaudy cloth attached to long sticks"— have been used throughout the ages to communicate ideas and to arouse emotions. Flags have been the visible symbols used to unite groups and to lead them in those causes which they held to be important. From those colorful medieval "favors" bestowed upon chosen knights by ladies of the court to today's more contemporary banners carried by bands, drill teams, scouting units and military units, flags historically have been designed and stitched by women. Along with these colorful favors or banners bestowed on departing loved ones by sweethearts, wives and mothers were the special packets of food lovingly prepared and intended to sustain them in battle and to remind them of home.

Artist Don Collins of Austin has combined all these elements in the cover design for *Ready to Serve*. The patriot is answering the call to defend his home, wife, children, and his freedom to work and live in peace; the wife is sustaining her husband with food for the battle and her home with courage; and the Lone Star Flag, symbolizing the Republic of Texas, flies in the background above a landscape dear to the Texan's heart—bluebonnets, lush wild flowers, oak trees, rolling hills, and native crops.

Ready to Serve is a collection of recipes and items of historical interest, compiled and presented by members of the Texas National Guard Auxiliary of Austin. The Military History Committee of the National Guard Association of Texas assisted with the research. The recipes found here reflect the diversity of the state's heritage. They have been chosen with care and are presented with pride—in the same spirit that is the heritage of the state militia, the Texas National Guard which stands *Ready to Serve!*

Texas National Guard Auxiliary of Austin
Cookbook Committee
Mrs. Lewis O. King (Pat), Chairman
Mrs. J. Travis Blakeslee (Gladys)
Mrs. Walter J. Dingler (Gayle)
Mrs. Richard E. Harrison (Nancy)
Mrs. James C. Ragan (Joyce)
Mrs. L. James Starr, Jr. (Jo Ann)
Mrs. Leonard T. Tallas (Jean)

The Battle Flags . . .

At least ten battle flags or colors have been documented as having been designed specifically for use by the citizen soldiers who fought for the independence of Texas.

Six of the ten flags were designed and stitched by wives and sweethearts of the men who fought for the Texan cause or by other ladies who expressed their patriotic support in this colorful manner.

Bruce Marshall, prize-winning artist who is best known for his renderings of early Texas historical scenes, was commissioned to paint scenes depicting these ten battle flags. Signed and numbered prints were produced in an art portfolio in 1975. Brigadier General Jay A. Matthews, Jr., Editor and Publisher of Presidial Press, has graciously given his consent for the reproduction of the paintings and descriptive copy in this book.

It is particularly significant that some of the same women (members of the Texas National Guard Auxiliary of Austin) who assisted in the reproduction of six sets of the ten battle flags of Texas in 1973-74 for use by color bearing units of the Texas National Guard also have been instrumental in the design and preparation of this cookbook.

The ten flags reproduced throughout the book are:

> The Gonzales Flag
> The Flag of the New Orleans Greys
> The Flag of the Harrisburg Volunteers
> The Flag of the Lynchburg Volunteers
> Captain Brown's Flag of the Bloody Sword
> The Flag of the Georgia Volunteers
> The Flag of the Alabama Volunteers
> The San Jacinto Flag
> The Flag of the San Felipe Volunteers
> Hawkins' Flag of the Texas Navy

The flags have inspired us. The foods have sustained and pleased us. The Cookbook Committee sincerely hopes that this taste of Texas, when it is *Ready to Serve,* will be your sustenance and pleasure.

The Lone Star Flag

The beautiful, inspiring flag that waves over Texas today, was created and officially dedicated only after a score of other flags had first been the banners under which Texans had so valiantly fought for freedom.

The Lone Star flag was designed by Dr. Charles B. Stewart, second signer of the Texas Declaration of Independence and long a devoted Texas citizen and patriot. The Lone Star flag was approved, first by a committee composed by seven signers of the Texas Declaration of Independence, namely: Lorenzo de Zavala, William B. Scates, Thomas Barnett, Sterling C. Robertson, Thomas J. Gazley and Richard Ellis. The red, white and blue flag, with but a single star in its union of blue, was officially designated in 1839.

CHARLES E. GILBERT, JR.
A CONCISE HISTORY OF EARLY TEXAS

Contents

I Am A Guard Wife

It was my hand that caught up the plow my husband let fall when he answered the call at Lexington and Concord. Through the dark years of our country's birth I fought too ★ working the land ★ rearing the children ★ nursing the sick and wounded. Conservator of the life for which he fought ★ For I am a Guard Wife, and I am proud. For two hundred years in every armed conflict, I have said good-bye with aching heart and smiling face when my husband went to war. I knew the perilous days of 1812 and suffered the searing agony of the Civil War. Through the holocaust of two World Wars, I waited ★ lonely and fearful. Yet I never despaired for I knew the stubborn will of the Guardsman. I know the shining courage which makes him so valiant a soldier ★ and I have matched it with my woman's courage that deals with living ★ not dying ★ shouldering added responsibilities ★ holding the family together ★ bolstering morale. Preserver of the American ideal in a world at war. ❧

I am a Guard Wife, and I am proud. ❧

In peace, I work beside my civilian soldier to build a better world. I put aside the annoyances of drill week-ends and camp periods ★ for I know that these make him the bone and sinew of our country's defenses. I know he is learning the skills and discipline that make him ready in emergencies. When he protects others from danger ★ preserves the peace ★ or gives comfort and aid in disaster ★ I understand and give him my support. For that has always been my job ★ nurturer, comforter the healer. ❧

I am a Guard Wife, and I am proud. ❧

When I hear fearful talk of abuse of power growing into dictatorship or read stories of military take-overs ★ I am not afraid for my country. For I knew the Guard ★ trained, skilled, and strong ★ each man matured and strengthened in the home I have built ★ to be tough ★ independent thinking and self-reliant. Civilian builder ★ Soldier protector ★ Custodian of Democracy. And by his side I stand ★ wife of Heroes ★ Mother of Generations ★ Keeper of Ideals ★ Custodian of the Future. I do not fear for America ★ For I am a Guard Wife, and I am proud. ❧

HARRIET A. DAFFRON, WIFE, IOWA ARNG

Yvonne Wallace's Crab Mousse

Serves 6 to 8

2	tablespoons butter
2	tablespoons flour
1½	cups chicken stock
1	package unflavored gelatin
½	cup white wine
½	cup mayonnaise
2	cups cooked crab meat

Tabasco sauce
Salt
Pepper
1   cup whipping cream,
        whipped to soft peaks
Thin cucumber slices for garnish

Melt butter in a saucepan on medium heat; stir in flour to make a paste. Add chicken stock a little at a time, stirring well after each addition. Cook until sauce is medium-thick. Sprinkle gelatin over wine in a small pan and dissolve over a pan of hot water; then stir wine into first saucepan along with the mayonnaise. Flake the crab meat and stir into the sauce. Add Tabasco, salt and pepper to taste, and mix. Refrigerate until mixture is almost set. Fold in whipped cream. Pour into soufflé dish or one-quart mold which has been lightly greased. Cover and chill at least 2 hours, or until set. Garnish with thin cucumber slices.

Mrs. Carl D. Wallace (Yvonne)
Wife of the Adjutant General of
Tennessee

This recipe is from Yvonne's own cookbook called "Tennessee Living".

Chicken Waldorf Salad

Serves 6 to 8

1½	cups cooked chicken, diced (white meat is more attractive in salad)
⅔	cup whole green grapes, halved
½	cup pecans, chopped
⅔	cup celery, chopped
½	teaspoon salt
⅔	cup mayonnaise

Blend all ingredients together and chill before serving. Flavors blend better when made day before serving.

This is so good and easy.

Mrs. Preston Smith (Ima)
Wife of former Governor of Texas,
1969-1973

Seafood Dip

Serves 8 to 10

2	(8 ounce) packages cream cheese, cut in small squares
½	pound of crab meat or shrimp or lobster, cooked and cut up
4	ounces of clams, minced
1	medium onion, chopped
1	medium tomato, chopped
1	rib celery, chopped
3	cloves garlic, minced
5	banana peppers, seeded and chopped
4	torrido peppers, seeded and chopped
1	teaspoon lemon juice
1	teaspoon Tabasco sauce
⅛	teaspoon MSG (monosodium glutamate)
2	tablespoons ripe olives, chopped (optional)

Place all ingredients in double boiler and heat over hot water for one hour or until cheese is soft. Do Not Cook. After cheese is melted, fold ingredients together very lightly. Serve with potato chips, tortilla chips or crackers.

Mrs. Warren D. Hodges (Kathleen)
Wife of the Adjutant General of Maryland

Blue Cheese Dressing

Yields 2 cups

4	ounces blue cheese, approximately ¾ cup, crumbled (made in the good old USA)
1	cup mayonnaise
½	cup sour cream
½	clove garlic, minced
1	tablespoon wine vinegar
1	tablespoon lemon juice
1	teaspoon sugar

Combine blue cheese with other ingredients, mixing just to blend. This is not a smooth dressing. Cover and chill. Serve over tossed salad or lettuce wedges.

A few small lumps enhance the richness of taste . . . just like life.

Robert F. Ensslin, Jr.
The Adjutant General of Florida

Sausage Stuffed Mushrooms

Bake at 350° for 20 minutes
Yields 2 dozen

2 dozen fresh mushrooms (choose mushrooms equal in size and shape)
1 pound pork sausage (plain or hot)
1 teaspoon minced garlic
2 tablespoons chopped parsley
1½ cups grated sharp Cheddar cheese

Clean mushrooms thoroughly. Rinse and pat dry. Remove stems and chop stems. Set aside. Cook sausage until browned, stirring to crumble. Drain off drippings. Add chopped stems, garlic and parsley and sauté 3 minutes. Stir in cheese and mix well. Spoon mixture into mushroom caps and place in baking dish. Bake for 20 minutes.

May also be served on Melba toast rounds.

Mrs. William E. Ingram (Betty)
Wife of the Adjutant General of
North Carolina

St. Basil's Liver Pâté

1 pound Braunschweiger
1 teaspoon garlic juice
1 teaspoon sweet basil
3 tablespoons minced onion

TOPPING
1 (3 ounce) package cream cheese
⅛ teaspoon Tabasco sauce
1 teaspoon garlic juice
1 teaspoon mayonnaise

Combine Braunschweiger, garlic juice, sweet basil and onion. Mix thoroughly. Shape into ball or oblong roll. Wrap in plastic wrap and chill. Blend cream cheese, Tabasco, garlic juice and mayonnaise for topping pâté. Place well-chilled pâté on serving dish and cover with topping. Cover again with plastic wrap and chill before serving.

By flattening pâté in wide oval shape (about 1½ inches high), more area can be covered with cream cheese.

Mrs. John A. Wilson, III (Elizabeth)
Wife of the Adjutant General of
West Virginia

Chicken Little Fingers

Bake at 350° for 35 to 40 minutes
Serves 12 to 14

6	whole chicken breasts, boned and skinned
1½	cups buttermilk
2	tablespoons lemon juice
2	teaspoons Worcestershire sauce
1	teaspoon soy sauce
1	teaspoon paprika
1	teaspoon salt
1	teaspoon pepper
1	tablespoon Greek seasoning
2	cloves garlic, minced
2	cups soft bread crumbs
2	cups Ritz cracker crumbs
½	cup sesame seeds (optional)
½	cup melted butter
¼	cup melted shortening

PLUM SAUCE

1½	cups Red Plum jam
1½	tablespoons prepared mustard
1½	tablespoons horseradish
1½	teaspoons lemon juice

Day before use: Cut chicken into ½-inch strips. Combine buttermilk, lemon juice, Worcestershire sauce, soy sauce, seasonings and minced garlic. Mix well. Pour over chicken strips; cover and marinate overnight in refrigerator.

Two hours before serving: Drain chicken thoroughly. Combine crumbs, sesame seeds and coat chicken well. Place in 2 greased 9x13-inch baking dishes. Combine melted butter and shortening and drizzle over chicken. Bake for 35 to 40 minutes. Combine all sauce ingredients, place over low heat until warm. Serve chicken fingers on platter with Plum Sauce.

Mrs. LaVern Weber (Bette)
Wife of the Military Executive,
Reserve Forces Policy Board,
Office of the Secretary of Defense,
Former Chief, National Guard Bureau

Creamy Italian Salad Dressing

1	cup Hellmann's mayonnaise
½	cup sour cream
⅓	cup Italian garlic dressing
⅓	cup canned Parmesan cheese
⅓	teaspoon oregano
¼	teaspoon garlic powder or garlic salt

Blend mayonnaise and sour cream. Mix in garlic dressing. Add cheese, oregano and garlic and blend. Refrigerate and allow time for seasonings to blend before serving. Mix with greens, sprinkle more cheese on salad. Add garlic croutons.

Mrs. Roger W. Gilbert (Ruthie)
Wife of the Adjutant General of Iowa

Strawberry Delight Punch

Serves 24 (with seconds)

1   quart of tea (made up)
1½   cups sugar
2   small packages raspberry
      jello
4   cups hot water
1   (46 ounce) can pineapple
      juice
1   (6 ounce) can frozen
      orange juice (undiluted)
2   (10 ounce) packages
      frozen strawberries
1   quart gingerale, chilled

Dissolve sugar in tea. Dissolve jello in hot water and cool. Mix tea and jello and add chilled fruit juices. If cold juices are added before jello cools you will have lumps in the punch. Before serving add the strawberries and gingerale.

Freeze a ring of gingerale with fresh strawberries in it to float in punch bowl. This will chill the punch and not dilute the mixture. Makes a very attractive punch bowl.

Mrs. Willie L. Scott (Billie)
Wife of the Adjutant General of Texas,
1979 to present

Cheese-Mushroom-Pastrami Quiche

Bake at 350° for 35 to 40 minutes
Serves 6 to 8

1   (8 ounce) carton whipping
      cream, whipped
3   eggs, slightly beaten
Parsley to taste
1   cup grated cheese,
      Cheddar or Muenster
1   medium onion, chopped
2   tablespoons butter
½   pound fresh mushrooms,
      sliced
6   ounces pastrami, remove
      fat and cut into bite-
      size pieces
1   9-inch pie shell, unbaked
Paprika

Combine cream, eggs, parsley, cheese, salt and pepper; set aside. Sauté chopped onion, sliced mushrooms and pastrami in butter until onion is soft. Spread half of the pastrami-mushroom mixture on bottom of pie shell, pour on half of the cheese-cream mixture. Then add remaining pastrami and pour on remaining cheese-cream mixture. Sprinkle with paprika. Bake for 35 to 40 minutes; top should be brown and center firm when shook. Let stand 10 minutes before cutting.

Mrs. John Blatsos (Aphrodite)
Wife of the Adjutant General of
New Hampshire

Orange-Rice Salad Orientale

Serves 6 to 8

3   cups cooked rice, cooled
1   (8 ounce) can water
       chestnuts, drained and
       sliced
3   Florida oranges, divided
1   tablespoon vinegar
⅓   cup vegetable oil
3   tablespoons catsup
2   tablespoons soy sauce
2   tablespoons minced onion
1   tablespoon sugar
½   teaspoon ground ginger
3 to 4 drops hot pepper sauce
4   ounces fresh snow peas
       OR
1   (6 ounce) package frozen
       snow peas, thawed and
       rinsed in hot water; dry
       and chill

Combine rice and water chestnuts. Squeeze juice from half of one of the oranges. Combine juice, vinegar, oil, catsup, soy sauce, onion, sugar, ginger and pepper sauce. Pour over rice and water chestnuts; toss to combine. Peel and thinly slice remaining oranges. Pour boiling water over snow peas and let stand 1 minute; drain, dry and chill. Spoon half of rice mixture into serving bowl. Cover with a layer of half of the snow peas and orange slices. Spoon remaining rice mixture over top. Arrange remaining snow peas and orange slices in a decorative design on top.

This is a pretty dish to take on a picnic or to a church supper.

Mrs. Robert F. Ensslin, Jr. (Fae)
Wife of the Adjutant General of Florida

Fae emphasized on her recipe FLORIDA oranges, so we included it . . . reluctantly!!!

Chuck Roast Barbecue

1   boned chuck roast, 2½-3
       inches thick
Salt and pepper to taste
½   cup soy sauce
1   cup orange juice
1   tablespoon lemon juice
1   teaspoon sugar
1   clove garlic, minced
1   teaspoon ground ginger

Sprinkle roast with salt and pepper and place in a shallow glass container. Combine remaining ingredients and pour over meat. Marinate at least 12 hours turning several times during this period. Grill meat 4-5 inches from hot coals, 20 minutes on each side. Cut in thin slices across the grain.

Mrs. James W. Duffy (Barbara)
Wife of the Adjutant General of Montana

Rich Luncheon Salad

Serves 6 to 8

4 egg yolks, beaten
½ cup half and half cream
Juice of 1 lemon
1 (8 ounce) carton whipping cream, whipped
1 (17 ounce) can sweet white cherries, pitted and drained
1 (20 ounce) can pineapple chunks, drained
¼ pound marshmallows, cut into small pieces
¼ pound blanched almond slivers

Combine egg yolks, cream and lemon juice in top of double boiler. Cook over hot water until thick and coats the spoon. Allow to cool completely. Then add whipped cream. Combine all ingredients with dressing and let stand in refrigerator overnight before serving.

This is a handy and satisfying salad for a busy-day luncheon as it can be made the day before serving.

Mrs. Thomas S. Bishop (Bettymarie)
Wife of former Adjutant General of Texas,
1962-1969 and 1973-1979

Molded Cranberry Salad

Serves 6 to 8

2 cups cranberries
1¼ cups cold water
1 cup sugar
1 envelope unflavored gelatin
½ cup chopped celery
½ cup chopped pecans or walnuts
¼ teaspoon salt

Cook cranberries in 1 cup of water for 20 minutes. Stir in sugar and cook 5 minutes longer. Soften gelatin in ¼ cup cold water; add to hot cranberries and stir until dissolved. Set aside to cool. When mixture begins to thicken, add chopped celery, nuts and salt. Turn into mold that has been rinsed with cold water. Chill in refrigerator until firm. Unmold on serving plate. Garnish with salad greens if desired.

This is decorative and delicious for the holidays or whenever you serve chicken or turkey.

Mrs. Lyndon B. Johnson (Lady Bird)
Wife of former President of the
United States, 1963-1969

Crabmeat Imperial Special

Bake at 375° for 15 to 20 minutes
Serves 4

1	egg
2	tablespoons mayonnaise
2	teaspoons Worcestershire sauce
½	teaspoon salt
¼	teaspoon white pepper
1	pound fresh crabmeat
¼	cup finely chopped Bell pepper
¼	cup finely chopped red Bell pepper
2	teaspoons butter, softened
4	medium crab or scallop shells, cleaned
2	tablespoons butter, cut in small pieces

In a deep bowl, beat egg lightly with a wire whisk. Add mayonnaise, Worcestershire, salt and pepper, then beat until mixture is smooth. Add crabmeat and green and red peppers and toss lightly but thoroughly. With a pastry brush spread softened butter over crab shells. Spoon crab mixture into buttered shells evenly, mounding centers lightly. Dot tops with pieces of butter. Bake at 375° for 15 to 20 minutes, then place under hot broiler for 30 seconds to brown the tops. Serve immediately directly from the shells.

Mrs. Christopher S. Bond (Carolyn)
Wife of the Governor of Missouri

Orange Biscuits

Bake at 450° for 20 minutes
Serves 8

2	cups flour
4	tablespoons sugar
4	tablespoons Butter Flavor Crisco
1	teaspoon salt
2½	teaspoons baking powder
¾	cup liquid (*half* milk and *half* orange juice)

Rind of one orange, grated

Sift dry ingredients together. Cut in shortening and add orange rind. Pour liquid all at one time, mix lightly, just enough to bind ingredients together. Roll ¾-inch thick on lightly floured board. Cut with biscuit cutter. Bake for 20 minutes or until golden brown.

Mrs. John B. Connally (Nellie)
Wife of former Governor of Texas,
1963-1969

Scotch Pheasant

1	pheasant, quartered
4	tablespoons butter
¾	cup Scotch whiskey
¾	cup strong chicken consommé
1	tablespoon flour
1	(8 ounce) carton whipping cream, scalded
2	ounces sherry

Sauté floured pheasant quarters in butter until golden brown. Pour Scotch over pheasant. Cook 5 minutes over medium heat until liquor has evaporated. Add consommé. Cover tightly, turn down heat and simmer at low temperature 1 hour or until meat is tender. Remove pheasant and crisp in broiler very quickly – do not let pheasant dry out. Mix flour with juices in pan. Add ¼ cup water; cook for several minutes stirring mixture slowly. Stir the cream and sherry into the gravy and simmer 5 minutes. Pour over the crisped pheasant pieces and serve at once.

Chicken is also good if pheasant is not available.

Mrs. Willard D. "Bill" Hill (Barbara)
Wife of the Assistant Adjutant General of
Texas (Army)

Rice Pudding

Bake at 300° for 30 minutes
Serves 6 to 8

1½	cups cooked rice
1	cup sugar
1	teaspoon nutmeg
1	teaspoon allspice
½	cup milk
4	eggs, well beaten
¼	pound butter or margarine, melted

Combine all ingredients, mixing well. Pour into lightly greased baking dish. Bake about 30 minutes. Serve with cream or ice cream.

This recipe was submitted in memory of her parents by Celeste Berry Riley of Austin, daughter of General and Mrs. K. L. Berry, former Adjutant General of Texas, 1947-1961. General Berry is one of the most highly decorated Generals in history.

Sourdough Rolls

Place rolls in cold oven
Bake at 325°

1	package dry yeast
2	tablespoons *warm* water
6	cups flour
2⅓	cups buttermilk
4	tablespoons sugar
1	tablespoon salt
2	tablespoons baking powder
½	teaspoon baking soda
⅓	cup shortening

Dissolve yeast in warm water (110°) and set aside. Put 6 cups flour in large bowl and make well in center. Add all other ingredients and mix until all flour is used. Add yeast mixture. Mix well. Cover with towel and let stand for 5-7 hours; until is smells sour. Put in refrigerator in covered bowl or plastic bag for 2 days. Make rolls by pinching off golf ball size pieces and patting out on greased and floured baking pan. Let rise for 5-7 hours. Bake until rolls are saddle brown.

Serve with Red-Eye Gravy.

PRESTON SMITH'S RED-EYE GRAVY

1	tablespoon bacon or ham drippings
1	cup black coffee
1	tablespoon sugar

Blend all ingredients in heavy skillet and bring to boil. Stir constantly. Boil a few minutes to let flavors blend. Gravy will not be thick.

Ross Ayers
Former Adjutant General of Texas,
1969-1973

Willie's Bell Pepper Rings

1	egg, beaten
1	cup milk
Flour	
Salt and pepper to taste	
Bell peppers, cleaned and sliced into rings	
Hot oil	

Combine beaten egg and milk. Combine flour, salt and pepper. Dip pepper rings into flour mixture, then into egg mixture and back into flour. Fry in hot oil until brown. Serve hot.

These, of course, are better when they are fresh out of your garden . . . like mine!!

Willie L. Scott
The Adjutant General of Texas,
1979 to present

Pumpkin Date Nut Bread

Bake at 350° for 1 hour
Yields 4 loaves

4   cups sugar
1   (29 ounce) can pumpkin
3   eggs
1   cup vegetable oil
5   cups all-purpose flour
1   tablespoon baking soda
2   teaspoons cinnamon
1½   teaspoons ground cloves
1   teaspoon salt
2   cups coarsely chopped
       dates
2   cups coarsely chopped
       toasted walnuts

Combine sugar, pumpkin and eggs in large bowl. Beat until well blended. Add oil and beat to combine. Blend in flour, soda, cinnamon, cloves and salt thoroughly. Stir in dates and nuts. Fill prepared pans ¾ full to allow for rising during baking. Bake about 1 hour or until toothpick inserted near center of loaf comes out clean and bread has pulled away slightly from sides of pan. Bread may be baked in 1 pound coffee cans, 8x4-inch loaf pans, ring mold, muffin tins or other small pans. Test after 20 minutes for doneness in small pans.

Mrs. Joseph M. Lank (Virginia)
Wife of the Adjutant General of Delaware

Shrimp Newberg

Serves 4 to 6

1   stick butter
1   pint half and half cream
Flour to thicken to medium
       thick white sauce
1   tablespoon catsup
1   teaspoon Tabasco sauce
¼   teaspoon Worcestershire
       sauce
Salt and white pepper to taste
       (depends on how
       salty the shrimp is)
¼   cup Vermouth
1½   pounds shrimp, cleaned
       and boiled
1   large can Chow Mein
       Noodles, heated

Mix butter, cream and enough flour to make white sauce. Blend in catsup, Tabasco, Worcestershire sauce, salt, pepper and Vermouth. Next add boiled shrimp and simmer *only* until thoroughly heated. Serve over heated Chow Mein Noodles.

Good with green salad, hot rolls and dessert.

Mrs. Ansel M. Stroud, Jr. (Barbara)
Wife of the Adjutant General of Louisiana

Brisket a la Supreme

Roast at 325° for 2½ to 3 hours
Serves 8 to 10

4-5 pound beef brisket
½ teaspoon salt
Pepper to taste
Garlic powder to taste
1 medium onion, sliced
½ cup catsup
2 tablespoons mustard
¼-½ cup red wine
1 cup water
1 small can sliced
mushrooms

Season meat with salt, pepper and garlic powder. Sauté onion in roasting pan. In separate bowl mix catsup and mustard well. Add wine, water and mushrooms. Place brisket in roaster with onions on top. Pour mixture over meat. Roast, covered, at 325° for 2½ to 3 hours. Remove meat from sauce to let stand. (You get nicer slices when meat is allowed to cool.) Remove fat from sauce. Slice meat and serve cold or reheated in sauce.

Sliced thinly this goes a long way for a buffet. May be frozen.

Mrs. George E. Coates (Betty)
Wife of the Adjutant General of
Washington

Quick Beef Stroganoff

Serves 4 to 5

1 pound round or sirloin
steak, ¼-inch thick
¼ cup butter
6 ounces mushrooms, sliced
(about 2 cups)
½ cup chopped onion
1 can condensed beef broth
2½ tablespoons flour (mixed
with enough beef broth
to make thin paste)
Salt and pepper to taste
1 (8 ounce) carton sour
cream

Trim fat from meat. Cut meat diagonally across grain in strips, ¼-inch wide. (Strips should be very thin.) Brown quickly in butter. Push meat to one side; add mushrooms and onion; cook just till tender. Add broth; heat just to boiling. Add flour paste and stir until mixture thickens. Season to taste. Blend in sour cream and cook only until heated. Serve over hot buttered noodles.

Mrs. Edward C. Binder (Roma)
Wife of the Adjutant General of Nebraska

Bourbon Meatballs

1½ pounds ground beef
1   slice white bread,
        crumbled (no crust)
1   tablespoon catsup
1   egg
½   teaspoon salt
¼   teaspoon pepper
Oil for frying, if needed

Mix all ingredients. Form into small balls approximately 1-inch in diameter. Brown meatballs in oil. Remove from heat and set aside.

BOURBON SAUCE

2   tablespoons butter or oil
1   small onion, diced
1   clove garlic, minced
1   tablespoon flour
¼   teaspoon salt
1   teaspoon dry mustard
¼   teaspoon oregano
1   beef bouillon cube
1   cup boiling water
½   cup bourbon

Sauté onion and garlic in oil until brown. Add flour and mix. Add salt, mustard and oregano stirring constantly. Add bouillon and water stirring until slightly thickened. Add bourbon and bring to a boil. Add meatballs and simmer 30 to 45 minutes on low heat. Serve over cooked rice.

Mrs. James L. Spence (Esther)
Wife of the Adjutant General of Wyoming

Zesty Asparagus

2   (15 ounce) cans extra
        long, green, asparagus
        spears, drained
¼   cup vinegar
¼   cup vegetable oil
2   tablespoons chopped
        onion
1   tablespoon diced pimiento
½   teaspoon salt
⅛   teaspoon pepper
¼   teaspoon sugar

Gently place asparagus spears in shallow container. Blend remaining ingredients thoroughly and pour over asparagus. Cover and chill at least 6 hours. Check to see that all asparagus is covered with marinade. Be very careful with turning asparagus as it tends to tear apart easily. Drain and serve cold.

Mrs. E. H. "Mickey" Walker, Jr. (Tuta)
Wife of the Chief of National Guard
Bureau, Washington, D.C.

6 Minute Cheese Soufflé

Bake at 375° for 40 to 50 minutes
Serves 6

1	tablespoon butter, softened
6	eggs
¼	cup grated Parmesan cheese
½	teaspoon prepared mustard
½	cup cream
½	teaspoon salt
¼	teaspoon white pepper
½	pound sharp Cheddar cheese
11	ounces cream cheese

Put eggs, Parmesan, mustard, cream, salt and pepper in electric blender and swirl until smooth. Cut Cheddar cheese into pieces and add piece by piece into container with motor running. Do the same with cream cheese. When all cheese has been added, whirl mixture at high speed for 5 seconds. Pour into a buttered 5-cup soufflé dish. Bake for approximately 45 minutes for soft center and another 5 minutes for firmer center. This can be prepared and held in soufflé dish without refrigeration for 1-2 hours.

Milk may be used instead of cream with equally good results.

Mrs. Bruce Jacobs (Shirley)
Wife of the Deputy Executive Vice
President, National Guard Association
of the United States
Washington, D.C.

Baja California Chicken

Bake at 350° for 10 minutes
8 Servings

8	boned chicken breasts
	Seasoning salt and pepper, to taste
2	cloves garlic, crushed
4	tablespoons olive oil
4	tablespoons tarragon vinegar
⅔	cup dry sherry

Sprinkle chicken with seasoning salt and pepper. Crush garlic into oil and vinegar in a skillet. Sauté chicken pieces until golden brown, turning frequently. Remove; place in a baking dish. Pour sherry over pieces and place in oven for 10 minutes.

Mrs. Ronald Reagan (Nancy)
Wife of the President of the
United States, 1980 to present

Cranberried Chicken

Bake at 425° for 1 hour
Serves 6 to 8

4	tablespoons soy sauce
4	tablespoons lemon juice
½	teaspoon garlic powder
½	cup margarine
1	(16 ounce) can whole berry cranberries
6-8	chicken breasts, split

Combine first 5 ingredients in saucepan and bring to boil. Place chicken breasts in baking pan, skin side down. Cover with sauce and bake for 30 minutes. Turn chicken and bake 30 minutes more, basting about four times during baking.

Delicious!

Mrs. Leonard Holland (Bernice)
Wife of former Adjutant General of
Rhode Island

Mississippi Mud Cake

Bake at 350° for 35 to 45 minutes

2	sticks margarine or butter
½	cup cocoa
2	cups sugar
4	eggs, slightly beaten
1½	cups flour
⅛	teaspoon salt
1½	cups chopped pecans
1	teaspoon vanilla
1	cup miniature marshmallows

Chocolate Frosting
  (recipe follows)

Melt butter and cocoa together. Remove from heat and stir in sugar and eggs. Mix well. Add flour, salt, nuts and vanilla. Mix well. Spoon batter into a greased 13x9-inch pan and bake at 350° for 35 to 45 minutes. Sprinkle marshmallows on top of warm cake and cover with Chocolate Frosting.

CHOCOLATE FROSTING

½	stick margarine or butter
⅓	cup cocoa
1	(16 ounce) box powdered sugar
½	cup milk

Melt margarine, add powdered sugar and cocoa. Gradually add milk and mix until smooth. Spread over hot cake and marshmallows.

Mrs. Cohen E. Robertson (Elizabeth)
Wife of former Adjutant General of
Mississippi

Tarragon Chicken with Turkish Pilaf

Serves 6 to 8

3	whole chicken breasts, split
6	chicken thighs
2	tablespoons shortening
2	teaspoons salt
1	medium onion, sliced
3	tablespoons flour
1	cup chicken broth
1	bay leaf
1¼	teaspoons tarragon leaves, crushed
¼	teaspoon pepper
1	(8 ounce) carton sour cream

Place salted chicken in a heavy Dutch oven container and brown in shortening. Remove chicken. Sauté onion until golden. Do not overcook. Remove onions. Blend flour with ½ of broth and stir in with pan drippings. Add remaining broth and bay leaf. Add chicken and onions. Cover and simmer 25 minutes or until tender. Add tarragon and pepper; simmer 5 minutes longer. Remove bay leaf. Stir in sour cream and simmer just until heated. Do not boil sour cream.

TURKISH PILAF

1	cup long grain rice, uncooked
Water to cover	
2	tablespoons butter
1	teaspoon salt
1	teaspoon pepper (use full amount)
2½	cups chicken stock, boiling
2	tablespoons butter

Soak rice 30 minutes. Drain. Sauté rice in butter until dry and starting to stick. Add salt, pepper and stock. Cover and simmer 20 minutes. Remove from heat; add butter and let stand 5 minutes. Toss gently with fork.

These two dishes are great served together and with an avocado-grapefruit salad.

Mrs. Herbert R. Temple, Jr. (Pat)
Wife of Director, Army National Guard
National Guard Bureau
Washington, D.C.

The description of the flag of the United States is most vivid in its National Anthem. In June of 1777, the Congress adopted a flag of 13 stripes of alternate red and white with a union of blue. Thirteen stars, white on the blue field, would represent the new constellation. In 1818, Peter Wendover succeeded in getting Congress to pass a flag law which provided for the addition of new stars to represent new states as they joined, while retaining the original thirteen stripes to represent the original colonies. When the United States annexed Texas after ten years of hot debate on both sides, the number of stars in the blue field was raised to 28 and the American colors began flying over Texas, along with the single star of the state flag.

Seafood Rice

Bake at 350° for 30 minutes
Serves 8 to 10

4	cups cooked rice
2	cups minced celery
1	cup minced onion
1	cup minced Bell pepper
2	(8 ounce) cans sliced water chestnuts, drained
¼	teaspoon salt
¼	teaspoon pepper
1½	cups mayonnaise
1½	cups tomato juice
1	(2 ounce) jar diced pimientos
2	(1 pound) packages frozen shrimp, cooked
1	(6 ounce) package frozen King crab, cooked
½	cup almonds, slivered
1	tablespoon butter
1	cup grated Cheddar cheese

Paprika

Mix rice, celery, onion, Bell pepper, water chestnuts, salt, pepper, mayonnaise and tomato juice. Next carefully blend in pimientos, shrimp and crab meat. Mix only until blended. Pour into a greased 4-quart casserole and bake for 30 minutes. Sauté the almonds in butter, just until light tan. Drain off butter and sprinkle almonds and grated cheese over the casserole. Sprinkle paprika liberally over all and return to oven for additional 10 minutes or until cheese is melted.

This is a great luncheon dish with either a green salad or fresh fruit in season.

Mrs. Richard M. Scott (Flo)
Wife of the Adjutant General of Pennsylvania

Buckeye Balls

1½	cups creamy peanut butter
½	cup butter or margarine
1	teaspoon vanilla
1	(16 ounce) package powdered sugar
1	(6 ounce) package chocolate chips
2	tablespoons shortening

Mix peanut butter, margarine, vanilla and powdered sugar until thoroughly blended. It will be a very stiff batter. Roll into 1-inch balls. At this point, they may need to be refrigerated in order to dip better. Melt chocolate chips with shortening. Place a toothpick in a ball and dip ½ way into melted chocolate, leaving a small portion without chocolate. Let drain on waxed paper.

Mrs. Raymond R. Galloway (Peggy)
Wife of the Adjutant General of Ohio

Stuffed Clams

Bake at 350° for 20 minutes

2	cups minced onions
¼	cup minced garlic
2½	sticks butter
1	teaspoon red pepper
1	teaspoon oregano
1	tablespoon minced parsley
1	teaspoon minced dill weed
1	teaspoon salt
1	quart clam liquor
1	quart clams, minced in food processor (24 Quahogs=1 quart)
2	(14 ounce) packages stuffing mix, less 1 cup, herb or plain
¾	cup grated Parmesan or Romano cheese

In Dutch oven, sauté onions and garlic in butter but do not brown. Add pepper, oregano, parsley, dill weed, salt and clam liquor and bring to boil. Add minced clams. Clean processor out with ½ cup of water and add to clam mixture. Bring to a slow rolling boil then remove from heat. Do not overcook clams as they get tough. Add stuffing mix and cheese and mix well but lightly. Taste to adjust seasonings. Mixture should be very moist — sticky but not sloppy. Cool. Stuff prepared shells. (see below) Sprinkle paprika on top. Heat to serve. Stuffed shells may be frozen; allow to thaw and then heat as indicated.

To clean shells, break them in half, scrub them and clean muscle out.

Mrs. John F. Gore (Georgia)
Wife of the Adjutant General of
Connecticut

France gave up her claims to Texas in 1803 as a part of the Louisiana purchase and settlement. However, the French influence is still apparent in the names of many Texas heroes—James Bonham, the Baron de Bastrop and Henri Castro. In parts of East Texas, French creole cooking and rich chicory-flavored coffee are found in abundance and in the recipes which instruct us to "sauté" our onions and celery as a beginning to many excellent dishes.

Smothered Quail

3 tablespoons butter
1 medium onion, finely
  chopped
½ pound fresh mushrooms,
  sliced
3 tablespoons butter, plus 1
  tablespoon oil
8 to 12 quail breasts
½ cup dry white wine or
  vermouth
1 cup half and half cream
1 (10 ounce) can cream of
  mushroom soup

In heavy skillet melt 3 tablespoons butter. Sauté onion and mushrooms until tender. Remove from skillet. Add additional butter and oil; sauté breasts until brown. Remove from pan, pour off remaining fat. Add white wine, scrape up particles on bottom of skillet. Add soup, onions, mushrooms and cream. Stir until well blended. Return breasts to skillet, spooning sauce over, cover and simmer for 30 minutes or until tender. (Chicken breasts may be substituted.)

Mrs. Mark White (Linda Gale)
Wife of the Governor of Texas,
1983 to present

Baked Artichoke Hearts

Bake at 325° for 20 minutes
Serves 6 to 8

2 (9 ounce) packages frozen
  artichoke hearts
3 tablespoons butter or
  margarine
1 medium onion, chopped
2 tablespoons flour
1⅓ cups milk
¾ teaspoon oregano leaves
3 hard-boiled eggs,
  chopped
Salt and pepper to taste
1 cup grated Cheddar
  cheese
Paprika

Cook artichokes according to package directions; drain well. Melt butter in 3-quart pan; sauté onions until limp. Stir in flour and cook until bubbly. Gradually add milk and cook until thickened. Remove from heat. Mix in oregano, eggs, artichokes, salt and pepper. Spoon into a shallow 1½-quart casserole and sprinkle with cheese and paprika. Bake uncovered 20 minutes. If made ahead and refrigerated bake for approximately 35 minutes.

Mrs. William F. Engel (Sharon)
Wife of former Adjutant General of
Nevada

Vermont Baked Beans

Bake at 275° for 6 to 8 hours
Serves 8 to 10

2	pounds dried navy beans
1	large onion, peeled but left whole
1	tablespoon salt
¾	cup maple syrup
1	teaspoon dry mustard
½	pound salt pork, a ham bone or bacon end

Wash beans and cover with cold water to soak overnight. The next morning, remove any floating beans and drain. Put the beans in a pan and cover with water. Simmer until the skins split; about 1½ hours. Do not drain. Put the onion in the bottom of a bean pot or a large, deep, oven-proof casserole dish. Add the beans and their liquid. Combine salt, maple syrup and mustard with 1 cup boiling water and pour over beans. Cut gashes in salt pork or bacon about ½ inch apart but not through the rind. Place meat into beans with only rind exposed. Cover pot and cook *very slowly* at 275° for 6 to 8 hours. Do not stir but peek at the beans every hour or two and add water if they start to look dry.

Of course, Vermont is famous for maple syrup and it does give a special flavor of its own. This is a good recipe for a big family.

Mrs. Donald E. Edwards (Wibs)
Wife of the Adjutant General of Vermont

Puerto Rican Style Beans

Serves 6

2	tablespoons olive oil or cooking oil
2	ounces smoked ham or bacon, cut in small pieces
1	medium tomato, chopped
1	medium onion, chopped
1	small Bell pepper, finely chopped
2	small sweet peppers, finely chopped
1	tablespoon finely minced garlic
⅛	teaspoon ground oregano
4	leaves of cilantro, finely minced
4	tablespoons tomato sauce or spaghetti sauce
1½	teaspoons salt
½	teaspoon sugar
¼	pound yellow squash, cut in small pieces
1	(15 ounce) can red kidney (or pink) beans, drained but save liquid

Sauté ham, tomato, onion, peppers and garlic in oil just until limp. Do not brown. Then add oregano, cilantro, tomato sauce, salt, sugar, squash, the liquid from beans and enough water to fill the bean can. Cook over medium-low heat for 5 to 8 minutes. Add the beans and cook for 5 minutes longer.

This is a very fast dish to prepare; however, you must insure that the sauce does not thicken too much or is too watery. There should be about 1 to 1½ more sauce than beans. Add more tomato sauce if necessary.

This is traditionally served in Puerto Rico with white rice and any kind of pork or beef.

Mrs. Orlando Llenza (Krystyna)
Wife of former Adjutant General of Puerto Rico

Cheese Cornbread

Bake at 375° for 30 minutes
Serves 8

1	cup yellow cornmeal
1	cup all-purpose flour, sifted
¼	cup sugar
½	teaspoon salt
4	teaspoons baking powder
1½	cups grated sharp Cheddar cheese
1	egg
1	cup milk
¼	cup soft shortening

Sift together cornmeal, flour, sugar, salt and baking powder. Add cheese. Add egg, milk and shortening. Beat with a rotary beater about 1 minute until smooth. Do Not Overbeat. Pour in a greased 8-inch pan. Bake for 30 minutes. Cut in squares and serve hot.

Mrs. Allan Shivers (Marialice)
Wife of former Governor of Texas,
1949-1957

Party Potatoes

Bake at 350°
Serves 8 to 10

8	large or 10 medium potatoes, peeled
1	(8 ounce) carton sour cream
1	(8 ounce) package cream cheese, room temperature
1	teaspoon onion salt
1	teaspoon garlic salt
Butter	
Paprika	

Boil potatoes and drain. Beat sour cream and softened cream cheese until blended. Add drained potatoes gradually, whipping constantly until blended. Season with onion and garlic salt. Spoon mixture into ungreased casserole dish. Dot with butter and sprinkle with paprika. Brown in a 350° oven. This is even more delicious if refrigerated 24 hours; then you would need to bake it for approximately 45 minutes.

Mrs. Paul R. Day (Mary)
Wife of the Adjutant General of Maine

Minnesota Wild Rice

Bake at 350° for 1½ hours
Serves 6 to 8

1	cup uncooked wild rice
¼	cup butter or margarine
½	cup slivered almonds
2	tablespoons chopped chives or tops of green onions
1	(8 ounce) can mushroom stems and pieces
3	cups chicken broth (3 bouillon cubes in 3 cups boiling water acceptable)

Wash and drain rice in cold water. Melt butter in large skillet. Add rice, almonds, chives and mushrooms; cook and stir until almonds are golden brown; about 20 minutes. Pour rice mixture in a greased 1½-quart casserole. Heat broth to a boil, stir into rice mixture. Cover tightly and bake about 1½ hours or until all liquid is absorbed and rice is tender and fluffy.

Mrs. James G. Sieben (Charlotte)
Wife of the Adjutant General of
Minnesota

Chicken Long Rice

5   bundles Chinese long rice (threads)
3   pounds chicken thighs
3   (14½ ounce) cans chicken broth
Garlic salt to taste
1   piece ginger root, mashed
⅛   teaspoon ajinomoto
1   cup chopped green onion
2   sprigs Chinese parsley

In large saucepan soak long rice for about 1 hour in water. Drain. Remove skins from chicken thighs and simmer thighs, garlic salt, ginger root and ajinomoto in chicken broth for approximately 1 to 1½ hours or until tender. Add long rice after cutting in 2-inch lengths. Cook for 25 to 30 minutes and add green onions just before serving. Garnish with Chinese parsley.

Mrs. Alexis T. Lum (Momi)
Wife of the Adjutant General of Hawaii

Barley Casserole

Bake at 350° for 1 hour
Serves 16

½   cup butter or margarine
1   medium onion, chopped
1   cup quick-cooking pearl barley
1   cup slivered almonds
1   (2 ounce) package onion soup mix
2   cups chicken broth
1   (4 ounce) can mushrooms, sliced, with juice
1   (4 ounce) can water chestnuts, drained and sliced

Sauté butter, onion and barley until light golden in color. Add ½ cup almonds, dry soup mix and chicken broth. Add mushrooms and juice to the barley. Add water chestnuts and stir well. Turn into a 2-quart deep casserole dish, top with ½ cup slivered almonds, cover and bake for 1 hour. Remove cover the last 15 minutes of baking. Add more broth if the mixture gets too dry. This may be prepared ahead of time and refrigerated before baking. Doubled, this makes a 9x13-inch pan size.

To be used in place of potatoes or rice dish.

Mrs. Ralph T. Tice (Nadine)
Wife of the Adjutant General of Kansas

Pasta with Anchovy Sauce

Serves 4 to 6

1	cup bread crumbs (set aside)
4	cans anchovies, do not drain
1	tablespoon garlic powder
¼	cup olive oil
½	cup water
2	ribs celery, chopped
½	medium onion, chopped
4	teaspoons chopped parsley
½	cup grated Romano or Parmesan cheese
½	cup dry white wine, optional
1	pound vermicelli, cooked

Sauté all ingredients, except bread crumbs, until well blended and soft. Pour over vermicelli and top with bread crumbs. You may substitute 2 cans of chopped clams for anchovies.

This is a traditional Italian dish served with the traditional seafood dinner on Christmas Eve.

Mrs. Vernon Andrews (Grace)
Wife of the Adjutant General of Michigan

Briscoe Picosa (Hot Sauce)

8	fresh green chili peppers (or fresh jalapeños)
1	clove garlic
1	teaspoon lemon juice
1	teaspoon Mazola oil
Salt to taste	
1	(28 ounce) can whole peeled tomatoes, drained

Boil chilies in enough water to cover until they become dull green. Drain and place in blender or processor to grind. Add oil, lemon juice and salt and grind until blended. Add drained tomatoes and blend until thoroughly mixed. Stores indefinitely in refrigerator.

I make a gallon at a time since my family uses it on everything. I serve tortilla chips as a snack accompaniment.

Mrs. Dolph Briscoe (Janey)
Wife of former Governor of Texas,
1973-1979

Jalapeño Jelly

Yields 12 to 14 half-pints

1½ cups Bell pepper (about 8 small) seeded and cut fine
½ cup jalapeño peppers
3 cups cider vinegar
12 cups sugar
2 bottles Certo
Green coloring (optional)

Place peppers in blender with 1 cup vinegar at high speed. Blend well. Pour into saucepan, rinse blender with remaining vinegar and add to peppers. Add sugar and bring to rolling boil that you cannot stir down. Remove from heat. Let stand 5 minutes, skim off foam, if necessary. Pour in Certo and add coloring, if desired. It should be a pretty green color. Pour into 12 to 14 sterilized ½-pint jars and seal.

Willard D. "Bill" Hill
Assistant Adjutant General of Texas
(Army)

Freezer Strawberry Jam

Yields 2 pints

3 pints strawberries
3 cups sugar
1 (3 ounce) package strawberry flavored gelatin

Rinse and hull strawberries. Place in saucepan and crush with potato masher. Pour the sugar on strawberries; let stand uncovered 4 hours. Heat the strawberry mixture to boiling over high heat, stirring constantly. Reduce heat to medium; simmer 10 minutes, stirring frequently. Stir in the gelatin. Remove pan from heat and let stand 30 minutes. Spoon mixture into containers, leaving ½-inch space at the top. Let stand until room temperature. Cover with the lids. Jam will thicken when cold. Store in freezer or refrigerator.

Great recipe for children to help with.

Mrs. John L. France (Carole)
Wife of the Adjutant General of Colorado

Swedish Mustard

Yields 1 pint

3 egg yolks
¾ cup whipping cream
¼ cup vinegar plus 1
   tablespoon
1 (2 ounce) can dry mustard
1 teaspoon salt
2 tablespoons cornstarch
1¼ cup brown sugar

In saucepan mix egg yolks and whipping cream. Add other ingredients and blend well. Cook over low heat stirring constantly until mixture reaches a full rolling boil. Remove from heat and cover with lid. When cool, pour into small mixer bowl and beat with electric beater until light colored. Pour into covered jar and store in the refrigerator.

This keeps for months in the refrigerator. It is good with ham, turkey or any kind of sandwich.

Mrs. C. Emerson Murry (Donna)
Wife of the Adjutant General of
North Dakota

"Debbie" Cake

Bake at 350° for 45 minutes

1½ sticks margarine
3 eggs
1 box yellow cake mix
1 (16 ounce) box powdered
   sugar
1 (8 ounce) package cream
   cheese, softened

Melt 1 stick margarine in a 9x13-inch pan. Cream one well beaten egg and cake mix into melted butter. Pat this mixture in the pan as you would a pie crust. Set aside.

Cream together powdered sugar, softened cream cheese, ½ stick margarine and 2 eggs. Pour this over cake mixture in pan. Bake at 350° for 45 minutes. Do not overbake.

Mrs. Jimmie "Red" Jones (Inez)
Wife of the Adjutant General of Arkansas

14-Karat Cake

Bake at 350° for 35 to 40 minutes

2	cups flour
2	teaspoons baking powder
1½	teaspoons baking soda
2	teaspoons cinnamon
2	cups sugar
1½	cups Mazola salad oil
4	eggs
1½	teaspoons salt
2	cups finely grated carrots
1	(8¾ ounce) can crushed pineapple, drained
½	cup chopped pecans
1	(3¼ ounce) can flaked coconut

Sift flour, baking powder, soda and cinnamon in large mixing bowl. Add sugar, oil, salt and eggs mixing thoroughly. Next add carrots, drained pineapple, pecans and coconut stirring just until mixed. Pour into 3 greased 9-inch cake pans. Bake at 350° for 35 to 40 minutes. Cool on racks and frost.

FROSTING

½	cup margarine, softened
1	(8 ounce) package cream cheese, softened
1	(16 ounce) package powdered sugar
1	teaspoon vanilla
	Chopped pecans

Blend all ingredients, except pecans, thoroughly. Spread on cooled layers. Sprinkle chopped pecans on top.

This will keep 2 to 3 weeks in refrigerator. Absolutely delicious, but sinfully rich. Only 607 calories per slice if cut into 16 slices!!

Variation — try baking the Karat Cake in a greased and floured tube or Bundt pan and serve warm with the following Rum Sauce.

Yields 2 cups

RUM SAUCE

1	cup firmly packed dark brown sugar
½	cup dark corn syrup
½	cup half and half cream
¼	cup butter
¼	cup light rum
1	teaspoon vanilla

In a 2-quart saucepan over low heat, stir together constantly the sugar, corn syrup, cream and butter until boiling. Cool to warm, stirring occasionally. Stir in rum and vanilla. Serve warm with Karat Cake. Sauce may be made ahead, stored in the refrigerator and reheated gently.

Just enjoy . . . don't ask about the calories!!

Mrs. John Phipps (Pauline)
Wife of former Adjutant General of
Illinois

Bourbon Cake

Bake at 350° for 1 hour

2 cups self-rising flour
2 cups sugar
1 teaspoon cinnamon
1 teaspoon cloves
1 cup Wesson oil
3 eggs, beaten
2 small jars Gerber's strained plums (baby food)
1 cup chopped nuts

In large mixing bowl combine all dry ingredients. Add oil and beaten eggs alternately. Mix only until blended. Do not overbeat. Add strained plums and nuts. Mix only until blended. Pour into well greased and floured tube or Bundt pan and bake 1 hour. Let cake set 5 to 10 minutes before turning onto cake plate.

GLAZE

⅓ cup powdered sugar
Bourbon

Mix powdered sugar and bourbon, adjusting amount of bourbon to right consistency for pouring over cake. Pour over warm cake.

Men love this cake so it will not last long.

Mrs. James E. Taylor (Estelle)
Wife of former Adjutant General of Texas, 1961

Sour Cream Pound Cake

Bake at 350° for 1 hour

1 cup margarine, softened
½ cup shortening
3 cups sugar
6 eggs
3 cups flour
¼ teaspoon soda
¼ teaspoon salt
1 (8 ounce) carton sour cream
1 teaspoon vanilla
1 teaspoon orange extract
1 teaspoon butter flavoring
1 teaspoon lemon extract

Cream margarine, shortening and sugar together. Add eggs one at a time, blending well after each one. Add flour, soda and salt and beat thoroughly. Blend in sour cream and flavorings and mix well. Pour into a well greased and floured Bundt pan and bake at 350° for 1 hour. DO NOT PEEK FOR FIRST 30 MINUTES!

Mrs. Robert M. Morgan (Ladean)
Wife of the Adjutant General of Oklahoma

Truly Different Cupcakes

Bake at 325° for 35 minutes
Yields 18 cupcakes

4	squares semi-sweet chocolate
1	cup margarine
1½	cups chopped pecans
1¾	cups sugar
1	cup unsifted flour
4	large eggs
1	teaspoon vanilla

Melt chocolate in heavy saucepan. Add margarine and nuts and stir until margarine is melted and pecans are well coated. In large mixing bowl combine sugar, eggs, flour and vanilla. Mix *only* until blended. *Do not beat.* Add chocolate mixture and again mix carefully. Fill paper cups in muffin tins approximately ⅔'s full and bake for 35 minutes.

Mrs. Charles M. Kiefner (Marilyn)
Wife of the Adjutant General of Missouri

Frozen Lemon Custard Pie

Serves 6 to 8

3	eggs, separated
½	cup sugar
4	tablespoons lemon juice
1	(8 ounce) carton whipping cream, whipped
1	vanilla wafer crumb crust or one of your choice

Cook egg yolks and sugar in saucepan over medium heat, beating constantly, until thick and frothy. Remove from heat, stir in lemon juice and cool. Beat egg whites until stiff peaks form. Fold in stiffly beaten egg white and whipped cream. Spoon into crumb crust and freeze. Serve frozen, garnished with fresh strawberries. This can be served as a custard with a cookie accompaniment.

This is my husband's favorite dessert.

Mrs. T. Eston Marchant (Caroline)
Wife of the Adjutant General of
South Carolina

35

My Favorite Cookie

Bake at 350° for 10 to 12 minutes
Yields 18 dozen, small

2	sticks margarine, softened
1	cup sugar
1	cup brown sugar
2	eggs, well beaten
1	teaspoon soda
1	teaspoon salt
1	teaspoon vanilla extract
2	cups chopped pecans
4	cups flour

Cream margarine and sugar (both white and brown) in large mixing bowl. Add the beaten eggs, soda, salt and vanilla. Mix in pecans and flour until all is thoroughly mixed. Divide the dough into 6 parts and shape each on a piece of waxed paper. Shape each part on the waxed paper into a long roll, working the dough so that the roll will be round and compact. Store in the refrigerator until cold and firm. Slice in thin slices and cook on the waxed paper, that dough was rolled in, on a cookie sheet. Bake 10 to12 minutes or until light brown. Let cookies cool on waxed paper on a cooling rack. Will keep indefinitely in cookie jar but are better fresh from the oven.

This recipe is from my Great-Aunt Jenny.

Mrs. Price Daniel (Jean)
Wife of former Governor of Texas,
1957-1963

Mrs. Jean Daniel is the great-great-granddaughter of General Sam Houston who served twice as President of The Republic of Texas, 1836-1838 and 1841-1844, and also as Governor of Texas, 1859-1861.

Pecan Tassies

Bake at 325° for 25 minutes

PASTRY
1½   cups flour
2   (3 ounce) packages cream
     cheese, softened
½   stick butter, softened

PECAN FILLING

2   eggs
4   tablespoons butter, melted
⅛   teaspoon salt
1½   cups brown sugar
2   teaspoons vanilla
1½   cups pecans, coarsely
     chopped

To prepare pastry, cut cream cheese and butter into small portions. Whip with mixer on medium speed until light and fluffy. Add flour in thirds and mix well after each third is added. Form 3 dozen small balls about 1-inch in size. Press into small muffin tins, bottoms and sides, to form a tart shape. To prepare filling, beat eggs lightly, add sugar, butter, vanilla and salt and beat well. Divide pecans in half, fill pastry cup with half. Fill cups with egg mixture and top with remaining half of pecans. Bake at 325° for 25 minutes. Cool and remove from pans carefully. These may be frozen for a month in freezer.

Mrs. William P. Clements, Jr. (Rita)
Wife of former Governor of Texas,
1979 to 1983

Peach Cobbler

Bake at 300° for 20 to 30 minutes
Serves 6

1   (29 ounce) can sliced
     peaches, drained
2   cups sugar
1   stick butter, softened
2   eggs
¾   cup flour

Pour drained peaches into square baking dish. Pour 1 cup of sugar over peaches. Cream butter and remaining 1 cup sugar; add eggs and beat well. Add flour and mix thoroughly. Spread batter over peaches. Bake for 20 to 30 minutes.

Mrs. William A. Hornsby (Betty)
Wife of the Adjutant General of Alabama

Avocado Pie

Serves 6 to 8

2½   very ripe avocados
1   (13 ounce) can sweetened condensed milk
½   cup bottled lemon juice
1   (9-inch) graham cracker crumb pie crust
Whipped cream
Garnishes of almonds or slivered chocolate

Peel, seed and cut up avocados into blender. Add condensed milk and lemon juice and mix until smooth. Pour into crust. Decorate with whipped cream and garnish with slivered almonds and/or shaved chocolate. Refrigerate.

This pie is rich and delicious but very perishable.

Mrs. Willard A. Shank (Elizabeth)
Wife of the Adjutant General of California

Kentucky Racetrack Pie

Bake at 350° for 40 to 50 minutes

¼   cup butter or margarine, softened
1   cup sugar
3   eggs, beaten
¾   cup light corn syrup
¼   teaspoon salt
1   teaspoon vanilla
¾   cup chocolate chips
3   tablespoons bourbon (Kentucky)
½   cup chopped pecans
1   9-inch pie shell, unbaked

In large mixing bowl, cream butter and sugar. Add eggs, syrup, salt and vanilla. Mix well. Stir in chocolate chips, bourbon and pecans. Pour into unbaked pie shell. Bake for 40 to 50 minutes.

Mrs. Billy G. Wellman (Betty)
Wife of the Adjutant General of Kentucky

"Linn County" Chocolate Pie

3	tablespoons butter, softened
1	cup sugar
¼	cup flour
2	egg yolks, well beaten
1¼	cups milk
2	squares semi-sweet chocolate
1	teaspoon vanilla
1	9-inch pie shell, baked
1	(8 ounce) carton whipping cream, whipped

Grated chocolate

Cream butter and sugar thoroughly. Gradually add flour, beating well. Slowly add egg yolks, milk and broken pieces of chocolate. Cook mixture in double boiler until thick, stirring frequently. Add vanilla and beat well. Pour into baked pie shell. Top with whipped cream and grated chocolate.

My mother has made this pie since I was a child growing up in Linn County. Mine never was so good until I found the secret—she beats the very "puddin" out of it before she fills the pie shell!

Mrs. Richard A. Miller (Maryann)
Wife of the Adjutant General of Oregon

French Strawberry Glazed Pie

Serves 8

1	quart strawberries
1	cup water
1	cup sugar
3	tablespoons cornstarch
1	(8 ounce) carton whipping cream, whipped
1	9-inch pie shell, baked

Simmer 1 cup strawberries and ⅔ cup water for 3 minutes. Blend in sugar, cornstarch and ⅓ cup water. Boil 1 minute, stirring constantly. Cool well. Put 2½ cups strawberries in pie shell. Cover with glaze, making sure edges are sealed. Whip cream, sweeten to taste, and spread over top.

Try it—you'll love it!

Mrs. John G. Castles (Towlesey)
Wife of the Adjutant General of Virginia

Provo Ice Cream

Serves 12

1½   cups boiling water
1   small package flavored
     gelatin, any flavor you
     desire
2   cups sugar
3   cups crushed fruit, chilled,
     any kind except fresh
     pineapple
2   cups evaporated milk,
     chilled
2   cups milk, chilled
1   (8 ounce) carton whipping
     cream

Dissolve gelatin and sugar with boiling water in mixing bowl. Chill but do not let gelatin congeal. In gallon ice cream freezer, pour fruit and all of the milk. Add chilled gelatin mixture. Stir and freeze. Takes about 45 minutes in electric freezer.

Mrs. John L. Matthews (Darlene)
Wife of the Adjutant General of Utah

Apricot Delight

Serves 6 to 8

1   (8 ounce) package dried
     apricots
⅔   cup water
⅓   cup sugar
1½   tablespoons orange juice
½   teaspoon brandy extract
1   (8 ounce) carton whipping
     cream, whipped

Combine apricots, water and sugar in a small saucepan. Bring to a boil, lower heat and simmer about 10 to 12 minutes. Pureé in blender. Stir in juice and brandy extract. Cool. Whip cream until stiff peaks form and fold in apricot mixture. Chill. If desired, garnish with uncooked apricot for each serving.

Mrs. Francis R. Gerard (Yolanda)
Wife of the Adjutant General of
New Jersey

Trifle au Poire

Serves 8

1	(29 ounce) can pear halves, drained
1	cup almond slivers
1	(4¾ ounce) package regular vanilla pudding (not instant)
1	Sara Lee Butter Pound Cake
¼	cup cointreau or Triple Sec liquor, or to taste
1	(8 ounce) carton whipping cream, whipped

8" diameter heavy crystal
    trifle bowl

Drain pear halves, slice and set aside. Save juice for something else. Toast almonds on cookie sheet at 350° until lightly browned. Cook pudding according to directions on package and refrigerate. Slice cake into ¾-inch slices and line bottom of trifle bowl. Sprinkle with ½ the liquor. Layer with pear slices, ½ the custard and ⅓ of the almond slivers. Repeat layers and cover with plastic wrap to keep film from forming and chill several hours in refrigerator. One hour before serving, whip cream with a teaspoonful of sugar added and pipe on top of trifle. Sprinkle with last ⅓ of almond slivers.

This is an original recipe . . . hope you enjoy it.

Mrs. Robert H. Neitz (Laura)
Wife of the Adjutant General of Guam

Persimmon Pudding

Serves 6 to 8

2	cups persimmon pulp
¼	cup sugar
1	packet graham crackers, crushed but not too fine
2 to 3 cups cut marshmallows (large ones cut are best)
1	cup chopped nuts

Whipped cream

Combine pulp and sugar, stir in graham cracker crumbs. This mixture should be stiff. Add marshmallows and nuts. Place in a 2-quart dish. Refrigerate, then serve with whipped cream.

The longer this sets, the better it is!

Mrs. Alfred F. Ahner (Betty)
Wife of the Adjutant General of Indiana

Raspberry Time Squares

Bake at 350° for 25 minutes

1	egg
1	tablespoon milk
1	cup flour
½	cup butter or margarine, softened
1	teaspoon baking powder
¾	cup raspberry jam
1	egg
1	teaspoon vanilla
1	cup sugar
1½	cups coconut
¼	cup butter or margarine, melted

Beat 1 egg and milk. Add flour, ½ cup softened butter and baking powder and mix well. Spread in greased 8 or 9-inch baking pan. Spread raspberry jam over the crust mixture. Set aside. Mix 1 egg, vanilla and sugar together; add coconut and melted butter. Spread this mixture over jam. Bake at 350° until lightly browned, about 25 minutes. Cut into squares.

Mrs. Vito Castellano (Lynda)
Wife of the Adjutant General of New York

Chocolate Bavarian Cream

2	squares unsweetened chocolate
1	cup milk
⅓	cup sugar
1	envelope gelatin
¼	cup water
1	teaspoon vanilla
1	(8 ounce) carton whipping cream, whipped

In saucepan melt chocolate squares, stir in sugar and milk and heat. Do Not Boil. Remove from heat. Soften gelatin in water and add to heated chocolate mixture. Place over ice until slightly thickened, stirring occasionally. Add vanilla. Fold in whipped cream. Serve in large bowl or individual serving dishes. Garnish as desired.

Mrs. Josh Morriss, Sr. (Mabel)
Former wife of Beauford Jester
(deceased)
Governor of Texas, 1947-1949

Rum Bavarian

Serves 8

1½	tablespoons gelatin
¼	cup cold water
¼	cup boiling water
½	cup sugar
⅓	cup rum
4	tablespoons bourbon
2	egg whites
2	(8 ounce) cartons whipping cream, whipped

GARNISH

1	(8 ounce) carton whipping cream, whipped
¼	cup sugar
1	tablespoon vanilla
¼	cup rum
½	cup finely slivered almonds
Grated nutmeg	

Soak the gelatin in cold water for 5 minutes. Dissolve in the boiling water and stir until completely clear. Stir in ½ cup sugar, rum and bourbon. Continue to stir until sugar is dissolved. Strain and cool. When mixture begins to thicken, beat with a wire whisk or rotary beater until frothy. Beat 2 egg whites until stiff and fold into gelatin mixture. Beat 2 cups of the whipping cream until stiff peaks form. Add cream to the mixture, 2 tablespoons at a time, blending each addition thoroughly. Pour into a rinsed, well chilled mold or individual dessert glasses. Refrigerate at least 4 hours. When ready to serve, unmold and garnish with 1 cup whipping cream beaten until stiff peaks form, sweetened with ¼ cup sugar and the vanilla and rum. Sprinkle with almonds and dust with nutmeg.

Mrs. Ronald F. Williamson (Betsi)
Wife of the Adjutant General of
South Dakota

Apple Cider Punch

Serves 20 to 25

4	cups apple cider
2	cups cranberry juice
1	cup orange juice
1	(12 ounce) can apricot nectar
1	cup sugar
2	sticks cinnamon

Mix together in large pan and simmer for 20 minutes. Remove cinnamon sticks and pour into punch bowl. Decorate punch by floating orange slices studded with cloves.

Mrs. W. David Counts (Mary)
Knox City

Banana Punch

6	cups water
3	cups sugar
5	bananas (3 cans banana baby food may be substituted)
1	(12 ounce) can frozen orange juice
1	(46 ounce) can pineapple juice

Juice of 2 lemons

4	(28 or 32 ounce) bottles of ginger ale

Heat water and sugar until dissolved. Blend bananas in blender. Combine bananas, orange juice, pineapple juice and lemon juice and add sugar water. Cool and freeze 4 hours before serving. Remove from freezer and thaw until mushy. Place in punch bowl and pour in ginger ale. Punch should be like slush. Punch concentrate - before adding ginger ale - makes a little over a gallon and may be kept in freezer for months.

Mrs. Curtiss R. Waggoner (Sheila)
Austin

"Border" Buttermilk

1	(6 ounce) can frozen pink lemonade, undiluted
1	(6 ounce) can rum or tequila

Blender of ice

Mix in blender and sip SLOWLY.

David L. Tumlinson
Brownsville

Our friends at the Brownsville Chamber of Commerce are famous for hosting many receptions with this drink to introduce visitors to the "border".

Big Red Holiday Punch

Serves 18 to 20

1 (12 ounce) can frozen lemonade
4 (12 ounce) cans water
1 (10 to 15 ounce) carton frozen sliced sweetened strawberries
Red food coloring
1 quart Big Red soda pop

Mix together lemonade, water, strawberries and add a few drops of red food coloring. Chill. Pour into punch bowl. When ready to serve, add 1 chilled quart bottle of Big Red soda pop.

To keep punch icy cold and flavorful, pour Big Red into ice cube trays and add Big Red cubes to your Holiday Punch.

Mrs. Harold Loftis (Billie)
Austin

Christmas Wassail

Serves 20

2 quarts sweet apple cider
2 cups orange juice
1 cup pineapple juice
1 tablespoon whole cloves (tied in a bag)
½ cup pure honey
½ cup fresh lemon juice
1 stick whole cinnamon

Mix all ingredients and heat to boiling point. Simmer slowly for 20 minutes. Remove cloves and cinnamon stick. Serve in mugs. You may freeze any left over. Add sugar, if needed, for a sweeter drink.

Perk Punch

2¼ cups pineapple-grapefruit juice
1¾ cup water
2 cups cranberry juice
¼ teaspoon salt
½ cup light brown sugar
1 tablespoon whole cloves
3 cinnamon sticks
½ teaspoon whole allspice

In bottom of 8 cup percolator put pineapple-grapefruit juice, water, cranberry juice, salt and brown sugar. In basket of percolator put cloves, cinnamon and allspice. Then perk as you would coffee. Remove basket and serve.

Mrs. Walter J. Dingler (Gayle)
Austin

45

Party Punch

Serves 35 (4 ounce cups)

1   (6 ounce) can frozen
    orange juice
1   (6 ounce) can frozen
    lemonade
1   (6 ounce) can frozen
    limeade
1   (46 ounce) can pineapple
    juice
1   pint cranberry juice
2   quarts ginger ale
1   quart cool water
1   quart sparkling water
Crushed ice

Mix all ingredients and pour into punch bowl. Serve.

Mrs. Bobby Ingram (Dorothy)
Smithville

Southern Coffee Punch

Serves 15 to 18

2   quarts strong cold coffee
1   pint cold milk (or Half and
    Half)
2   teaspoons Kahlúa
½   cup sugar
1   quart coffee ice cream,
    softened
½   pint whipping cream,
    whipped

Combine cold coffee, milk, Kahlúa and sugar in large bowl. Stir until sugar is dissolved. Chill thoroughly. To serve, pour mixture over dips of ice cream in punch bowl. Top with mounds of whipped cream. Sprinkle lightly with nutmeg.

Variations: For mocha punch, substitute chocolate ice cream, vanilla and sprinkle with cinnamon instead of nutmeg.

I never have leftovers when I serve this punch!

Mrs. L. James Starr, Jr. (Jo Ann)
Austin

Special Shower Punch

3	cups sugar
3	cups water
2	small packages flavored gelatin (1 peach and 1 apricot is good)
1	(12 ounce) can frozen lemonade
1	(46 ounce) can pineapple juice
1	(1 ounce) bottle almond extract
3	quarts ginger ale, chilled

Bring sugar and water to a boil and stir to dissolve sugar; remove from heat and add Jello. Stir until Jello is dissolved. Add lemonade, pineapple juice and almond extract. Mix and refrigerate to cool. Just before serving, pour into punch bowl and add chilled ginger ale and ice.

Make an ice ring using ginger ale and maraschino cherries—it looks so special and will not dilute the punch.

Cookbook Committee

Champagne Sherbet Punch

Serves 50

2	cups reconstituted lemon juice
1	(46 ounce) can pineapple juice
3	quarts club soda
3	gallons lime sherbet, softened
6	quarts dry champagne

Mix lemon juice and pineapple juice in punch bowl. Add soda and sherbet and stir gently. Pour in champagne when ready to serve.

Brunch Punch

Serves 15

1	quart coffee (ready to serve)
½	gallon coffee ice cream, softened
½	cup rum
	Whipped cream (if desired)

In punch bowl, mix coffee, ice cream and rum and blend. If whipped cream is desired, place dollops of cream on top of punch.

Mrs. R. V. Miller (Dick)
Austin

47

Promotion Punch

Serves 20

2   **liters champagne**
2   **quarts ginger ale**
1   **liter white wine**

Chill and just before serving; combine all ingredients. Mix. Float a large chunk of dry ice in the bowl to keep punch chilled — or make your own special ice ring.

Recommended for any promotion party — from private to general!

Mrs. Jack T. Martin (Shirley)
Beaumont

Daiquiri

2   **(6 ounce) cans frozen limeade**
1   **(6 ounce) can frozen pink lemonade**
7   **(6 ounce) cans water**
½   **cup grenadine syrup**
3   **(6 ounce) cans light rum (using lemonade can to measure)**

Mix together and let freeze for a day. Stir occasionally until ready to serve.

Frozen Piña Colada

Serves 2

1   **pint pineapple sherbet, softened**
3   **tablespoons pineapple juice**
4   **tablespoons orange juice**
3   **tablespoons Coco Lopez Cream of Coconut**
4   **tablespoons rum**
4   **tablespoons vodka**

Combine all ingredients in blender. Blend until mixture is smooth and sherbet blended. Garnish each glass with pineapple wedge and maraschino cherry.

Mrs. Mike Beal (Sherilyn)
Plano

After Dinner Dessert Drink

Serves 8 to 10

1	shot glass (1½ ounce) Cointreau
1	shot glass Benedictine
4	shot glasses Kahlúa
2	dips vanilla ice cream, per person
3 to 4	handfuls broken vanilla wafers

Mix together and serve in champagne or wine glass.

John D. Mahaffey
Springfield, Missouri

Apricot Brandy

1½	pounds dried apricots
1¾	cups sugar
1	quart vodka

Place, but do not mix, ingredients in a ½-gallon, flat topped, glass jar. Jar must be washed and sterilized. Turn the jar twice a day (allowing jar to set on its top for half the day) for 8 days and your first batch is ready. You may use the same apricots (more sugar and vodka) to make the second batch. Let the second batch set 12 to 14 days. Then bottle.

Jewell D. Luersen
Austin

Slush

1	(12 ounce) can frozen lemonade
1	(12 ounce) can frozen orange juice
¾	cup sugar
1	cup strong tea
3½	cups water
1½	cups vodka
	7-Up

Combine all ingredients, except 7-Up and pour into airtight container and allow to freeze. It will not freeze solid, but will be slushy. Scoop about ½ cup of Slush into an old fashioned glass and add 7-Up. Stir.

This is a mild drink and especially nice to keep on hand around the holidays.

Mrs. Don Fiero (Pat)
Leander

49

Kahlúa

2	cups water
4	cups sugar
1	(2 ounce) jar instant coffee
1	split vanilla bean
20	ounces brandy (cheapest you can find)

Pour water in large pot, add sugar and bring to a slight boil and add instant coffee; stir until dissolved. Cool slightly, pour into a 1½ gallon sterilized bottle. Add vanilla bean and brandy. Place bottle into a large brown paper bag and put into a dark place for 30 days before serving.

Jewell D. Luersen
Austin

Wine and Food

Which Wine to Serve—There is no strict code of rules for which wine goes with what food. There are those who prefer to drink a white wine or Rosé with everything; others who customarily serve white wine with white meat, red wine with red meat, and Rosé for everything else. Certain time-honored pairings, however, that have evolved over the years indicate specific wines bring out the best with a particular dish. In general, beef and lamb dishes that are spicy are complimented by a hearty red wine, while a delicate white wine should be served with lightly flavored poultry and seafood. Rosés are extremely versatile and may be served with a wide variety of foods. There are so many excellent wines available, both domestic and imported, so experiment and discover your own secret to success.

Chilling Wine

Type	Serving and Storage Temperatures
Red	60-70 degrees
Rosé	45-50 degrees
White	45-50 degrees
Sparkling	40-45 degrees
Dessert	60-70 degrees

Storing Wine—Corked bottles should be stored on their sides so that the cork will stay moist and firmly in place to keep air out of the wine. Extreme heat, vibration and direct sunlight can also be injurious to wine. The ideal temperature for storing is a constant one between 50 and 60 degrees. Once opened, table wines will keep for several days if tightly closed and refrigerated.

Mustang Grape Wine

3   (¼ ounce) packages dry
        yeast
2   cups warm distilled water
2   gallons mustang grape
        juice
10   pounds sugar
1½   gallons distilled water
5-gallon container
4   feet of ¼-inch flexible
        plastic tubing

Dissolve yeast in 2 cups warm distilled water. Pour into 5-gallon container (distilled water jug works best) the dissolved yeast mixture, grape juice, sugar and 1½ gallons distilled water. It is very important to leave sufficient space in the jug to allow the wine to expand and "work" - approximately space for one additional gallon. Place a 4-foot length of ¼-inch flexible plastic tubing into the jug above the liquid. Allow the other end of the tubing to run into a 1-gallon container filled ⅓ full with water. This will allow for gas to escape and any liquid to run off caused by the wine while it is working. Seal the top of the 5-gallon jug as tightly as possible to keep air out of the wine. This can be accomplished with a piece of plastic, rubber bands and plastic tape. Place jug in a cool place—temperature between 65° and 80°—and allow wine to work approximately 3 weeks. Now, wine is ready to be bottled. Plastic tubing can be used to syphon the wine into wine bottles. Do not syphon liquid below the bottom 2 inches of the jug. Enjoy!

Richard E. Harrison
Austin

Margaritas

1   (6 ounce) can frozen lime
        juice
1   juice can tequila
½   juice can (3 ounce) triple
        sec (orange liqueur)

Put ingredients in blender and fill blender with ice; blend till slushy. Serve in salt rimmed glasses.

Mrs. Harold Blackshear (Marilyn)
San Antonio

Whiskey Sour

1   (12 ounce) can frozen
        orange juice
1   (12 ounce) can frozen
        lemonade
1   quart 7-Up
3   (12 ounce) cans water
1½ to 2 (12 ounce) cans
        whiskey (using lemon-
        ade can to measure)

Mix well. Keep in freezer. Serve at slush consistency.

Almond Tea

Serves 15 to 20

2½   cups sugar
6   cups water
½   cup lemon juice
1½   teaspoons almond extract
1½   teaspoons vanilla extract
3   cups strong tea
½   cup Tang (orange instant
        breakfast drink mix)
3   cups water
1   (46 ounce) can pineapple
        juice

Simmer sugar, water and lemon juice for 5 minutes, then cool. Add the remaining ingredients. Serve hot or cold.

This is a favorite of my 5-year old daughter and my 86-year old grandma!

Mrs. Billy B. Pope (Vanessa)
Greenville

Egg Nog

6   eggs, separated
1   cup sugar
1   (8 ounce) carton whipping
        cream
Milk
Nutmeg

Beat egg whites until stiff peaks form. Set aside. In another bowl, beat egg yolks, sugar and whipping cream until light and fluffy. Fold in stiffly beaten egg whites and add milk until consistency you desire. Chill. Pour into cups and sprinkle with nutmeg.

Mrs. Roy Hamor (Laverne)
Austin

Hot Buttered Rum Mix

1   **pound butter, softened**
1   **(16 ounce) package light brown sugar**
1   **(16 ounce) package powdered sugar**
2   **teaspoons nutmeg**
2   **teaspoons cinnamon**
1   **quart of quality vanilla ice cream, softened but not melted**

Soften butter and mix in dry ingredients, then add softened ice cream. Mix. Place in freezer container. For one drink, place one tablespoon of mix in mug. Add 1½ ounces rum and fill mug with hot water. Mixture can be kept in freezer as it does not get rock hard and can be spooned out as needed.

Mrs. Jack Fisher (Alyne)
Austin

Spiced Tea Mix

Yields 3 pints of mix

1   **(1 pound, 11 ounce) jar Tang (orange drink mix)**
2   **(3 ounce) packages sweetened lemonade mix**
1   **cup instant tea**
1   **cup sugar**
½   **teaspoon ground cloves**
½   **teaspoon cinnamon**

Mix all ingredients thoroughly and store in an airtight container. To prepare tea, use 2 or 3 heaping teaspoons in a cup of boiling water.

For a change, add 1 heaping teaspoon mix to 1 cup hot apple cider....delicious!!!

Mrs. Les Gallatin (Kathy)
Austin

Hot Chocolate Mix

2   **pound box Nestle's Quik chocolate**
1   **(8 quart) package powdered milk**
2   **cups sugar**
1   **teaspoon salt**
1   **large bottle of Pream or Coffeemate**

Combine all ingredients and store in airtight container. As needed, place ⅓ cup or 2 tablespoons per cup of hot water.

Mrs. Harold Loftis (Billie)
Austin

Blue Cheese Cake

Bake at 300° for 60 to 70 minutes
Serves a large party

2   (8 ounce) packages cream
      cheese, softened
8   ounces blue or Roquefort
      cheese, crumbled
2½   cups sour cream (divide
      into 1 and 1½ cups)
⅛   teaspoon white pepper
3   eggs
½   cup finely chopped pecans
¼   cup minced green onions
Red Bell peppers or whole
      pimientos
Green onion tops

In large bowl of electric mixer, beat the 3 cheeses together until light and fluffy, about 5 minutes. Mix in 1 cup of the sour cream and add pepper. Add eggs, one at a time, beating well after each addition. Stir in pecans and minced onion until well combined. Pour mixture into buttered 9-inch springform pan. Bake at 300° for 60 to 70 minutes, until knife inserted in center comes out clean. Remove from oven and let stand 5 minutes. Spread remaining 1½ cups sour cream over top and return to oven 10 minutes. Cool completely on wire rack and refrigerate at least 3 hours or overnight. Remove sides of springform pan and place cake and bottom of pan on serving platter. Decorate top with flowers cut from red Bell peppers or pimientos and stems of flowers made from green onion tops. Serve with crackers or rye bread.

Mexican Dip

4   large tomatoes
8 to 10 green onions
1   (8 ounce) can chopped
      green chilies
1   (8 ounce) can chopped
      ripe olives
2   tablespoons olive oil
2   tablespoons salad vinegar
⅛   teaspoon garlic salt

Chop tomatoes into very small pieces. Chop green onions including the tops. Stir in remaining ingredients. Chill and serve with tortilla chips.

This is a good appetizer before barbecue or Mexican food.

Mrs. Don Fiero (Pat)
Leander

Cheese Krispies

Bake at 350° for 15 minutes
Yields 5 to 6 dozen

2 sticks margarine, softened
10 ounces grated sharp
cheese
2 cups flour
¼ teaspoon cayenne pepper
¼ teaspoon salt
2 cups Rice Krispies

Mix together margarine and cheese. Sift flour, cayenne pepper and salt; add to cheese mixture. Add Rice Krispies and mix. Roll into small balls and press flat with a fork. Bake at 350° for 15 minutes or until done.

Mrs. J. Travis Blakeslee (Gladys)
Austin

Parmesan Cheese Rounds

⅓ cup grated Parmesan
cheese, canned or
fresh
¾ cup mayonnaise
½ cup chopped onion
⅛ teaspoon Worcestershire
sauce
Salt
Pepper
2 packages rye rounds or
1 loaf rye, white or
whole wheat bread

Combine Parmesan cheese, mayonnaise, onions, Worcestershire sauce, salt and pepper, and mix well. Spread on bread and broil until golden brown and puffy. If loaf bread is used, remove crusts and cut into four squares.

Quick fixings for unexpected guests!

Mrs. Robert Hefford (Valerie)
Austin

Chili Bean Dip

1 (15 ounce) can chili with
beans
1 (10 ounce) package frozen
Welsh Rarebit
1 teaspoon Worcestershire
Several drops Tabasco
¼ teaspoon garlic powder

Pour chili into skillet and mash beans with fork. Add remaining ingredients. Cook and stir until blended and heated thoroughly. Serve hot with corn chips.

Mrs. Henry Fouts (Gladis)
Austin

Cheese Puffs

Bake at 350° for 15 minutes

3   loaves Pepperidge Farm sandwich bread
1   pound margarine
4   jars Kraft Old English Cheese Spread, room temperature
1½   teaspoons Worcestershire sauce
1   teaspoon Tabasco sauce
1   teaspoon onion powder
⅛   teaspoon cayenne pepper
Dill weed seed

Cut off crusts of 2½ loaves bread, 3 slices at a time. Mix together with electric hand mixer margarine, cheese spread, Worcestershire, Tabasco, onion powder and cayenne pepper. Beat until consistency of icing. Spread mixture between 3 slices of bread. Stack the 3 slices of bread and cut into quarters. Spread each square with "icing" over top and sides; each square will be 3 slices thick. Freeze on cookie sheet; when frozen place in plastic bag for convenience. *Do not thaw* before baking. Bake at 350° for 15 minutes. Serve warm.

Tamale Tidbits

Bake at 350° for 20 minutes
Yields 90

2   cups crumbled cornbread
1   (10 ounce) can mild enchilada sauce
½   teaspoon salt
1½   pounds ground beef (uncooked)
1   (8 ounce) can tomato sauce
½   cup (2 ounces) grated Monterey Jack cheese

Combine cornbread crumbs, ½ cup enchilada sauce and salt. Add ground beef and mix well. Shape into 1-inch balls. Place in shallow baking pan. Bake uncovered at 350° for 18 to 20 minutes or until done. Meanwhile, in small saucepan, heat together tomato sauce and the remaining enchilada sauce. After meatballs have cooked, place them in chafing dish and pour sauce on top; sprinkle with grated cheese. Keep warm over low heat and serve with wooden picks.

Mrs. J. Travis Blakeslee (Gladys)
Austin

Fried Cheese

8	ounces baby Swiss cheese, grated
8	ounces Cheddar cheese, grated
8	ounces cream cheese, softened

Pecans, finely chopped
2 to 3	teaspoons milk
2	large eggs, beaten
4	tablespoons cornmeal
2	cups flour

Black pepper
Garlic powder
Oregano
Vegetable oil

Thoroughly mix the 3 cheeses. Roll into 1½-inch balls. Roll each ball in chopped pecans and place balls in the freezer for 10 minutes while getting the other ingredients ready. Combine milk and eggs; beat well and set aside. Combine cornmeal, flour and black pepper, garlic powder and oregano to taste. Mix well. Dip cheese balls in egg mixture and then in dry mixture; then dip again in egg mixture and in dry mixture. Fry in hot vegetable oil until brown.

South-of-the-Border Dip

Bake at 350° for 15 to 20 minutes

1	(8 ounce) package cream cheese, softened
1	large can Frito jalapeño bean dip
20	drops Tabasco
1	(8 ounce) carton sour cream
½	package taco seasoning
½	cup sliced green onions
1½	cups grated Monterey Jack and Cheddar cheese, combined

Mix together cream cheese, bean dip, Tabasco, sour cream, taco seasoning and green onions. Bake at 350° for 15 to 20 minutes. Add grated cheese the last 5 or 6 minutes of baking time. Serve warm with corn chips. Dip may need stirring as it sets.

Mrs. John Bottoms (Diane)
Austin

The Mexican influence continues to contribute significantly to the taste of everyday life in Texas—especially to the diet. Tacos, tamales, enchiladas and chile are all common. In turn, the Mexican-Texan owes much to the first inhabitants of the land—the Indian tribes who cultivated the corn which is the basis for much "Tex-Mex" food and who also gave Texas its name and its motto.

Hot Cheese Ball

Serves 20

2 pounds Velveeta cheese, softened
1 (3 ounce) package cream cheese, softened
2 tablespoons parsley flakes
2 tablespoons garlic powder
2 tablespoons cayenne pepper
1 (8 ounce) can chopped ripe olives
1 cup chopped nuts
3 jalapeño peppers, chopped (optional)
Chili powder
Paprika

After both cheeses set at room temperature, mix with parsley flakes, garlic powder, cayenne, olives and nuts. Roll into two large balls or four logs. Roll in mixture of chili powder and paprika or chili powder and cayenne. Cover with plastic wrap and refrigerate for several hours. Cheese balls will keep in refrigerator for about two months.

Mrs. Clyde Phillips (Betty)
Dallas

Texas Cannon Balls

Bake at 350°

1 (1 pound) package Smokets
1 jar Old English cheese spread
½ cup margarine
¼ teaspoon Tabasco
1 cup minus 2 tablespoons flour

Cut each sausage into 6 or 8 pieces. Cook slightly in skillet. Drain on paper towel. Blend remaining ingredients together with pastry blender. Pinch off enough dough to wrap around each piece of sausage. Bake at 350° until golden brown.

These can be frozen before baking by placing them on a cookie sheet in the freezer until sausage-cheese balls are firm; then store in freezer bags for future use.

Variation - Substitute stuffed or ripe olives instead of Smokets.

Mrs. James C. Ragan (Joyce)
Round Rock

Olive-Cheese Puffs

Bake at 400° for 10 to 15 minutes
Yields 24

1	cup sharp Cheddar cheese, grated
3	tablespoons butter
½	cup flour
⅛	teaspoon salt
½	teaspoon paprika
24	stuffed olives

Blend cheese and butter. Stir in flour, salt and paprika and mix well. Wrap 1 teaspoon of cheese dough around each olive. Place on ungreased cookie sheet and bake at 400° for 10 to 15 minutes until lightly browned. Serve warm.

Olive-cheese puffs can be frozen before cooking.

Mrs. John Muegge (Marjie)
Austin

Italian Chicken Livers

Serves 10

Olive oil
1	pound chicken livers
1	(16 ounce) can stewed tomatoes
1½	tablespoons ground oregano
1	teaspoon garlic powder
½	teaspoon salt
½	teaspoon pepper
1	loaf crusty French or Italian bread cut into bite-size servings

Cover bottom of skillet with olive oil and heat. Rinse livers in cold running water until water is clear. Sauté livers until they blanch or begin to turn light and are firm. Stir in tomatoes and all seasonings. Simmer 1 hour until most of liquid is absorbed. If livers do not cook into tiny pieces, stir or chop so that they are very small pieces. Serve in chafing dish surrounded by small pieces of crusty bread. Place a spreader in chafing dish so that liver can be spread on bread.

Very Italian! "I can't believe it's chicken liver."

Mrs. L. James Starr, Jr. (Jo Ann)
Austin

Pineapple-Cheese Balls

2   (8 ounce) packages cream
    cheese, softened
1   (8 ounce) can crushed
    pineapple, drained well
½   cup chopped Bell pepper
4   tablespoons chopped
    onion
1   teaspoon seasoned salt
2   cups chopped nuts

Combine cream cheese and drained crushed pineapple. Mix well. Add chopped Bell pepper, onion and seasoned salt. Form mixture into one large cheese ball or into bite-size balls. Roll balls in chopped nuts. Cover in foil and chill 2 to 3 hours before using.

Mrs. O. B. "Jack" Franks (Opal)
Austin

Mrs. James T. Dennis (Mavis)
Bedford

Artichoke Dip

Yields 1 cup

1   (15 ounce) can artichoke
    hearts, drained
⅓   cup mayonnaise
1   tablespoon chopped onion
Juice of ½ medium lemon
3 or 4 slices bacon, cooked
    crisp and chopped
⅛   teaspoon salt
⅛   teaspoon pepper
Tabasco

Chop artichoke hearts. Add mayonnaise, chopped onion, lemon juice and bacon; mix well. Add salt, pepper and Tabasco to taste; chill. Serve with crackers, corn chips or raw vegetables for dipping.

Mrs. Allan Shivers (Marialice)
Austin

Corn Dip

2   (12 ounce) cans Mexicorn,
    drained
1   cup sour cream
1   cup mayonnaise
1   small onion, chopped
1   (10 ounce) package
    Cheddar cheese, grated
1   can green chilies, chopped
2   jalapeños, chopped
    (optional)

Combine all ingredients and mix well. Serve with tortilla chips.

Avocado Dip

Serves 8 to 10

2	small ripe avocados, peeled and cut up
1	medium tomato, peeled and cut up
½	cup sour cream
½	small onion
2	tablespoons chopped green chilies, drained
2	tablespoons lemon juice
½	teaspoon salt
1	tablespoon chopped chives (optional)

Place all ingredients in food processor and blend until smooth. Cover and chill at least 1 hour. Sprinkle with chives. Serve with raw vegetables or corn chips.

Mrs. Jerry Garlington (Melvia)
Plano

Chicken Curry Balls

Yields 6 dozen

1	(8 ounce) package cream cheese
¼	cup mayonnaise
2	cups cooked, chopped chicken
1½	cups chopped almonds
3	tablespoons chopped chutney
¼	teaspoon salt
2	teaspoons curry powder
Grated coconut	

Cream thoroughly cream cheese and mayonnaise. Stir in chicken, almonds, chutney, salt and curry powder. Chill. Shape in bite-size balls. Roll each ball in grated coconut. Cover and chill until ready to serve.

Mrs. Jack T. Martin (Shirley)
Beaumont

61

Broccoli Dip

Serves 8 to 10

1	(10 ounce) package frozen chopped broccoli
2	tablespoons butter
½	large onion, chopped
3	ribs celery, chopped
1	(8 ounce) roll garlic cheese
1	(10½ ounce) can cream of mushroom soup
1	(4 ounce) can mushrooms
⅛	teaspoon Tabasco
⅛	teaspoon cayenne pepper
⅛	teaspoon Worcestershire sauce

Cook broccoli according to package directions. Drain well. Melt butter and sauté chopped onions and celery. Combine all ingredients and cook over low heat to melt cheese and blend. Stir well. Serve in chafing dish with toasted bread.

Roberta Bell
Portland

Cueso Extraordinaire

Serves 15

2	pounds Velveeta cheese
1½	pounds lean ground beef
1	teaspoon garlic powder
1	teaspoon onion salt
½	teaspoon pepper
1	(8 ounce) can chopped green chilies
1	(10 ounce) can Old El Paso mild enchilada sauce

Melt cheese in double boiler. While cheese is melting, brown meat in skillet. Drain all grease from meat and add garlic, onion salt, pepper, green chilies and enchilada sauce. Mix thoroughly and simmer 15 minutes. Combine meat mixture with melted cheese. Stir. Serve hot with tortilla chips.

(Cheese can be melted in a crock pot. Use about 4 tablespoons milk with cheese to prevent it from scorching. After meat mixture has simmered, add to cheese in crock pot and serve from crock pot. Cueso Extraordinaire!)

Mrs. Royce Ivory (Sharyn)
Lubbock

Hot Crab Cheese Dip

Yields 2½ cups

1 (5 ounce) jar sharp American cheese
1 (8 ounce) package cream cheese
1 (7 ounce) can crab meat (drained and flaked)
¼ cup milk
½ teaspoon Worcestershire sauce
¼ teaspoon garlic salt
½ teaspoon cayenne pepper

Use a double boiler and in top portion combine American cheese and cream cheese; stir constantly until well blended. Add crab meat, milk, Worcestershire, garlic salt and cayenne. Heat until well blended. Pour into fondue pot or chafing dish to keep warm. If dip thickens during serving, add milk and stir well.

Regular crackers will become soggy when used for this dip.

Mrs. Arthur G. Coley (Susie)
San Antonio

Tex-Mex Layered Dip

2 large cans bean dip with jalapeños
1 cup sour cream
½ cup salad dressing
1 package taco seasoning mix
3 medium avocados
Juice of ½ medium lemon
⅛ teaspoon salt
⅛ teaspoon pepper
2 cups shredded lettuce
3 medium tomatoes, seeded and chopped
1 cup chopped green onions with tops
1 can ripe olives, pitted and sliced
1 cup grated Cheddar cheese

Spread bean dip on large platter. Blend sour cream, salad dressing and taco seasoning, and spread on top of bean dip. Mash peeled and seeded avocados with lemon juice, salt and pepper. Spread avocado mixture over sour cream layer. Place lettuce over the avocado layer and sprinkle with tomatoes, green onions and ripe olives. Cover with grated cheese. Chill well and serve with tortilla chips or crackers.

Mrs. Don Fiero (Pat)
Leander

APPETIZERS

63

Pico de Gallo

3	ripe avocados
2	tablespoons fresh cilantro, finely chopped
3	tablespoons finely chopped onion
1	cup diced tomatoes
½	teaspoon white pepper
1	tablespoon white vinegar
3	tablespoons olive oil

Juice of ½ lime

2	serrano peppers, finely chopped

Juice of 1 clove of fresh garlic, pressed

1	package tostados

Peel and chop the avocados into small chunks into a bowl. Add the remaining ingredients, except tostados, and toss gently to mix. Refrigerate to let the flavors blend. Serve with tostados.

Cocktail Meatballs

Serves 15

1	jar Del Monte chili sauce
1	(10 ounce) jar grape jelly
2	pounds lean ground beef

Mix chili sauce and grape jelly in saucepan. Bring to a boil. Make bite-size meatballs and drop into sauce—add enough meatballs to cover bottom of saucepan. After meatballs have cooked about 5 minutes, remove from sauce and add another batch to cover bottom of saucepan. Continue until all have been slightly cooked. Then place all meatballs back into pan and cook UNCOVERED for about 40 minutes at simmer.

This recipe can be doubled, tripled, etc., and frozen. Meatballs are even better after freezing and can be kept in freezer up to 6 months.

Mrs. Clyde Phillips (Betty)
Dallas

The Gonzales Flag

The Texans rallied quickly to support the defiance of the settlement of Gonzales to demands of its Mexican military commander for surrender of an old cannon which had been loaned long before for defense against marauding Indians. As the volunteer Texas Army grew, Cynthia Burns and Evaline DeWitt undertook to provide the troops with a flag. The flag was fashioned from a length of cotton cloth. Painted in black upon it was a picture of the old cannon. Above the cannon was painted a lone star and below, the lettering "Come and Take It." Thus, there appeared in the field the first battle ensign of the Texas Revolution.

BANNER OF THE TEXAS VOLUNTEER ARMY OF THE PEOPLE
The Gonzales Flag

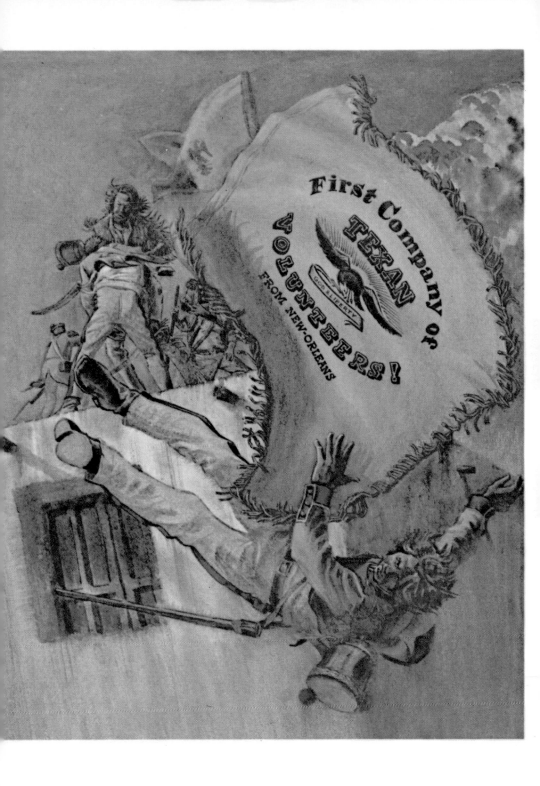

FLAG OF THE LOUISIANA VOLUNTEERS
The New Orleans Grey Flag

The Flag of the New Orleans Greys

As early as October 1835, Adolphus Sterne and the people of New Orleans were enthusiastically supporting the Texan cause. Two companies of volunteers were raised and departed for Texas. One company, called the First, under Captain T. H. Breece, traveled by land and the other moved by sea. "The First Company of Texan Volunteers from New Orleans" was met by a delegation of ladies of East Texas who had made a flag of blue silk with an eagle design and lettering identifying the company. The flag flew at the Siege of Bexar. Although most members of the company joined the ill-fated Matamoros Expedition, the flag remained in San Antonio to fly over the battlements of the Alamo until it was torn down by the victorious Mexican troops and sent to Mexico City. It is displayed in the Castle of Chapultepec there.

Rotel Beef Dip

Serves 8 to 10

2　(8 ounce) packages cream
　　cheese
1　(10 ounce) can Rotel
　　tomatoes with green
　　chilies, chopped
1　(2½ ounce) jar dried beef,
　　chopped
¼　cup minced onion
　　(optional)

Blend all ingredients together until smooth. Chill and serve with tortilla chips.

Mrs. Leonard Illtis (Gerri)
Elgin

Tweedle Dum Dip

Yields 1⅔ cups

½　pound Velveeta cheese
2　tablespoons milk
½　cup sour cream
2　tablespoons finely
　　chopped Bell pepper
1　tablespoon finely chopped
　　onion
1　tablespoon chopped
　　pimiento

Over low heat blend cheese and milk and stir until smooth. Add remaining ingredients and mix well. Heat thoroughly and serve warm. Fresh vegetables are good with this dip.

Mrs. George Bowers (Jonnie)
Austin

Caviar Pie

6　hard-boiled eggs
1½　tablespoons mayonnaise
1　cup sour cream
1½　teaspoons grated onion
Salt
White pepper
1　(2 ounce) jar caviar
Parsley

Finely grate eggs and mix with mayonnaise, sour cream, grated onion and salt and pepper to taste. Mound on serving platter. Cover top with caviar and garnish around base of mound with parsley. Serve with toast rounds or crackers.

Mrs. Crawford Martin (Margaret)
Austin

Sausage Dip

1	pound ground beef
1	pound sausage
2	pounds Velveeta cheese
1	medium onion, chopped
1	(10 ounce) can Rotel tomatoes
1	(10½ ounce) can mushroom soup
2	chili peppers or jalapeño peppers
1	teaspoon garlic powder

Cook ground beef and sausage and drain well. Use a double boiler and in top portion melt cheese. Add beef and sausage and stir well. Add chopped onion, Rotel tomatoes, mushroom soup, peppers and garlic powder. Blend well. Serve hot.

Mrs. Leonard Tallas (Jean)
Austin

Sherry-Crab Dip

½	cup butter
¼	cup chopped green onions
¼	cup chopped parsley
2	tablespoons flour
1	cup evaporated milk
4 to 5 ounces grated Swiss cheese	
2	cans claw crab meat
2	tablespoons cooking sherry
Cayenne pepper	

Melt butter and sauté onions and parsley. Add flour and blend well. Stir in milk and add cheese, cooking until melted (stir constantly). Add crab meat and sherry. Season with cayenne pepper to taste. Serve in a chafing dish with crackers.

Mrs. Ron Brissette (Kerin)
Austin

Sausage Pinwheels

Bake at 400° for 10 to 15 minutes

2	cups Bisquick
4	tablespoons margarine
½	cup milk
1	pound sausage, mild or hot, room temperature

Cut Bisquick and margarine together and add milk. Roll dough out into a rectangle and pat sausage onto dough to within ½-inch of edge. Roll up jelly-roll fashion, wrap in plastic wrap and freeze. When ready to use, set out about 20 minutes or until partially thawed, slice ¼ to ½-inch thick and bake for 10 to 15 minutes. They do not slice well if the roll is completely thawed.

Mrs. Rufus Spraberry (Doris)
Abilene

Tapenade Dip for Vegetables

1 (6½ ounce) can solid-pack
   white tuna, drained
4 anchovy filets
1 tablespoon anchovy oil
4 tablespoons chopped ripe
   olives
½ small onion, grated
2 cloves garlic, crushed
½ cup chopped celery
¼ cup cubed, cooked potato
½ teaspoon Worcestershire
   sauce
Juice of 1 lemon
Dash Tabasco
⅛ teaspoon freshly ground
   pepper
½ cup mayonnaise

Blend all ingredients in blender until smooth. Serve in a vegetable shell (cabbage, eggplant, etc.), surrounded by vegetables as dippers.

Mrs. Rufus G. Martin (Dee)
Alexandria, Virginia

Spinach Balls

Bake at 350° for 20 minutes
Yields 7 dozen

1 (20 ounce) package frozen
   spinach
2 cups herb stuffing mix
1 medium onion, finely
   chopped
½ cup grated Parmesan
   cheese
½ teaspoon garlic salt
¼ teaspoon thyme
½ teaspoon pepper
½ teaspoon Accent
4 eggs, beaten
½ pound butter, melted

Cook spinach according to package directions; drain and pat dry. Toss all ingredients with spinach and chill. Form into small balls and bake at 350° for 20 minutes.

Spinach balls may be frozen on baking sheet; then drop in freezer containers. Remove from freezer, bake and serve.

Mrs. Jackie D. Stephenson (Mary)
San Marcos

Mrs. Jack Redmond (Sue)
Houston

Vegetable Dip

2	eggs, beaten
2	tablespoons sugar
2	tablespoons vinegar
2	(3 ounce) packages cream cheese
¼	cup chopped onion
¼	cup chopped Bell pepper

In top portion of double boiler, mix together eggs, sugar and vinegar. Stir and cook until thick. Remove from heat and add cream cheese, onion and Bell pepper. Chill and serve with celery, carrots, cauli-flower, Bell pepper or cucumber sticks.

Mrs. Joe Gartman (Vonnie)
Leander

Zesty Vegetable Dip

1	cup sour cream
1	cup Hellmann's mayonnaise
2	tablespoons parsley flakes
1	tablespoon green onion flakes
1	teaspoon dill weed
1	teaspoon garlic salt
1	teaspoon Beau Monde
1	teaspoon Accent
2	drops Tabasco

Mix all ingredients together. Chill in air-tight container overnight. Raw vegetables such as celery, cauliflower, cherry tomatoes, mushrooms, carrots, Bell peppers and olives are very good with this dip.

Glenn Whatley
Waco

Hot Crab Dip

Bake at 350° for 15 minutes

1	(8 ounce) package cream cheese, softened
½	stick butter, softened
2	cans crab meat, drained and rinsed

Combine cheese and butter until well blended. Stir in crab meat carefully. Spoon into casserole dish and bake for 15 minutes. Serve hot with crackers.

Mrs. Robert Preston (Judy)
Indian Mills, New Jersey

Ham Balls with Mustard-Dill Sauce

Bake at 350° for 30 to 40 minutes

1	pound ground ham
1	pound ground pork
½	cup corn flake crumbs, finely crushed
¼	cup chopped onion
½	cup milk
2	eggs
1	teaspoon prepared mustard
⅛	teaspoon pepper

Combine meats, crumbs, onion, milk, eggs, mustard and pepper; mix well. Shape into 24 large balls. Place on shallow greased baking pan. Bake at 350° for 30 to 40 minutes. Drain grease from meatballs and cover with mustard-dill sauce. For cocktail buffet, form meatballs into bite-size portions and reduce baking time; serve in chafing dish in sauce.

MUSTARD-DILL SAUCE

2	tablespoons butter
2	tablespoons flour
½	teaspoon salt
1	cup milk
½	cup sour cream
1	tablespoon prepared mustard
¼	teaspoon dill seed

Melt butter; stir in flour and salt; add milk; cook, stirring constantly until thick and smooth. Stir in sour cream, mustard and dill seed. Heat slowly to serving temperature. Makes 1½ cups sauce.

Mrs. John Bottoms (Diane)
Austin

Chili-Cheese Canapes

Bake at 450° for 5 to 8 minutes
Yields 8 dozen

⅓	cup grated Parmesan cheese
½	cup mayonnaise
1	(4 ounce) can green chilies, seeded and minced
1	tablespoon chopped pimiento
2	jalapeño peppers (optional)

Mix all ingredients together and spread mixture on party wheat or rye bread. Place on cookie sheet and bake at 450° for 5 to 8 minutes until brown. Serve hot.

Mrs. Harry Smith (Ginny)
Austin

Tuna Chip Balls

Bake at 475° for 10 minutes
Serves 8 to 10

1	can grated tuna
½	can beef consommé
1	egg, beaten
¼	cup mayonnaise or salad dressing
1	tablespoon mustard
1	cup herb stuffing mix
2	tablespoons parsley flakes
½	cup chopped onion
1	medium package potato chips, crushed

Blend tuna, consommé, egg, mayonnaise, mustard, herb stuffing, parsley flakes and onion. Form into bite-size balls and roll balls in crushed potato chips. Bake at 475° for 10 minutes. Serve hot.

Mrs. Clyde Phillips (Betty)
Dallas

Chili Dip

4	medium tomatoes, diced
2	large Bell peppers, diced
1	medium onion, diced
2	tablespoons jalapeños, diced
2	(8 ounce) cans tomato sauce
	Salt
	Pepper
	Garlic salt
	Sugar

In a large bowl dice tomatoes, Bell peppers, onion, and jalapeños. Stir in tomato sauce and add salt, pepper, garlic salt and sugar to taste. Serve with tortilla chips.

Chili dip may be spread over a platter of tortilla chips and topped with a cheese sauce. Delicious!

Mrs. Stephen Pennington (Cathy)
Weatherford

Marinated Mushrooms

Yields 2 cups

⅓	cup red wine vinegar
⅓	cup salad oil
1	small onion, chopped
1	teaspoon salt
2	teaspoons dried parsley
1	teaspoon mustard
1	tablespoon brown sugar
2	(6 ounce) cans mushrooms, drained

In a saucepan add vinegar, salad oil, chopped onion, salt, parsley, mustard and brown sugar. Bring to boil and then add drained mushrooms. Simmer 5 minutes. Chill in covered bowl stirring occasionally. Yields 2 cups.

Mrs. Herbert G. Purtle (Jan)
Austin

Salmon Mold

Bake at 350° for 1 hour
Serves 20

5   slices white bread
2/3   cup milk
1   (15½ ounce) can pink
    salmon
3   egg yolks
1   tablespoon Worcestershire
    sauce
⅛   teaspoon salt
⅛   teaspoon pepper
3   egg whites

TOPPING

Mayonnaise
Frozen green peas
Pimientos

Remove crusts from bread and dip slices in milk. Place bread, salmon, egg yolks, Worcestershire sauce, salt and pepper in blender. Blend on high speed for 10 seconds. Beat egg whites until stiff. Fold egg whites into salmon mixture. Pour into greased mold. Bake at 350° for 1 hour. After baking, cool and turn out of mold. Frost with mayonnaise and decorate with frozen green peas, which have been cooked according to package directions, and pimientos.

This is an attractive dish baked in fish-shaped mold. If shape breaks or does not unmold "perfectly," mold it together and cover with mayonnaise--no one will ever know!

Mrs. Bruce Jacobs (Shirley)
Washington, D. C.

Old English Cheese Ball

4   (3 ounce) packages cream
    cheese, softened
2   small jars Old English
    sharp cheese, softened
1   cup chopped walnuts

Blend together cream cheese and Old English sharp cheese. Chill. Form into ball and roll in chopped walnuts.

Mrs. Woody Paige (Margaret)
Borger

Crab Roll

Serves 8 to 12

1 (8 ounce) package cream cheese
1 teaspoon mustard
2 teaspoons horseradish
3 tablespoons butter
1 teaspoon Worcestershire sauce
½ to 1 pound crab meat or shrimp
Seafood sauce

Blend cream cheese, mustard, horseradish, butter and Worcestershire. Form into a long roll. Finely chop crab meat or shrimp. Roll cream cheese roll in crab meat or shrimp. Before serving pour bottled seafood sauce over the roll. Serve with crackers.

Chipped beef, which has been cut into small pieces and sautéed in butter, may be substituted for the crab meat or shrimp.

Mrs. Richard A. Miller (Maryann)
Clackamas, Oregon

Dilled Shrimp Spread

Yields 1 cup

1 (4½ ounce) can shrimp, drained
1 (8 ounce) package cream cheese, softened
1 tablespoon mayonnaise
¼ to ½ teaspoon garlic powder
1 tablespoon catsup
1½ teaspoon Worcestershire sauce
1 teaspoon lemon juice
2 tablespoons chopped onion
1 teaspoon dill seeds

Chop shrimp, reserving several whole ones for garnish. Combine cream cheese, mayonnaise, garlic powder, catsup, Worcestershire sauce, lemon juice and onion. Blend well. Add chopped shrimp. Chill several hours or overnight. Shape as desired and garnish with whole shrimp and dill seeds.

Glenn Whatley
Waco

Bambini

Bake at 350° for 20 minutes
Yields 20 turnovers

1	cup ricotta cheese
½	cup coarsely grated mozzarella cheese
¼	cup grated fresh Parmesan cheese
1	(10 ounce) package large flakey refrigerator biscuits
20	very thin slices pepperoni (half of 3½ ounce package)

Combine the 3 cheeses in a small bowl and mix. Halve each biscuit by layers, forming 20 thin biscuits. Gently shape each round into an oval shape. Place a slice of pepperoni slightly off center on dough. Top with about 1 level tablespoon of cheese mixture. Moisten edges; fold dough over to enclose filling, pinching edges carefully to seal. After filling all biscuits, place on lightly greased baking sheet and bake at 350° for 20 minutes. Serve warm.

Salmon Cheese Ball

Serves 10

1	(7¾ ounce) can salmon
1	(8 ounce) package cream cheese, softened
½	cup grated Cheddar cheese
¼	cup chopped stuffed green olives
4 slices crisp bacon or 2	tablespoons bacon bits
2	tablespoons minced onion
Tabasco sauce	
⅓	cup minced fresh parsley

Drain salmon and flake. Combine the salmon with all other ingredients except parsley. Chill until firm and then shape into ball. Roll in parsley. Serve with crackers.

Salmon-cheese ball may be prepared in advance and frozen. Thaw 6 hours in refrigerator until ready to serve.

Mrs. Douglass Cheshire (Joanne)
Dallas

Broccoli Beignets

1	package frozen broccoli (2 cups chopped small)
1	stick butter
1	cup water
1	teaspoon salt
⅛	teaspoon garlic powder
1	cup sifted all-purpose flour
4	eggs
Vegetable oil	
½	cup grated Parmesan cheese

Cook broccoli according to package directions until tender. Drain well and mash or chop finely. Set aside. Combine butter, water, salt and garlic powder in large saucepan. Heat until water is boiling and butter is melted. Add flour all at once and remove from heat. Stir mixture quickly with a wooden spoon until dough leaves sides of pan and forms ball. Add eggs, one at a time, beating well after each addition until mixture is smooth. Stir broccoli into dough and chill 2 hours or overnight. Pour vegetable oil into deep fry pan or saucepan to make a 3-inch depth. Heat oil to 375°. Scoop up a heaping teaspoon of dough and push it into the oil with another spoon. Do not crowd. When beignets are puffed and brown, remove with a slotted spoon to paper towel to drain. Sprinkle with Parmesan cheese and serve piping hot.

Beignets can be fried and frozen. Reheat in 350° oven and then sprinkle with Parmesan cheese.

Mrs. Lewis King (Pat)
Austin

Carrot Balls

1	pound carrots, cooked and mashed
2	eggs, well beaten
2	tablespoons all-purpose flour
1	tablespoon margarine, melted
½	teaspoon salt
Vegetable oil	

Combine carrots, eggs, flour, margarine and salt. Mix well. Shape into 1-inch balls and fry in deep oil until golden brown. Drain.

Jo's Party Puffs

Bake at 425° for 10 minutes then at 350° until done
Yields 6 dozen

1 cup water
½ cup butter, margarine or
 shortening
¼ teaspoon salt
1 cup flour, sifted
4 eggs

These are well worth the time it takes to make them, for all the "oohs" and "aahs" you will receive.

Bring water, margarine and salt to boiling point in medium saucepan. Add flour all at once. Stir quickly over heat until mixture leaves sides of pan and forms a ball. Continue cooking about 3 minutes more, mashing dough against sides of pan. Remove from heat and beat 2 or 3 minutes to cool mixture. Add eggs one at a time, beating thoroughly after each addition. Continue beating until mixture is smooth and shiny. Drop dough by *level* teaspoons to make bite-size puffs. Bake at 425° for 10 minutes on greased baking sheets. Then lower oven to 350° and bake until done. Cool. Slit or cut off top and fill with either nutted chicken filling or cheese filling.

After filling, these can be frozen in well-sealed foil for up to 1 month. Before serving, remove foil and thaw 1 hour at room temperature. Bake at 450° for 3 minutes.

NUTTED CHICKEN FILLING

Yields 2 cups

2 tablespoons butter or
 margarine
1 cup finely chopped pecans
1⅓ cups finely chopped
 cooked chicken
¼ cup mayonnaise
1 (3 ounce) package cream
 cheese, softened
¼ teaspoon salt
½ teaspoon nutmeg
½ teaspoon grated lemon rind

Melt butter in skillet. Add pecans and cook over low heat until lightly browned. Cool. Combine with remaining ingredients. Fill puffs and replace tops.

Mrs. L. James Starr, Jr. (Jo Ann)
Austin

Spinach Dip

Serves 8 to 10

1 (10 ounce) package frozen chopped spinach, thawed
1 package Knorr's vegetable soup mix
8 ounces sour cream
8 ounces mayonnaise
3 chopped green onions
2 tablespoons minced parsley
1 (8 ounce) can water chestnuts, finely chopped
Round French or Dutch bread

Drain spinach very well and mix with soup mix, sour cream, mayonnaise, green onions, parsley and water chestnuts. Hollow out the bread and toast lightly. Spoon the dip into the bread cavity and serve with toasted bread chunks, melba toast or wheat crackers.

Mrs. William L. Seals (Betty)
Austin

Stuffed Jalapeños

1 (11 ounce) can whole jalapeños (mild or hot)
1 (8 ounce) package cream cheese
¾ cup grated Cheddar cheese, softened
6 green onions, finely diced
⅛ teaspoon garlic salt

Drain, seed and halve jalapeños. (Jalapeños can be soaked in ice water for 1 hour before stuffing—this supposedly makes them mild!) Soften cream cheese at room temperature and blend in Cheddar cheese. Add onions and garlic salt. Stuff drained jalapeño boats with cheese mixture. Refrigerate at least 30 minutes before serving.

Pickled Eggs and Onions

Serves 12

3	cups white vinegar
2	tablespoons mustard
1	cup sugar
1	tablespoon salt
1	tablespoon celery seed
1	teaspoon mustard seed (optional)
½	cup water
6	whole cloves
2	medium onions, sliced
12	small eggs, hard-boiled and shelled

Simmer vinegar, mustard, sugar, salt, celery seed, mustard seed and water for 10 minutes. Add 6 whole cloves and cool to room temperature. Slice 2 onions into rings and place in jar or suitable container with cover. Add eggs and liquid. Refrigerate overnight. These will keep for several days in the refrigerator.

Pickled eggs and onions are great for cocktail parties or picnics. Men especially like them.

Mrs. C. Emerson Murry (Donna)
Bismarck, North Dakota

Fruit Frappé

Serves 6 to 12

2	large oranges
2	large lemons
2	bananas
¼	cup sugar
1	(8 ounce) can crushed pineapple
2	cups ginger ale

Combine juice and grated rind of lemons and oranges, bananas cut finely, and remainder of ingredients. Freeze, stirring occasionally. Partially thaw to a slushy consistency for serving. Add cherries for color, if desired. Can be frozen for several weeks and can be refrozen.

Great for appetizer, brunch or salad — especially in the summer!

Mrs. Jim Daniel (Julia Ann)
Little Rock, Arkansas

Swiss Fondue

2	pounds Swiss cheese, grated
6	tablespoons flour
1	garlic clove, cut
4	cups dry white wine
6	tablespoons brandy
½	teaspoon ground nutmeg

Pepper

Combine cheese and flour and mix until cheese is coated with flour. Rub inside of large fondue pot with garlic. Pour wine into fondue pot and heat until bubbles of wine rise to the surface. Stir in cheese, a little at a time, and continue stirring until all cheese is thoroughly melted and mixture starts to bubble. Add brandy, nutmeg and pepper. To serve, dip pieces of French bread, cubes of ham or slices of apples into fondue. Be creative!

The fondue could be made in the top of a double boiler and poured into a chafing dish or fondue pot for serving.

Mrs. Thomas E. Williams (Jody)
Round Rock

Toasted Asparagus Pick-Ups

Bake at 400°

1	slice white bread for each spear of asparagus
1	(3 ounce) package cream cheese
2	tablespoons mayonnaise
1	(15 ounce) can asparagus spears

Melted butter

Remove crust from very fresh bread slices. Blend cream cheese and mayonnaise until it is spreadable. Spread on bread slices; place asparagus spear at one end. Roll up and place on cookie sheet, seam down. Brush with melted butter. (Can be frozen at this point and baked later.) Bake at 400° until golden brown.

Delicious alone or served with salads.

Mrs. Walter J. Dingler (Gayle)
Austin

NGAT Conference Zesty Pecans

Bake at 300° for 15 minutes

¼ cup butter
1½ teaspoons chili powder
1 teaspoon Worcestershire sauce
½ teaspoon cayenne pepper
½ teaspoon garlic salt
4 cups pecan halves

Melt butter and combine chili powder, Worcestershire, cayenne pepper and garlic salt. In a large bowl, pour mixture over pecans. Toss well to coat completely. Spread pecans evenly on a baking sheet and bake at 300° for 15 minutes. Bake until pecans are crisp inside, not brown. Stir at least twice during baking time.

John Henry
San Angelo

Spiced Pecans

1 cup sugar
1 teaspoon salt
½ teaspoon each nutmeg and cloves
2 teaspoons cinnamon
¼ cup water
½ pound pecans

Mix all ingredients except nuts. Cook until syrup forms a soft ball when tested in cold water. Add pecans. Remove from heat and stir until sugary. Spread on waxed paper or platter. Break apart when cool.

Mrs. Robert L. Stockton (Sylvia)
Waco

Party Pizza

Bake at 350° for 10 to 15 minutes

2 pounds hot sausage
1 pound grated Velveeta cheese
½ teaspoon oregano
½ teaspoon garlic powder
Several drops Tabasco

Cook sausage in skillet until lightly brown. Drain very well. Add cheese and seasonings. Mix well. Spread mixture on thin party rye bread. Bake at 350° for 10 to 15 minutes. Freezes well.

Mrs. Vernon Scofield (Audrey)
Austin

79

Broccoli Cheese Soup

2	quarts chicken stock *or*
2	quarts water and 4 chicken bouillon cubes
1	cup chopped celery
½	cup chopped onion
1	pound fresh broccoli *or*
1	large bag frozen broccoli cuts
½	cup flour
2	cups milk
2	cup grated American cheese

Salt and pepper to taste

Bring chicken stock to a boil and add celery, onion and broccoli. Cook until vegetables are tender. Reduce heat; add milk and cheese. Make a thickening of the flour and some milk and add to soup until desired consistency. DO NOT BOIL.

Variation: After vegetables are tender, pureé in blender for a smooth soup.

Mrs. Don Fiero (Pat)
Leander

Canadian Cheese Soup

¼	cup butter
½	cup diced onion
½	cup diced celery
½	cup diced carrot
¼	cup flour
1½	tablespoons cornstarch
1	pint chicken broth (or bouillon cubes mixed as directed)
1	quart milk
⅛	teaspoon soda
½	pound Velveeta cheese
1	teaspoon parsley

Salt and pepper

Melt butter, add vegetables and sauté. Add flour and cornstarch. Add stock and milk. Add soda, cheese and seasonings. Heat thoroughly but do not boil.

Mrs. James B. McGoodwin (Jane)
Fort Worth

Chicken Corn Chowder

Serves 4 to 6

¾   **cup chopped celery and
     tops**
¾   **cup chopped onions**
¼   **cup butter or margarine**
1¼ **cups milk (or more for
     thinner soup)**
2   **cans cream of chicken
     soup**
1   **(17 ounce) can creamed
     corn**
½   **teaspoon basil**
½   **teaspoon salt**
⅛   **teaspoon pepper**

Sauté celery and onions in butter until tender. Add milk, soup, corn and seasonings. Heat, stirring occasionally, until chowder is hot, but not boiling.

Great on a soup and sandwich evening.

Mrs. Ron Brissette (Kerin)
Austin

Potato Cheddar Soup

Yields 2½ cups

2   **slices bacon**
½   **cup chopped onion**
1   **(10 ounce) can cream of
     potato soup**
½   **cup diced American
     cheese**
½   **teaspoon thyme**
1   **cup milk**

Cook bacon till crisp. Crumble. Discard all but 1 tablespoon fat. Add onion and cook 5 minutes. Add soup, bacon, cheese and thyme. Gradually stir in milk. Cook until heated, but do not boil.

Mrs. Billy B. Pope (Vanessa)
Greenville

During its period of settlement, the most universal crop of the southern United States was, without question, corn. It was found in the field and on the table of the humblest yeoman and the richest planter. Cornbread, hominy, and corn on the cob were familiar dishes.
—Terry G. Jordan, German Seed in Texas Soil, p. 66

German Potato Soup

Serves 8

7	slices bacon
3	medium onions, chopped
6	fresh mushrooms, chopped
4½	tablespoons flour
9	cups bouillon
6	large red potatoes, thinly sliced
3	egg yolks
1½	cups sour cream
2	tablespoons fresh parsley, minced
2	tablespoons basil

Dice bacon and sauté in a large kettle. Add mushrooms and onions and sauté until soft. Blend in flour. Add bouillon and potatoes. Cook until done, about 1 hour. Beat egg yolks. Mix with sour cream. Add parsley and basil. *Gradually* add to hot broth. Cook and stir until yolks are cooked and soup is hot through, about 5 minutes. DO NOT BOIL.

Delicious with cheese popovers.

Mrs. Lewis Stephens (Nancy)
Dallas

Yellow Squash Soup

Serves 6

½	cup finely chopped white onion
½	stick butter
2	pounds yellow squash, diced
4	cups chicken broth
1	cup half and half cream
¼	teaspoon thyme
¼	teaspoon tarragon

In a saucepan sauté onion in butter until soft. Stir in squash and chicken stock. Bring to a boil, turn down heat and simmer, covered, for 30 minutes or until vegetables are soft. Pureé the mixture in a blender and return it to the pan. Stir in cream, thyme, tarragon and salt and pepper to taste. When the soup is hot, transfer it into heated (if wintertime) bowls. Top with a very thin slice of squash for decoration.

This is a lovely soup, good in summer as well as winter.

Mrs. Jay Matthews (Babs)
Austin

French Onion Soup

Bake at 425° for 10 minutes
Serves 6

2	medium Sweet Spanish onions (5 cups onion rings)
¼	cup butter
2	tablespoons flour
2	(10 ounce) cans condensed beef bouillon
2½	cups water or ½ water and ½ dry white wine
6	slices French bread, cut 1-inch thick
½	cup grated Parmesan cheese
½	cup grated Swiss cheese

Peel and slice onions and separate into rings. Sauté in butter until soft and golden. Stir in flour. Gradually add bouillon and water or wine. Bring to boil and simmer 20 minutes. Meanwhile, toast bread lightly. Place soup in 6 ovenproof bowls, over bread. Sprinkle with cheeses. Bake for 10 minutes.

Microwave: Melt butter, stir in onions. Cover and cook on high for 10 to 12 minutes. Stir after 5 minutes. Stir in flour, gradually add bouillon and water. Cover and cook on high for 8 to 10 minutes until boiling. Continue cooking on medium for 5 minutes. Place toasted bread in bowls. Ladle soup over toast. Sprinkle with cheeses. Microwave for 2 to 3 minutes until cheese melts.

Mrs. James M. Hamilton ('Cille)
Austin

Chili Excellent

2	pounds lean ground beef
1	teaspoon salt
1	teaspoon pepper
¼	cup corn oil
3	heaping tablespoons chili powder
1	teaspoon cumin
½	teaspoon cayenne pepper
½	teaspoon garlic powder or garlic juice
5	(8 ounce) cans tomato sauce
½	cup chopped fresh onion

In stew pot cook ground beef, salt and pepper in oil, until lightly browned. Add all other ingredients and cook *slowly* for 2 to 3 hours.

Harold Groner
Dallas

Onion Wine Soup

Serves 6 to 8

¼ cup butter
5 large onions, chopped
5 cups beef broth
½ cup celery leaves
1 large potato, sliced
1 cup dry white wine
1 tablespoon vinegar
2 teaspoons sugar
1 cup half and half cream
1 tablespoon minced
   parsley
Salt and pepper

Melt butter in large saucepan. Add chopped onion and mix well. Add beef broth, celery leaves and potato. Bring to boiling. Cover and simmer for 30 minutes. Pureé mixture in a blender. Return to saucepan and blend in wine, vinegar and sugar. Bring to boiling and simmer 5 minutes. Stir in cream, parsley and salt and pepper to taste. Heat thoroughly but do not boil.

Mrs. Ronald Reagan (Nancy)
Washington, D.C. and California

Corn Soup

1 stick butter
2 (10 ounce) packages
   frozen corn, rinsed and
   drained thoroughly
4 cups milk
Salt and pepper to taste
   (don't overdo salt if
   chips are salty)
1 (3 ounce) can chopped
   green chilies
8 ounces Monterey Jack
   cheese, grated
Tortilla chips, crushed

Melt butter in large saucepan, do not brown. Pour 2 cups milk and corn in blender and pureé. (You may need to do this in small amounts at a time.) Add corn mixture, salt, pepper and remaining 2 cups milk to butter. Bring to a boil and cook till slightly thick, about 5 minutes. (Mixture will not get real thick.) In each serving bowl put approximately ½ cup grated cheese. Pour hot soup over cheese. Sprinkle crushed chips on top and spoon a little green chilies on top of chips. Serve immediately. The cheese helps thicken the soup.

Mrs. Lewis King (Pat)
Austin

Macho Gazpacho

Yields 10 1-cup servings

2	pounds ripe tomatoes
2	Bell peppers, halved and seeded
1	medium onion
1	large cucumber, halved and seeded
1	medium zucchini, cut into chunks
1	green onion, quartered
1	rib celery, cut into chunks
1	(6 ounce) jar marinated artichoke hearts in oil
2	canned pimientos
1½	cups tomato juice
¼	cup red wine vinegar
1	teaspoon pepper
¼ to ½	teaspoon oregano
1	teaspoon Italian seasoning
¼	teaspoon rosemary
¼	teaspoon thyme
⅛	teaspoon salt
¼	teaspoon liquid red pepper seasoning

Croutons

Coarsely chop enough tomatoes, Bell peppers, onion and cucumber to make ½ cup each. Reserve for garnish. Cut remaining tomatoes, Bell peppers, onion and cucumber into chunks. Place half in container of electric blender with half the zucchini, green onion, celery, undrained artichoke hearts and pimiento; whirl until smooth. Transfer to a large bowl. Repeat with remaining vegetables. Stir in tomato juice, vinegar, pepper, oregano, Italian seasoning, rosemary, thyme, salt and red pepper seasoning. Cover and refrigerate several hours. Serve with reserved vegetables and croutons.

Scandinavian Fruit Soup

Serves 8 to 10

1	(8 ounce) package mixed dried fruits, cut into small pieces
2½	cups water
½	teaspoon ground cinnamon
1	(3 ounce) package cherry-flavored gelatin
3	cups orange juice

Sour cream

Combine dried fruit, water and cinnamon in large saucepan and bring to a boil. Cover, reduce heat and simmer 20 minutes. Remove from heat and pureé in blender, a little at a time. Stir in gelatin until dissolved; add orange juice. Chill. Serve soup cold topped with sour cream.

Rich, tart and delicious.

Swedish Fruit Soup (Fruktsoppa)

Yields 4 quarts

1   (8 ounce) package pitted prunes
1   cup raisins
1   cup currants
1   cup dried apricots or dried peaches
10   cups water
1   orange, cut in small pieces (pulp and rind)
1   large apple, diced
3 to 5 rings pineapple, diced
1   tablespoon butter
¼   cup brown sugar, packed
1   tablespoon lemon juice
1   pint grape juice or 2 cups canned blueberries

Wash fruit thoroughly. In large dutch oven, combine prunes, raisins, currants, apricots and water. Soak overnight. Simmer mixture for 30 to 45 minutes or until fruit is tender. While simmering, add orange, apple, pineapple, butter, brown sugar and lemon and grape juices. Add enough water to make 4 quarts.

To serve soup hot: Add 2 tablespoons flour mixed with ½ cup cold water to make smooth consistency. Add to soup and stir well to thicken slightly.

To serve soup cold: Immediately after removing from stove add 1 (3 ounce) package lemon flavored gelatin or 2 tablespoons Knox gelatin dissolved in 4 tablespoons cold water. Stir well and chill.

Fruit soup is equally delicious served hot or cold.

As a child, I remember this soup being served for Sunday dinner.

Mrs. J. Travis Blakeslee (Gladys)
Austin

Bean Soup

1 pound pinto beans
1 medium onion, cut in 4 pieces
3 large cloves garlic
1 cup diced celery
½ bunch of cilantro (looks like parsley), diced
½ cup fresh raw cabbage, diced
4 fresh tomatoes, diced

Wash and cook beans in large saucepan. Add the onion and garlic to beans when they begin to boil. One-half hour before beans are done, add the celery and cilantro. Dice the cabbage and fresh tomatoes and mix in a salad bowl. Serve beans in soup bowls and add the cabbage salad to the beans. Serve with fresh hot corn bread.

Instead of the cabbage salad, you can substitute "Pico de Gallo".

Mrs. Ruben Torres (Olga)
Alice

Microwave Creamy Chicken Stew

Serves 4 to 6

2 medium potatoes, cut into 16 pieces
1 cup coarsely sliced celery
2 cups coarsely sliced carrots
1 large onion, cut in eighths
2 teaspoons salt
¼ teaspoon pepper
1 teaspoon ground sage
2½ to 3 pounds whole frying chicken, cut up
2 (10 ounce) cans cream of chicken soup
Parsley

Combine vegetables in layers in 4-quart glass Dutch oven. Season with salt, pepper and sage. Place chicken, skin side down and thick edge toward outside of dish, on top of vegetables. Cover with glass lid or plastic wrap. Microwave on High for 15 minutes. Drain and turn chicken over, pour soup over chicken, and cover again. Microwave on Simmer for 25 to 30 minutes or until fork tender. Let stand, covered, 5 minutes before serving. Garnish with snipped parsley.

Very good and easy!

Mrs. James T. Dennis (Mavis)
Bedford

Beer Beef Stew

Serves 4

1½	pounds beef cubes
2	tablespoons all-purpose flour
2	tablespoons oil
1	envelope beefy onion or onion soup mix
½	teaspoon caraway seeds
1	(12 ounce) can beer
½	cup water
4	medium potatoes, quartered
4	carrots, cut in 2-inch pieces
1	(10 ounce) package frozen cut green beans

Coat beef with flour. In large heavy skillet, heat oil and brown meat cubes. Add soup mix and caraway blended with beer and water. Bring to boil, then simmer covered for 30 minutes. Add potatoes and carrots and simmer, covered, 30 more minutes. Add green beans and simmer, covered, an additional 10 minutes or until beef and vegetables are tender.

"Blue Norther" Beef Stew

1½ to 2	pounds stew meat
2	tablespoons shortening
1	large onion, chopped
1	clove garlic
4	cups boiling water
1	tablespoon salt
1	tablespoon lemon juice
1	teaspoon sugar
1	teaspoon Worcestershire sauce
½	teaspoon pepper
1	teaspoon paprika
2	bay leaves
3 to 4	carrots
2	medium potatoes
2	ribs celery
½	cup cold water
¼	cup flour

In large Dutch oven, brown meat in shortening. Sauté onion and garlic just until onion is limp being careful not to brown garlic too much. Add water, salt, lemon juice, sugar, Worcestershire sauce, pepper, paprika and bay leaves and cook, covered, for 2 hours. Add vegetables which have been cut-up to desired size, and simmer 30 minutes longer or until vegetables are tender. Remove bay leaves. Thicken with cold water and flour made into a paste.

Serve with hot cornbread or ladled over split hot biscuits.

Cookbook Committee

Molasses Brown Bread

Bake at 325° for 45 minutes
Yields 3 loaves

2	packages dry yeast
2½	cups warm water
1	cup Grandma's molasses
½	cup sugar
2	teaspoons salt
4	tablespoons shortening, melted
2	cups wheat flour
7	cups white flour
2	cups raisins, optional

Dissolve yeast in ¼ cup warm water in a large mixing bowl. Measure molasses, sugar, salt, 2 tablespoons of the melted shortening, and the rest of the water into the bowl with the yeast. Sift and stir enough flour into the bowl to make a dough stiff enough to knead. Knead dough well to release bubbles. Wash bowl and grease well with melted shortening. Place dough in bowl and use rest of shortening to brush on top. Place in warm place and let rise until double in bulk. Knead dough in bowl and let rise again until double in bulk. Divide into three equal parts and knead well, then shape into loaves and place in greased bread pans. Let rise to double in bulk again and bake in 325° oven for 45 minutes.

Raisins are added with flour, if desired.

Mrs. George Peterson (Margie)
Austin

Aunt Mary's Mayonnaise Biscuits

Bake at 425° for 10 to 12 minutes

1	cup self-rising flour
1	tablespoon sugar
¼	cup mayonnaise
½	cup milk

Combine all ingredients and spoon into greased muffin tins. Bake at 425° for 10 to 12 minutes.

Very quick and easy and good!!

Mrs. Harold Groner (Mary)
Dallas

89

Bishop's Bread

Bake at 400° for 25 minutes
Serves 5 or more

2½ cups sifted flour
1¼ cups brown sugar, packed
½ teaspoon salt
½ cup butter or shortening
1 teaspoon baking powder
½ teaspoon soda
1 teaspoon cinnamon
1 egg, well beaten
¾ cup buttermilk or sour milk

Sift flour, measure. Add sugar and salt. Cut in shortening until mixture looks like coarse meal; reserve ¾ cup for top. To remainder, add baking powder, soda and cinnamon; then add beaten egg and sour milk. Beat until smooth. Turn into 2 greased 8x8x2-inch or 1 9x13x2-inch pan. Sprinkle with reserved ¾ cup of flour and shortening mixture. Sprinkle with additional cinnamon. Bake at 400° for 25 minutes.

I obtained this recipe while a student at Tarleton State University in the 1920's. This has become a family breakfast tradition for my Texas National Guard sons and grandsons.

Mrs. Luther J. Starr (Lucille)
College Station

Dilly Bread

Bake at 350° for 30 to 40 minutes

1 package dry yeast
¼ cup warm water
1 cup cottage cheese, room temperature
2 tablespoons sugar
1 tablespoon instant minced onion
1 tablespoon butter, melted
2 teaspoons dill seeds
1 teaspoon salt
¼ teaspoon soda
1 egg
2½ to 3 cups flour

Dissolve yeast in warm water and set aside. Combine cottage cheese, sugar, onion, melted butter, dill seeds, salt, soda and egg. Beat well. Add yeast mixture and then add enough flour to make a stiff dough. Beat again. Let rise to double in bulk in a warm place. Stir down and place in a greased baking pan. Let rise again. Bake at 350° for 30 to 40 minutes. Remove from oven and while still hot brush with butter and sprinkle with salt.

Spoon Bread

Bake at 425° for 50 minutes
Serves 4

4   cups milk
1   cup cornmeal
1   teaspoon salt
2   tablespoons butter
4   eggs

Heat milk in a double boiler; gradually stir in cornmeal mixed with
salt; cook, stirring, until smooth
and thick. Cover and cook until
consistency of mush. Remove
mush from heat; add butter. In
large bowl, beat eggs until well
blended; slowly stir in mush. Pour
into a well greased 1½ quart casserole. Bake 50 minutes. Eat
topped with butter.

Cookbook Committee

Mashed Potato Rolls

Bake at 350° for 20 minutes

1   package dry yeast
1½   cups lukewarm water
2   eggs, beaten
¾   cup mashed potatoes
¾   cup sugar
¾   cup shortening, melted
1   tablespoon salt
7½   cups flour (approximately)
Melted butter

Dissolve yeast in water. Add
beaten eggs, potatoes, sugar,
shortening, salt and flour to make
dough that handles easily. Knead
until smooth and does not stick to
hands. Let rise until double in
bulk. (about 1½ hours) Roll out
dough on lightly floured board.
Brush dough with melted butter.
Cut with biscuit cutter. Make
crease in dough with side of hand
in the center of each round.
Stretch out and fold over each
round. Seal edges together. Place
in slightly greased pan. Let rise
until double in size (about 1 hour).
Bake at 350° for 20 minutes. This
dough will keep in refrigerator but
you will need to let it rise about
1½ hours in warm oven.

Barbara O'Connell
Austin

Beer Biscuits

Bake at 425° for 15 minutes
Yields 6

1½   **cups Bisquick**
¾   **cup beer**
2   **tablespoons sugar**
⅛   **teaspoon salt**

Mix all ingredients together. Butter 6 muffin tins and drop dough in tins. Bake at 425° for 15 minutes. To double batter, use 1 full can of beer and double other ingredients.

These are so good and crunchy on the outside edges...might as well go ahead and double recipe.

Mrs. Gene Jackson (Marge)
Austin

Sourdough Biscuits

Bake at 425° for 15 to 20 minutes
Serves 8 to 10

1½   **packages dry yeast**
1   **cup warm water**
2   **cups buttermilk**
½   **cup Crisco oil**
3½   **teaspoons baking powder**
¼   **teaspoon soda**
2   **teaspoons salt**
1   **tablespoon sugar**
6 or 7 cups flour

In a large bowl dissolve yeast in warm water. Mix well and add: buttermilk, oil, baking powder, soda, salt and sugar. Mix well. Mix in 6 cups flour or more if needed to handle. Let rise 15 minutes before baking. Bake at 425° approximately 15 to 20 minutes.

Unused dough may be refrigerated in a covered bowl for a week. Better if you wait a day or two before using.

Mrs. Darrell Vinson (Anita)
Arlington

Beer Hush Puppies

Serves 6

2 cups yellow cornmeal
1 cup flour
1½ teaspoons baking powder
1½ teaspoons salt
1 medium onion, chopped fine
1 medium jalapeño pepper, chopped
Beer

Mix all ingredients together except beer. Gradually add enough beer to make a thin batter. Drop by teaspoon into hot grease. Should return to top of grease from 4 to 5 seconds (3 seconds, grease too hot, 7 seconds, grease not hot enough). Cook until brown.

Marvin Brown
Wake Village

Flour Tortillas

Yields 10 to 12

2 cups flour
1 teaspoon baking powder
¾ teaspoon salt
2 tablespoons shortening
½ to ¾ cups tepid water

Mix all dry ingredients, cut in shortening, mix with enough tepid water to form sticky dough. Knead on a floured board until dough is smooth. Cover with a moist cup towel and let stand for approximately 30 minutes. Divide into ten or twelve portions, knead each portion individually with both hands turning dough under as you turn it.* Roll with rolling pin on a floured surface. Turn a quarter of a turn after each stroke until desired size. Cook on a griddle over medium heat. Sear on one side, turn quickly to other side, turn back to original side. Place in foil to keep warm.

*To resemble a large stemless mushroom.

Mrs. Charles Kone (Minda)
La Pryor

93

One Hour Yeast Rolls

Bake at 400° for 15 to 20 minutes

2   packages dry yeast
¼   cup warm water
1½   cups buttermilk, lukewarm
3   tablespoons sugar
½   cup shortening, melted
4½   cups flour
½   teaspoon baking soda
1   teaspoon salt

Sprinkle yeast into warm water and dissolve. Add lukewarm buttermilk, sugar and melted shortening. Add dry ingredients and beat smooth with mixer and let stand 10 minutes. Roll out on floured surface and cut into desired shape. Place on lightly greased baking pan. Let rise about 30 minutes and bake for 15 to 20 minutes. (You may substitute same amount of milk soured with 1 tablespoon of vinegar in place of buttermilk.)

Mrs. Edmond Komandosky (Susan)
Taylor

Rio Frio Ranch Rolls

Bake at 350° for 20 minutes
Yields 2 to 3 dozen

1   cup boiling water
1   cup shortening
1   cup sugar
1½   teaspoons salt
2   eggs, beaten
2   packages dry yeast
1   cup warm water
6   cups flour, unsifted

In mixing bowl pour boiling water over shortening and dissolve. Blend in sugar and salt. When cool add eggs. Dissolve yeast in warm water; then add to mixture. Blend in flour a little at a time mixing well. Place in refrigerator. Roll out rolls on lightly floured board, cut and place on lightly greased pan. Let rise 1 to 2 hours before baking. Bake for 20 minutes.

The dough will keep in refrigerator for approximately a week and also makes marvelous cinnamon rolls. My family and friends like both.

Mrs. Dolph Briscoe (Janey)
Uvalde

Indian Fry Bread

3	cups flour*
1	tablespoon baking powder
½	teaspoon salt
¼	cup milk
1½	cups warm water

Combine dry ingredients in a large bowl. Add milk, blending thoroughly. Add warm water in small amounts and knead until soft but not sticky. (This can be done in food processor) Cover bowl and let stand for about 15 minutes. Pull off large egg-size balls of dough and roll or pat into rounds about ¼-inch thick. Punch hole in center of each round, to allow to puff.

In a heavy skillet fry rounds in shortening until bubbles appear on dough, turn and fry on other side until golden.

*Bread flour or Blue Bird Flour with a high gluten content works better.

Serve hot with honey or jam....delicious!!

Suzanne Ragan Crawford
Paige

Popovers

Bake at 375° for 45 to 50 minutes
Yields 1 dozen

1	cup flour
1	cup milk
1	tablespoon margarine
3	eggs
⅛	teaspoon salt

Place all ingredients in food processor. Mix continuously for 2½ minutes using food processor with steel blade on high speed. Pour into 12 greased muffin tins. Bake at 375° for 45 to 50 minutes. Serve immediately. (Recipe must be made with food processor. Do not use self-rising flour.)

Mrs. Richard Harrison (Nancy)
Austin

Amish Cornbread

Bake at 375°

½	cup sugar
2	eggs
1	stick margarine, melted
1	heaping teaspoon baking powder
1	teaspoon soda
¾	teaspoon salt
1	cup buttermilk
1⅓	cups cornmeal
1⅓	cups flour

Beat sugar and eggs and add melted margarine. Set aside. Mix baking powder, soda and salt into buttermilk. Mix cornmeal and flour and add alternately with buttermilk mixture to the egg mixture. Bake in lightly greased muffin tins or baking pan until golden brown.

Mrs. Raymond R. Galloway (Peggy)
Dublin, Ohio

Sweet Potato Biscuits

Bake at 400° for 10 minutes

6	rounded tablespoons shortening
⅓	cup sugar
3	cups flour
6	teaspoons baking powder
1¼	teaspoons salt
2	cups sweet potatoes, mashed
½ to ¾	cup milk

Combine dry ingredients. Cut shortening into dry ingredients until mealy. Add sweet potatoes and milk and mix well. Knead on floured board until smooth. Roll out and cut with biscuit cutter. Bake at 400° about 10 minutes.

Especially good with sausage or ham.

Leonard T. Tallas
Austin

NGAT Jalapeño Cornbread

Bake at 350° for 45 to 50 minutes

3 cups cornbread mix
2 cups milk
3-4 jalapeños, chopped
2½ cups grated Cheddar
  cheese
1 medium onion, chopped
  fine
½ cup oil
1 (16 ounce) can cream
  style corn
3 eggs, beaten

Blend all ingredients together. Pour into a greased 9x13-inch pan. Bake for 45 to 50 minutes.

NGAT Office Staff
Austin

Sausage and Pecan Cornbread Pie

Bake at 400° for 30 minutes
Serves 6

1 pound fresh pork sausage
1 cup yellow cornmeal
1 cup flour
¼ cup sugar
4 teaspoons baking powder
1 egg
1 cup milk
2 tablespoons oil
⅓ cup coarsely chopped
  pecans

In heavy skillet, brown sausage, separating into pieces. Drain grease and set aside. Sift together cornmeal, flour, sugar and baking powder. Add egg, milk and oil. Mix to combine thoroughly and fold in sausage and pecans. Turn batter into greased 9-inch glass pie plate. Bake at 400° for 30 minutes.

Spicy Monkey Bread Ring

Bake at 375° for 25 minutes

1   (13¾ ounce) package hot roll mix
¾   cup warm water
1   egg, slightly beaten
1   (1½ ounce) package burrito seasoning mix
3   tablespoons yellow cornmeal
2   tablespoons sesame seeds (optional)
2   tablespoons finely diced green chilies
2   tablespoons finely diced ripe olives
2   tablespoons finely diced pimientos
¼ to ½ cup butter, melted

In large mixing bowl, dissolve yeast from hot roll mix in warm water, according to package directions. Stir in egg. In another bowl, combine flour mixture from roll mix and burrito seasoning mix. Add to liquid mixture and stir until well mixed. Turn dough out on floured board and knead 1 minute. Place dough in large lightly greased bowl; turn once to grease the surface. Cover and let rise in warm place until double in size (about 45 minutes). In small bowl combine cornmeal and sesame seeds. In another small bowl, combine green chilies, olives and pimientos. Divide dough into 24 pieces, shaping into balls. Dip each ball into melted butter, then into cornmeal mixture to coat. Arrange 12 of the balls on bottom of well-greased 6½ quart ring mold. Sprinkle green chilies mixture evenly over rolls in the mold. Place remaining rolls over chilies, pressing slightly. Cover and let rise in warm place until doubled again. Bake for 15 minutes, covering with foil to prevent over-browning. Remove foil and bake 5 to 10 minutes longer, until golden brown and bread sounds hollow when tapped. Immediately turn out of pan; cool slightly.

Parkerhouse Easys

Bake at 400° for 12 to 15 minutes
Yields 2 dozen

1   **package dry yeast**
¼   **cup warm water**
1   **cup milk (scalded)**
¼   **cup margarine, softened**
½   **teaspoon salt**
½   **cup Jello Golden Egg**
      Custard mix
3½ to 4 cups flour

Soften yeast in warm water. In large mixing bowl combine hot milk, margarine and salt. Stir until margarine melts. Add custard mix and stir until dissolved. Cool to lukewarm. Add yeast mixture. Gradually add flour to form dough. Cover and let rise in warm place. Knead on lightly floured surface approximately 12 times. Roll out and cut with biscuit cutter. Fold rounded sides together forming semi-circle, pinching rounded sides together. Place on greased baking sheet and let rise again. Bake for 12 to 15 minutes or until brown.

These rolls are a pretty yellow and have a very unique flavor. The dough also makes good sweet rolls.

Mrs. Lewis King (Pat)
Austin

Raisin Loaf

Bake at 350° for 30 minutes
Yields 1 loaf

⅓   **cup margarine**
1⅔   **cups sugar**
2   **eggs**
¼   **cup milk**
1¾   **cups flour**
2   **teaspoons baking powder**
1   **teaspoon cinnamon**
1   **teaspoon allspice**
1   **cup raisins**

Blend margarine and sugar. Add eggs and milk, then stir in dry ingredients. Add raisins. Place in a greased and floured 9x13-inch pan. Bake at 350° for 30 minutes.

This is not a real sweet bread. Good for breakfast.

Mrs. Scott Bennett (Charlene)
Austin

Strawberry Bread and Spread

Bake at 350° for 1 hour
Yields 2 loaves

BREAD

3	cups flour
1	teaspoon baking soda
1	teaspoon cinnamon
2	cups sugar
1	teaspoon salt
2	(10 ounce) packages frozen strawberries, thawed
1¼	cup cooking oil
4	eggs, well beaten
¼	teaspoon red food coloring (optional)

Reserve ½ cup strawberry juice for spread. Mix all dry ingredients together. Make a hole in the center of the mixture. Pour strawberries, oil and eggs in the hole. Mix until all ingredients are thoroughly combined. (Don't use an electric mixer.) Add food coloring. Pour into 2 greased and floured loaf pans. Bake at 350° for 1 hour. Cool thoroughly.

SPREAD

½	cup strawberry juice
1	(8 ounce) package cream cheese, softened

Place ½ cup strawberry juice and cream cheese in deep bowl. Mix with electric mixer until spreading consistency. Spread on cooled bread.

Mrs. Morris Abercrombie (Barbara)
Sulphur Springs

Honey Oatmeal Hotcakes

2	eggs
2	cups buttermilk
1¼	cups flour
½	cup instant oatmeal, uncooked
¼	cup wheat germ
½	teaspoon salt
1	teaspoon baking soda
½	cup oil
3	tablespoons honey

Beat eggs and gradually stir in 1 cup of the buttermilk alternately with dry ingredients. Add oil. Add remaining cup of buttermilk and honey. Mix well. Cook on hot griddle.

Lewis King
Austin

Basic Sweet Dough

7½	cups flour
½	cup sugar
2	teaspoons salt
2	packages dry yeast
1	cup milk
1	cup water
½	cup butter or margarine
2	eggs

In large bowl of an electric mixer, measure 2 cups flour, sugar, salt and yeast. Place milk, water and butter in a small saucepan over low heat just until butter is melted. Temperature should be about 125°. Gradually add liquid to dry ingredients and beat 2 minutes at medium speed. Add eggs and ¾ cup flour or enough flour to make a thick batter. Beat at high speed 2 minutes. Gradually stir in just enough of the remaining flour to make a stiff dough. Turn out onto a floured board and knead 8 to 10 minutes, until dough is smooth and elastic, adding flour to board as needed to prevent dough from sticking. Smooth into a ball and place in a greased bowl. Turn once to bring greased side up. Cover with a damp cloth and let rise in a warm place (85°) until double in bulk, about 1 hour. Punch down, turn out onto a lightly floured board and knead a few minutes.

For use in recipe for Honey Buns; it also makes wonderful cinnamon rolls and coffee cakes.

Mrs. Louis Holder (Louise)
Many, Louisiana

Honey Buns

Bake at 375° for 25 minutes
Yields 15 buns

½ recipe Basic Sweet Dough
(see index)
½ cup butter or margarine,
melted
2 teaspoons cinnamon
½ cup chopped pecans
½ cup sugar
1 tablespoon honey

Roll dough into a 15x15-inch square. Brush with 2 tablespoons melted butter. Sprinkle with ¼ cup sugar and the cinnamon. Beginning with the wide side, roll tightly jellyroll fashion. Pinch edge to seal. Combine remaining butter, remaining sugar and honey. Spread evenly in bottom of a 13x9x2-inch baking pan. Arrange nuts evenly over sugar mixture. Cut roll into 1-inch slices. Place slices, cut side down, about 1-inch apart over nuts. Cover with waxed paper and a towel and let rise in a warm place (85°) until double in bulk, about 45 to 60 minutes. Bake for about 25 minutes. Remove from oven and immediately turn pan upside down on a flat tray. Let stand 1 minute then remove pan.

Mrs. Louis Holder (Louise)
Many, Louisiana

Blueberry Muffins

Bake at 375°
Yields 24 muffins

⅔ cup shortening
1 cup sugar
3 eggs
3 cups flour
2 heaping teaspoons baking
powder
1 teaspoon salt
1 cup milk
1 can blueberries, drained

Cream shortening and sugar. Add eggs, one at a time. Add sifted dry ingredients alternately with the milk. Fold in drained blueberries. Bake at 375° until golden brown. Makes approximately 2 dozen. This mixture will keep in the refrigerator two to three weeks.

Excellent with frozen or fresh blueberries.

Mrs. Walter J. Dingler (Gayle)
Austin

Cream Cheese Braids

Bake at 375° for 12 to 15 minutes
Yields 4 loaves

1   (8 ounce) carton sour
         cream
½   cup sugar
1   teaspoon salt
½   cup melted butter or
         margarine
2   packages dry yeast
½   cup warm water (105° to
         115°)
2   eggs, well beaten
4   cups all-purpose flour

Heat sour cream over low heat; stir in sugar, salt and butter; cool to lukewarm. Sprinkle yeast over warm water in a large mixing bowl, stirring until yeast dissolves. Add sour cream mixture, eggs, and flour; mix well. Cover tightly; refrigerate overnight.

The next day, divide dough into four equal parts; roll each part on a well-floured board into a 12x8-inch rectangle. Spread one-fourth of the Cream Cheese filling on each rectangle, roll up jellyroll fashion, beginning at long sides. Pinch edges together and fold ends under slightly; place rolls seam side down on greased baking sheets. Slit each loaf at 2-inch intervals about two-thirds of way through dough to resemble a braid. Cover and let rise in a warm place, free from drafts, until doubled in bulk (about 1 hour). Bake at 375° for 12 to 15 minutes. Cover with glaze while warm. This freezes well.

CREAM CHEESE FILLING

2   (8 ounce) packages cream
         cheese, softened
¾   cup sugar
1   egg, beaten
⅛   teaspoon salt
2   teaspoons vanilla extract

Combine cream cheese and sugar in a small mixing bowl. Add egg, salt and vanilla; mix well. Yield about 2 cups.

GLAZE

2   cups powdered sugar
4   tablespoons milk
2   teaspoons vanilla extract

Combine all ingredients in a small bowl; mix well.

John L. Dixon
Pasadena

103

Kolaches

Bake at 400° for 15 to 20 minutes

½ cup lukewarm water
1 soft yeast cake
½ teaspoon sugar
½ cup milk, scalded
½ cup shortening
½ cup sugar
2 teaspoons salt
2 eggs, beaten
5 cups flour, sifted
(Just enough flour
to make a soft smooth
dough)

Add yeast and sugar to water. Add milk to shortening, sugar and salt. When milk mixture is lukewarm, add yeast mixture, eggs and flour to make soft dough. Knead on lightly floured surface until smooth and elastic. Put in greased bowl; grease top and cover. Let rise in warm place until double in size. Using 1 large tablespoon dough at a time, flatten and spread on lightly floured surface until approximately 3 inches in diameter. Place a heaping teaspoon of filling in center; then bring sides together at the top and seal, covering all of the filling. Place a tablespoon of topping on each Kolache and place on greased baking sheet. Let rise until they have doubled in size. Bake at 400° for 15 to 20 minutes. Brush with melted margarine or butter and remove from pan. Serve warm with plenty of coffee.

Mrs. J. Travis Blakeslee (Gladys)
Austin

Fillings for Kolaches

APRICOT FILLING

| 1 | pound dried apricots |
| Enough water to cover apricots |
2	cups sugar
¼	teaspoon mace or
	½ teaspoon almond
	extract

Cook apricots in just enough water to cover until tender. About 20 minutes. Add sugar and cook 5 minutes longer or until thickened. Add mace or almond extract and mix well. Let cool.

CHEESE FILLING

| 1 | pound cottage cheese |
| 2 or 3 egg yolks |
1½	cups sugar
⅛	teaspoon salt
½	teaspoon lemon rind
1½	cups raisins (optional)
3	tablespoons butter or
	margarine

Combine in order listed.

PRUNE FILLING

| 1 | pound dried prunes |
| Enough water to cover prunes |
1½	cups sugar
3	tablespoons melted
	margarine or butter
½	teaspoon vanilla or
	½ teaspoon cinnamon

Cook prunes and water for about 20 minutes. Add sugar and butter and cook for additional 5 minutes. Add flavoring or cinnamon. Let cool.

Comment: Any dried fruit filling may be substituted. One can also use fresh fruits cooked and thickened.

Mrs. J. Travis Blakeslee (Gladys)
Austin

105

Nell's Cinnamon Rolls

Bake at 350°
Yields 1 dozen

1 cup milk
2 tablespoons sugar
2 tablespoons butter
1 teaspoon salt
1 package active dry yeast
¼ cup warm water
1 egg, well beaten
3½ cups flour
4 tablespoons butter
Cinnamon
Sugar
Raisins, optional
Nuts, optional

Scald milk, add butter, sugar and salt. Cool to lukewarm. Sprinkle yeast on warm water; let stand to soften, stir to dissolve. Add luke-warm milk to yeast mixture, add egg; stir to mix well. Add flour and stir well. Cover and let rise in warm place until doubled, 1 to 1½ hours. Punch down and turn onto floured surface.

Roll dough into rectangle about ¼-inch thick. Spread 4 table-spoons melted butter onto dough. Sprinkle with cinnamon and sugar to taste. Also, sprinkle on raisins and chopped nuts, if desired.

Roll dough starting on long edge, jelly-roll style. Cut in 2-inch slices. Place on greased baking sheet, cut side up, let rise 1 to 2 hours. Bake until slightly brown. Ice while hot.

ICING

1 box powdered sugar
2 tablespoons butter, melted
½ teaspoon vanilla
¼ cup milk

Blend until smooth. Pour on rolls while still hot. Makes 1 dozen large rolls.

Mrs. Walter J. Dingler (Gayle)
Austin

Cheesy Coffee Cake

Bake at 375° for 20 minutes

1	box Pillsbury Hot Roll Mix
½	cup sugar
2-3	tablespoons vegetable oil

Blend hot roll mix, sugar and oil together, following directions on box. Let rise according to directions. Spread dough on cookie sheet and pour filling over dough.

FILLING

2	(8 ounce) packages cream cheese, softened
4	eggs
⅔	cup sugar
½	teaspoon vanilla

In medium mixing bowl blend cream cheese, eggs, sugar and vanilla until thoroughly blended. Pour over dough.

TOPPING

1	stick of margarine, softened
1½	cups flour
1½	cups sugar
½	teaspoon vanilla

Mix until crumbly and spread over cream cheese mixture. Bake at 375° for 20 minutes.

Coffee Cake With Streusel Topping

Bake at 375° for 25 to 30 minutes
Serves 6

2	cups Pioneer Biscuit mix
⅓	cup sugar
¾	cup raisins
¾	cup chopped pecans
1	cup milk
1	egg, beaten
3	tablespoons butter, melted

Place biscuit mix, sugar, raisins and pecans into a mixing bowl. Add milk, egg and melted butter. Blend well. Pour into a greased 7x11-inch baking pan.

TOPPING

6	tablespoons sugar
6	tablespoons flour
3	tablespoons butter, melted
2	teaspoons cinnamon

Mix with a fork until crumbly. Spread over batter in pan. Bake for 25 to 30 minutes.

Mrs. David Tumlinson (Juanita)
Brownsville

Pineapple Fritters

Serves 4

1	cup flour
¼	teaspoon salt
1	teaspoon baking powder
⅓	cup sugar
1	egg, beaten
¼	cup milk
1	tablespoon cooking oil
1	cup crushed pineapple, drained well

Combine dry ingredients. Mix together egg, milk, oil and pineapple and lightly stir into dry mixture. Drop from a teaspoon into hot oil and fry until brown and cooked in center (3 to 5 minutes). Drain on paper towels and sprinkle with powdered sugar.

Great for breakfast with coffee or as a dessert.

Mrs. Louis Howard (Evelyn)
Garland

Apricot Bread

Bake at 350° for 55 minutes
Yields 1 loaf

1	(8 ounce) package dried apricots, in enough water to cover
1	cup sugar
2	tablespoons soft butter
1	egg
½	cup orange juice
¼	cup water
¼	teaspoon soda
1	teaspoon salt
2	teaspoons baking powder
2	cups flour
½	cup chopped nuts

Soak apricots in warm water for 30 minutes, drain and cut up fine. Cream butter and sugar, add egg, orange juice and water, blending well. Add dry ingredients making a smooth batter. Fold in chopped nuts and apricots. Pour in greased loaf pan. Bake at 350° for 55 minutes.

Mrs. John K. Gray, Jr. (Lynn)
Houston

Banana Bread

Bake at 325° for 40 minutes
Yields 1 loaf

1½ cups sugar
⅔ cup shortening
2 eggs
1 cup mashed bananas
4 tablespoons sour cream or
    buttermilk
2 cups flour
1 teaspoon soda
1 teaspoon almond extract
1 teaspoon vanilla
1 cup chopped nuts

Cream sugar and shortening until light and fluffy. Add eggs and mix well. Stir in bananas, add sour cream and the flour and soda which has been sifted together, beat well. Add almond extract, vanilla and nuts. Pour into greased and floured loaf pan (9x5x2½) or two 1 pound coffee cans. Bake at 325° for 40 minutes or until done.

Mrs. J. Travis Blakeslee (Gladys)
Austin

Raisin Bran Muffins

Bake at 400° for 15 to 20 minutes
Yields 6 dozen

1 (15 ounce) box Post's
    Raisin Bran
1 quart buttermilk
4 eggs
1 cup oil *or* melted
    shortening
2 tablespoons vanilla
5 cups flour
3½ cups sugar
5 teaspoons soda
1 teaspoon salt
1 cup chopped nuts

Mix bran and buttermilk and let soak for 5 minutes. Beat eggs and add to bran mixture; add oil and vanilla. Sift dry ingredients and add, mixing well. Fill greased muffin cups ⅔ full. Bake at 400° for 15 to 20 minutes.

This dough can be stored in the refrigerator for up to six weeks and baked as desired.

Edris Whitehall
Seabrook

109

Pumpkin Cakes

Bake at 325° for 20 minutes

1	cup brown sugar
½	cup margarine
1	egg
1	cup canned pumpkin
1	teaspoon soda
1	teaspoon baking powder
2	cups flour
1	teaspoon vanilla
1	cup chopped dates
1	cup chopped pecans

Cream sugar and margarine well. Beat in egg and pumpkin. Add sifted dry ingredients and vanilla and beat well. Fold in dates and pecans just until blended. Grease miniature muffin tins and drop by teaspoon to fill approximately ⅔ full. Bake for about 20 minutes. Do not overbake. Remove from tins to cool.

FROSTING

1	(3 ounce) package cream cheese, softened
1	cup powdered sugar
1	teaspoon vanilla

Mix together well and frost each cooled Pumpkin Cake.

Oatmeal Pancakes

Serves 4

2	eggs
1½	cups buttermilk (powdered buttermilk mixed with water works well)
1	cup quick cooking oats
1	cup all-purpose flour
½	cup sweet milk
¼	cup vegetable oil
2	tablespoons sugar
2	teaspoons baking powder
1	teaspoon baking soda
1	scant teaspoon salt

Beat eggs with hand beater till fluffy. Stir in remaining ingredients. (Very slow speed on mixer can be used.) For thinner pancakes stir in additional 2 to 4 tablespoons milk. Cook on hot griddle till puffed and dry around edges. Turn and cook other side.

May be served with any syrup, applesauce or fruit flavored syrup, but they are best sprinkled with powdered sugar.

Mrs. Harry Smith (Ginny)
Austin

Cranberry Coffee Cake

Bake at 350° for 1 hour

½ cup butter, softened
1 cup sugar
2 eggs
2 cups flour
1 teaspoon baking powder
1 teaspoon soda
½ teaspoon salt
1 (8 ounce) carton sour cream
1 tablespoon almond extract
1 (16 ounce) can whole berry
  cranberry sauce
½ cup chopped pecans

Cream butter; gradually add sugar beating until light and fluffy. Add eggs one at a time, beating well after each addition. Combine dry ingredients and add to sugar mixture alternately with sour cream beating well. Add almond extract and mix well. Spoon ⅓ of mixture into a greased and floured Bundt pan. Spread ⅓ sauce over center of batter. Repeat layers twice more, ending with cranberry sauce. Make sure not to get sauce on sides of pan. Sprinkle pecans over top. Bake and let cool 5 minutes before removing from pan. Drizzle with glaze.

GLAZE

¾ cup powdered sugar
1 teaspoon almond extract
1 tablespoon warm water

Mix until thoroughly blended and right consistency for pouring. Drizzle over cake.

Mrs. Lewis King (Pat)
Austin

Egg Salad Sandwiches

1 dozen boiled eggs,
  chopped
½ cup fresh parsley,
  chopped
4 or 5 green onions, chopped
  (tops too!)
1 (4 ounce) can chopped
  ripe olives
2 tablespoons mayonnaise
2 tablespoons mustard
Juice of 1 to 1½ fresh limes
Salt and pepper to taste

Mix all ingredients. Serve on whole wheat bread.

These sandwiches disappear instantly!

Mrs. Gerald W. McCoy (Nancy)
Austin

111

Pizza Bread Loaf

Bake at 350° for 20 minutes
Serves 10 to 12

2   packages Bridgeport
    frozen yeast bread
2   pounds hot sausage
1   (7 ounce) jar olives
2   (5 ounce) packages
    pepperoni
2   bunches green onions
1   pound Cheddar cheese,
    grated
1   pound Mozzarella cheese,
    grated
1   small can chopped
    mushrooms

Follow package directions for thawing bread loaves. Brown sausage and drain. Cut each loaf of bread in half. Stretch and roll dough and place on lightly greased cookie sheet. Layer all ingredients on dough. Sprinkle cheese on top of mixture. Fold sides to the middle, overlapping. Bake at 350°. Slice into individual servings.

Mrs. Cox R. Crider (Pam)
Mexia

Crab Cheese Filling

Yields 2 cups

1   cup creamed cottage
     cheese
½   teaspoon prepared
     mustard
1   tablespoon mayonnaise
1¼   cups flaked crabmeat

Mix all ingredients together well. Great on toast rounds.

Kay's Spam Sandwich Filling

1   large can Spam, grated
½   cup mayonnaise
⅓   cup minced onion
⅓   cup evaporated milk
1   tablespoon sweet pickle
     relish
¼   cup finely chopped Bell
     peppers
¼   teaspoon onion salt

Mix all ingredients together thoroughly.

Mrs. J. Travis Blakeslee (Gladys)
Austin

Avocado/Bacon Sandwich

Serves 2 to 3

6   slices bacon
1   medium avocado
1   medium tomato
Alfalfa sprouts
Lettuce
6   slices whole grain bread
     or
3   Pita bread
Mayonnaise
Salt and pepper, to taste

Fry bacon and drain well. Peel and slice the avocado. Peel and slice the tomato. Spread 3 slices of bread lightly with mayonnaise and layer with bacon, avocado, tomato, alfalfa sprouts and lettuce. Season with salt and pepper. Top each sandwich with another slice of bread and you are ready to serve. If using Pita bread follow same directions, stuffing ingredients in pockets.

Mrs. Walter J. Dingler (Gayle)
Austin

Cucumber Sandwiches

1   large cucumber
½   teaspoon salt
½   cup mayonnaise
1   loaf white bread

Peel cucumber and remove seeds. Cut into paper thin slices and place in ice water with ½ teaspoon of salt. Soak for 15 minutes, then drain well and pat dry with paper towels.

Trim crusts from bread slices and cut into desired shapes. Spread bread slices with mayonnaise, cover half the slices with cucumber slices. Top each with a slice of bread. Garnish with a small slice of cucumber on top of each sandwich. Cover with a slightly damp paper towel and plastic wrap and refrigerate until serving time.

Watercress Sandwiches

1	bunch watercress
6	slices brown or rye bread
2	tablespoons sweet butter
1	teaspoon lemon juice
Salt	

Wash watercress and remove stems. Pat leaves dry on a paper towel. Beat the butter and lemon juice together until smooth. Spread on bread.

Arrange enough watercress leaves to make a thin layer on half the bread slices. Sprinkle lightly with salt. Top with remaining slices. Cover with a damp paper towel and plastic wrap and chill. Garnish with remaining leaves just before serving.

Anchovy Cheese Filling

Yields 1½ cups

2	hard-boiled eggs
2	tablespoons minced anchovy fillets
1	tablespoon mayonnaise
1	cup creamed cottage cheese

Mix all ingredients together lightly.

Apricot Cheese Filling

Yields ¾ cup

¼	cup dried apricots
Water to cover apricots	
½	cup creamed cottage cheese
⅛	teaspoon salt

Soak apricots in water overnight or until tender. Drain. Cut fine with knife or kitchen scissors. Mix lightly with creamed cottage cheese and salt. Spread on bread, cut in finger size or desired shape.

Olive and Pecan Cheese Filling

Yields 2 cups

2	(8 ounce) packages cream cheese, softened
½	cup finely chopped pecans
1	cup chopped stuffed olives
¼ to ½ teaspoon garlic powder	
½	cup salad dressing

Mix all ingredients together in blender or food processor.

Basil Butter

4	tablespoons butter, softened
1 or 2 cloves garlic, minced	
1	teaspoon lemon juice
1	tablespoon finely chopped basil
Salt and pepper	

Cream the butter, beat in the garlic and lemon juice. Stir in the basil and season to taste with salt and pepper.

Black Olive Sandwich Spread

Yields 10 to 12 regular
size sandwiches

2	(8 ounce) packages cream cheese, softened
1	(4½ ounce) can ripe black olives
¼	teaspoon garlic powder
½	teaspoon Worcestershire sauce
¼	cup mayonnaise
½ to 1 cup ground pecans, optional	

Blend all ingredients and spread on white, wheat or rye bread. For party sandwiches: cut off crusts, spread and cut into fancy shapes. May be stored in covered container in refrigerator for several days.

Mrs. L. James Starr, Jr. (JoAnn)
Austin

Italian Sausage on a Bun

Serves 8 to 10 generously

2 to 3 pounds Italian sausage,
    browned and drained
    of fat
1   small stalk celery,
    chopped
4 to 5 onions, chopped
1   (28 ounce) can tomatoes
6   Bell peppers, chopped
4   large cloves of garlic,
    minced
Salt to taste

Combine all ingredients and simmer 1½ to 2 hours. Serve on hard rolls or buns.

Mrs. Bennie Adair (Carol)
Austin

Garlic Butter

5 or 6 cloves garlic, crushed
4   tablespoons butter,
    softened
Salt and pepper

Crush garlic with a garlic press into a paste. Cream the garlic into the softened butter and season with salt and pepper to taste.

Dried Beef and Cheese Filling

Yields 1 cup

¼   cup chopped dried beef
1   cup creamed cottage
    cheese

Mix ingredients together lightly. Spread on desired shaped bread, for party sandwiches, or on crackers. Also good for stuffing celery.

Baked Chicken Salad

Bake at 350° for 45 to 60 minutes
Serves 8

1	large hen, cooked until tender (reserve broth)
1	cup chopped celery
1	bunch green onions (including tops), chopped
4	hard-boiled eggs, chopped
2	tablespoons chopped parsley
1½	cups crushed potato chips
1	(10 ounce) can cream of mushroom soup
1	(10 ounce) can cream of chicken soup
¾	cup mayonnaise
1	can chicken broth

Remove skin and bones from chicken and chop into bite-size pieces. Dilute soups with chicken broth (reserved). Combine all ingredients except potato chips. Salad may be refrigerated at this point. Before baking add 1 cup crushed potato chips and mix well. Use remaining ½ cup potato chips as topping. Bake in buttered dish at 350 degrees for 45 to 60 minutes.

Mrs. Clarence Koehn (Mildred)
Houston

Chicken Salad Supreme

2½	cups cooked chicken, diced
1	cup chopped celery
1	cup sliced, white seedless grapes
½	cup slivered almonds, toasted (pecans may be substituted)
2	tablespoons minced parsley
1	teaspoon salt
1	cup mayonnaise
½	cup whipping cream, whipped

Combine all ingredients. Serve in lettuce cups. Garnish with sliced, stuffed olives or chopped ripe olives.

Mrs. William L. Seals (Betty)
Austin

Mexican Salad

Serves 4 to 6

1	pound ground beef
¼	cup chopped onion
3	cups kidney beans, drained
½	cup French dressing
½	cup water
1	tablespoon chili powder
4	cups shredded lettuce
½	cup sliced green onion
1	cup grated cheese

Fritos (optional)
Chopped avocado (optional)

Brown meat and onions. Drain well. Stir in beans, French dressing, water and chili powder. Simmer 15 minutes. Combine lettuce and onions in bowl. Add meat mixture and cheese. Toss all ingredients lightly, adding Fritos and avocados, if desired.

Mrs. Marvin Brown (Shirley)
Wake Village

Shrimp Aspic Ring

Serves 10 to 12

2	packages unflavored gelatin
½	cup water
1	cube beef bouillon
2	cups tomato juice
2	teaspoons prepared horseradish
2	teaspoons Worcestershire sauce
1	teaspoon salt
½	teaspoon celery salt
1	(7 ounce) bottle 7-Up
1	pound cooked shrimp

Soften gelatin in water. Add bouillon cube. Heat tomato juice to boiling and stir into gelatin until dissolved. Add horseradish, Worcestershire sauce, salt and celery salt. Cool slightly. Add 7-Up and pour half of mixture into 2-quart mold. Place in refrigerator until firm, arrange shrimp on top; add remaining mixture. Chill until firm. Garnish with shrimp.

Mrs. Lewis King (Pat)
Austin

Kansas Wheat-Shrimp Salad

Serves 12 to 16

1½ loaves Earthgrains Wheat
    bread (or 1 large loaf
    white bread)
1 medium onion, minced, or
    3 bunches of green
    onions, chopped
1 cup chopped celery
4 hard-boiled eggs, diced
5 cups boiled shrimp, or 4 (8
    ounce) cans shrimp
3 to 4 cups mayonnaise

Remove crusts from bread slices, butter on both sides and cube. Set aside. Combine onions, celery, eggs and shrimp. Add mayonnaise and mix well. Add bread cubes and stir until thoroughly combined. Chill well before serving.

Mrs. Ralph Tice (Nadine)
Topeka, Kansas

Molded Shrimp Salad

1 small package lemon
    flavored gelatin
1 (10 ounce) can tomato
    soup
1 teaspoon salt
3 teaspoons vinegar
½ cup chopped Bell pepper
¼ cup chopped onions
1 cup chopped celery
1 cup cottage cheese
1 cup mayonnaise
2 cups shrimp, cleaned and
    cooked

Heat gelatin and tomato soup until gelatin dissolves. Add salt and vinegar and allow to cool, then add Bell pepper, onions, celery, cheese, mayonnaise and shrimp. Refrigerate until congealed. Cut into squares and serve on lettuce leaves.

Tuna can be substituted for shrimp.

Mrs. George Bowers (Jonnie)
Austin

Mrs. John Waldrip (Gayle)
Austin

Layered Vegetable Salad

1	medium head lettuce, chopped
1	teaspoon salt
½	teaspoon pepper
2	teaspoons sugar (optional)
6	hard-boiled eggs, sliced
1	(10 ounce) package frozen peas, thawed
1	pound bacon, fried and crumbled
2	cups grated Swiss cheese
¼	cup sliced green onions, with tops
4	ribs celery, sliced

6-8 radishes, sliced (optional)

| 1 | cup fresh mushrooms, sliced |

2 or 3 medium carrots, grated

1	can sliced water chestnuts, drained
1	red onion, sliced into rings
1	Bell pepper, chopped
½	head cauliflower, broken in flowerets
1	(16 ounce) can asparagus spears, well drained

2 to 3 cups mayonnaise
Parmesan cheese and/or paprika, for garnish
Cheddar cheese, grated

Layer lettuce in large bowl. Sprinkle with salt and pepper (and sugar, if used). Make additional layers of any or all of the above ingredients, alternating colors and textures. Spread mayonnaise over top, completely sealing salad. Cover and refrigerate overnight. Sprinkle with Parmesan or Cheddar cheese and paprika before serving.

Variations of this salad were received from Mrs. Victor Byrd, Mrs. James Vercher, Mrs. Arthur Birdwell, Mrs. John Bottoms and Mrs. Benedict Cegelski. The Committee suggests that you choose the layers that most appeal to your family. Seven or eight layers are not too many!

Fruit/Crab Salad

1	medium sized pineapple
6	ounces crabmeat, flaked (frozen or canned)
⅔	cup finely chopped celery
½	cup seedless green grapes
3	tablespoons low-calorie mayonnaise
½	teaspoon curry powder
¼	cup chopped walnuts

Salt to taste

Slice pineapple lengthwise and remove meat; cut into cubes. Combine pineapple cubes, crabmeat, celery, grapes, mayonnaise and curry powder. Toss lightly, cover and refrigerate. At serving time, stir chopped walnuts into mixture. Add salt and additional curry powder to taste. Mound salad mixture into pineapple shells.

Mrs. John A. (Jack) Farrand (Phyllis)
Austin

Somen Salad & Sauce

Serves 10 to 12

1	package Somen (thin noodles), boiled
1	head lettuce, shredded
1	cup chopped ham or charsiu (Chinese red pork)
2	eggs, scrambled
3	chopped green onions
1	tablespoon cooking oil
2	tablespoons sesame oil
¼	cup shoyu (soy sauce)
½	cup vinegar
½	cup sugar

Spread cooked noodles in 9x13-inch pan. Garnish with lettuce, ham, eggs and green onions. Prepare sauce by combining cooking oil, sesame oil, shoyu, vinegar and sugar in jar and shaking well. Pour over salad and serve.

Mrs. Louis Miranda (Lorna)
Honolulu, Hawaii

Spinach Salad Supreme

Serves 6 to 8

1	pound fresh spinach
6	strips bacon
1	tablespoon bacon drippings
1	cup mayonnaise
1	teaspoon prepared mustard
½	teaspoon sugar
1	small onion, grated
¼	cup salad oil
¼	cup vinegar
¼	cup Parmesan cheese

Wash spinach three times. Dry, tear and chill for several hours. Fry bacon, reserving drippings. Break bacon into bits. Combine bacon drippings into mayonnaise. Add remaining ingredients and blend well. Toss dressing with spinach when ready to serve, adding bacon bits and additional cheese, if desired.

Additional ingredients such as sliced mushrooms, green onions, sliced ripe olives or chopped hard-boiled eggs may be added when ready to serve, if desired.

Mrs. George E. Coates (Betty)
Tacoma, Washington

Tuna-Macaroni Salad

Serves 10 to 12

1 (8 ounce) box elbow
   macaroni, cooked
1 tablespoon grated onion
2 tablespoons margarine or
   butter
2 cans tuna
1 cup diced cheddar cheese
½ cup chopped stuffed
   green olives
1 cup chopped celery
½ cup chopped pecans
2 tablespoons diced
   pimiento
3 or 4 boiled eggs, chopped
1 cup mayonnaise
½ teaspoon salt
½ teaspoon pepper

Add onion and butter to cooked macaroni and set aside. Combine tuna, cheese, olives, celery, pecans and pimiento. Chop eggs and add to tuna mixture. Add macaroni and combine with mayonnaise and seasonings. Mix well and refrigerate. Before serving, add additional mayonnaise and seasonings, if desired.

This makes a wonderful entrée or salad for a covered-dish luncheon or church supper.

Mrs. John Bottoms (Diane)
Austin

Artichoke-Rice Salad

½ to 1 cup mayonnaise
3 jars marinated artichokes
   (reserve liquid from one
   jar)
1 small can ripe olives,
   sliced
1 bunch green onions,
   chopped
1 Bell pepper, chopped
1 (4½ ounce) jar
   mushrooms, drained
   and sliced
1 box Chicken Rice-a-Roni,
   cooked according to
   directions

Combine mayonnaise with artichoke juice from one jar. Combine chopped artichokes, olives, onions, Bell pepper, mushrooms and rice. Blend dressing with rice mixture and refrigerate at least 12 hours before serving.

Mrs. Bobby W. Hodges (Lu)
Arlington

Mrs. Wallace Carlson (Ellen)
Austin

Mrs. Ed Balagia (Billie)
Austin

Broccoli-Cauliflower Salad

Serves 12 to 14

1	head cauliflower
1	bunch broccoli
½	cup chopped onion
1	cup mayonnaise
½	cup sour cream
1	tablespoon sugar
1	tablespoon vinegar
⅛	teaspoon Worcestershire sauce
⅛	teaspoon Tabasco sauce
½	teaspoon salt
¼	teaspoon pepper

Break cauliflower and broccoli into flowerets. Wash, drain well, and combine with onion. Blend remaining ingredients well and pour over vegetables. Cover and refrigerate overnight. Mix again before serving.

Mrs. Gary Covert (Susan)
Dallas

Slimming Chef's Salad

Serves 6 to 8

2	quarts mixed salad greens
1	cup shredded red cabbage
¼	pound mushrooms, sliced
½	cup chopped celery
2	tomatoes, cut into wedges
1	medium cucumber, sliced
1	small red onion, sliced
1	cup cooked turkey or chicken, cut into strips
3	ounces Swiss cheese, cut into strips
2	hard-boiled eggs, cut into wedges

Combine ingredients and serve, using favorite low-cal dressing.

Mrs. Edward C. Binder (Roma)
Lincoln, Nebraska

Chinese Sweet-Sour Vegetable Salad

Serves 10 to 12

1	(17 ounce) can LeSueur green peas, drained
1	(12 ounce) can shoe-peg corn, drained
1	cup chopped celery
¼	cup chopped Bell pepper
1	(16 ounce) can French-style green beans, drained
1	small jar chopped pimientos
¾	cup sugar
½	cup white vinegar
½	cup salad oil
½	teaspoon salt
¼	teaspoon pepper

In large bowl (with lid) combine peas, corn, celery, Bell pepper, green beans and pimientos. Mix sugar, vinegar, oil, salt and pepper together and pour over vegetables. Allow to marinate overnight in refrigerator before serving.

Mrs. Lewis King (Pat)
Austin

Copper Pennies

2	pounds carrots, sliced
⅛	teaspoon sugar
½	Bell pepper, sliced
½	medium onion, sliced
1	(10 ounce) can condensed tomato soup
½	cup vinegar
½	cup salad oil
¾	cup sugar
1	tablespoon mustard

Cook carrots in small amount of boiling, *sugared* water. Simmer about 20 minutes, covered, or until crisp tender. Drain. Combine onion, Bell pepper and carrots and set aside. In a saucepan, combine soup, vinegar, salad oil, sugar and mustard. Bring to a boil, stirring well. Pour over vegetables, toss lightly and refrigerate overnight.

Mrs. John Waldrip (Gayle)
Austin

Pea Salad

Serves 6 to 8

1 (17 ounce) can LeSueur English peas, well drained
1 medium onion, finely chopped
6 hard-boiled eggs, chopped
½ cup bacon bits (or more, if desired)
1 cup mayonnaise
1 cup grated Swiss cheese
Chopped lettuce

Mix first five ingredients. Pour over chopped lettuce, and top with cheese.

Mrs. Jack Davenport (Linda)
San Antonio

Italian Potato Salad

Serves 10 to 12

1 (2 pound) package frozen southern-style hash brown potatoes
1 (10 ounce) package frozen Italian green beans
1 teaspoon seasoned salt
⅔ cup bottled creamy Italian dressing
½ cup chopped celery
½ cup pitted Italian black olives, cut in half crosswise
2 tablespoons chopped green onion
¼ cup beef salami, diced
½ teaspoon salt
1 cup cherry tomatoes, halved
1 cup grated Provolone cheese
Romaine lettuce leaves

Cook potatoes and green beans in large skillet with seasoned salt and pepper in enough hot water to cover. Bring to boil and simmer 5 minutes, or until vegetables are crisp tender. Drain and chill. Combine dressing, celery, olives, onion, salami and salt in large bowl. Add vegetables and toss to coat with dressing. Fold in tomatoes and cheese. Chill several hours. To serve place in salad bowl lined with Romaine leaves.

Mrs. R. Bruce Harris (Georgia)
Austin

125

Janie's Hot Potato Salad

Serves 6 to 8

6	medium potatoes
1	tablespoon butter or margarine
¼	cup bacon bits (or 2 strips bacon, cooked and crumbled)
¼	cup chopped onion
1	teaspoon salt
¼	teaspoon pepper
2	medium tomatoes

Wash potatoes and cook until tender. Peel and cut into cubes and while still hot combine with butter, bacon bits, onion, salt and pepper. Mix well. Serve hot, garnished with tomato wedges.

Mrs. Jesse Lagunas (Janie)
Austin

Salad Marinduque

Serves 4

¾	cup sliced Bell pepper
¾	cup quartered tomatoes
¾	cup chopped onions
¾	cup chopped celery
1	cup regular Italian dressing
1½	cups plain yogurt

Combine all ingredients except yogurt and marinate overnight in refrigerator. When ready to serve, drain vegetables and stir in yogurt just until mixed. Serve chilled.

If you think your family doesn't like yogurt, don't tell them. They'll love it!

Mrs. Gary Voelker (Pat)
Garland

Marsha's Potato Salad

Serves 6 to 8

4	large potatoes
3	medium carrots, grated
5	hard-boiled eggs, chopped
¼	cup finely chopped onion
2	cups salad dressing
1	teaspoon salt

Boil potatoes with skins on and chill overnight. Peel cold potatoes and cut into bite-size pieces. Add remaining ingredients and thoroughly combine. Chill and serve.

Mrs. E. Lewis Boehm (Marsha)
Pearland

Rancho Salad

Serves 8 to 10

½   head lettuce, broken into
      bits
2   tomatoes, chopped
¼   cup chopped Bell pepper
      (optional)
1   (16 ounce) can ranch-style
      beans, drained
½   cup garlic-French salad
      dressing
1½   cups grated Longhorn
      cheese
1   (8 ounce) package Fritos,
      crushed

Combine lettuce, tomatoes and Bell pepper. Pour into 9x13-inch baking dish. Combine beans and dressing and pour over lettuce mixture. Cover and refrigerate overnight. Add grated cheese and crushed Fritos just before serving.

Mrs. Don McLain (Shirley)
Mesquite

Curried Rice Salad

Serves 10

1   cup rice, cooked as
      directed
1   cup mayonnaise
½   cup chutney (or sweet
      pickle relish)
1   teaspoon curry powder
1   cup chopped celery
1   (10 ounce) package frozen
      English peas, cooked
      and chilled
4   green onions, sliced
¼   teaspoon salt

Combine all ingredients and chill at least one hour before serving.

Serve in papaya halves, avocado halves, or tomato shells to accompany shrimp or other seafood, chicken or beef. Or add chicken or crab meat to salad and serve as luncheon dish.

Mrs. W. R. Morrison (Mavis)
Las Vegas, Nevada

Cole Slaw

Serves 6 to 8

½ cup salad oil
½ cup cider vinegar
1 teaspoon dry mustard
½ cup sugar
1 teaspoon salt
1 teaspoon celery salt
¼ teaspoon black pepper
1 large head of cabbage, shredded or 2 packages of prepared cole slaw mix
1 medium Bell pepper, chopped
1 medium onion, chopped
8 stuffed Spanish olives, chopped (optional)

Combine first 7 ingredients in saucepan and bring to boil. Combine cabbage, Bell pepper, onion and olives in large bowl. Pour hot dressing over vegetables. Cover and chill before serving.

This is better after 3 or 4 days!

Mrs. Curtiss Waggoner (Sheila)
Austin

Dutch Salad

Serves 10 to 12

1 (16 ounce) can sauerkraut, well drained
2 cups chopped celery
1 cup chopped onion
1 cup chopped Bell pepper
1 small jar chopped pimientos, drained
1½ cups sugar
¾ cup vinegar
¼ cup grated carrot (optional)
½ cup cauliflower flowerets, thinly sliced (optional)

Combine sauerkraut, celery, onions, Bell pepper and pimientos. In saucepan combine sugar and vinegar. Heat (do not boil) and pour over vegetables.

Keeps up to 6 weeks in refrigerator.

Mrs. A. W. VanCleave, III (Virginia)
San Antonio

The Flag of the Harrisburg Volunteers

The settlement of Harrisburg raised a company of volunteers to resist the threat of military occupation. Included in the company was Lieutenant Archaelaus B. Dodson whose bride, Sarah Rudolph Dodson, undertook to design a flag for her husband's company. The flag, a tri-color of red, white, and blue with a large white star in the blue field, flew at the head of the company as it marched to the aid of the threatened colonists of Gonzales and later at the Siege of Bexar.

FLAG OF THE HARRISBURG VOLUNTEERS
The Sarah Dodson Flag

FLAG OF THE LYNCHBURG VOLUNTEERS
Scott's Flag of Independence

The Flag of the Lynchburg Volunteers

William Scott, a wealthy settler from Kentucky, raised a company of 30 men at Lynchburg. Elected Captain, he trained the company at his home. He gave a yard of blue silk to Lieutenant James McGahey and instructed him to have it made into a flag for the company. McGahey, with the assistance of a Mrs. Lynch and an artist named Zanco, made the flag which featured a large white painted star and the lettering "Independence." The flag was carried at the Siege of Bexar and at the Battle of Conception, where Lieutenant McGahey was wounded. The flag passed into the keeping of Thomas Bell. It is believed that Scott's flag may have accompanied the ill-fated Matamoros Expedition.

Spinach-Pea Salad

Serves 12 to 14

1   (16 ounce) bag frozen
     peas
1   pound bacon, cooked,
     drained and crumbled
1   bunch green onions,
     chopped
½   pound fresh spinach,
     cleaned and torn into
     bite-sized pieces
1   can sliced water
     chestnuts, drained (or
     slivered almonds)
6   hard-boiled eggs,
     chopped
2   cups mayonnaise
1   cup sour cream
1   package Hidden Valley
     Ranch dressing mix

Layer in large bowl: frozen peas (do not cook), bacon, chopped green onions, spinach, water chestnuts or almonds, hard-boiled eggs. Mix together mayonnaise, sour cream and dressing mix and pour over salad. Refrigerate until serving.

Mrs. Ron Buettner (Cindy)
Victoria

Mrs. John Sockwell (Billie)
Arlington

Syrian Salad

Serves 8

½   cup bulgar (cracked
     wheat) or Taboli Mix
2   bunches fresh parsley
2 to 3 tomatoes
1   bunch green onions
¼   cup fresh lemon juice
¼   cup dried mint
3   tablespoons olive oil
⅛   teaspoon cinnamon
Salt and pepper to taste

Wash the cracked wheat under cold water. Soak in cold water ½ hour. (It is important that it absorb water and swell.) Drain and squeeze well. Finely chop parsley and onion in food processor or blender. Finely chop tomatoes. Mix all ingredients together and serve on lettuce leaves.

An unusual and highly nutritious Middle Eastern salad. Will stay fresh for several days. May be accompanied by warm Pita bread.

Mrs. Harry Steel (Louisa)
San Antonio

Mrs. Sam Cantu (Sandra)
Austin

Texas Tossed Salad

Serves 12 to 14

1	(16 ounce) package Velveeta cheese
⅓	cup evaporated milk
2	large tomatoes, chopped and drained
2	jalapeño peppers, chopped and drained
2	avocados, sliced
1	large onion, sliced
1	head lettuce, torn in bite-size pieces
1	(8 ounce) package Fritos

In top of double boiler, melt cheese and add milk to make smooth cheese sauce. Add more milk if necessary. Combine all other ingredients, including Fritos, and mix well. Add cheese sauce and serve immediately.

Mrs. George Bowers (Jonnie)
Austin

Creamy Vegetable Salad

Serves 8 to 10

1	(10 ounce) can tomato soup
1	(3 ounce) package cream cheese, softened
1	small package lemon flavored gelatin (or 1 envelope unflavored gelatin)
½	cup cold water
1	cup mayonnaise
½	cup finely chopped celery
½	cup finely chopped onion
½	cup finely chopped Bell pepper
1	small jar chopped pimientos
½	cup stuffed olives, chopped
½	cup finely chopped cucumber

Place soup in saucepan and bring to boil. Add cream cheese, stirring until well blended. Soften gelatin in cold water and stir into soup. Allow to cool, then add mayonnaise and chopped vegetables and mix well. Pour into an oiled 6-cup mold. Chill until firm.

This mold is especially good for ladies' luncheon. For variations, try adding a can of shrimp, a can of tuna, or a cup of finely chopped ham, corned beef or left-over roast beef.

Mrs. Vernon Scofield (Audrey)
Austin

Sinful Salad

Serves 4 to 6

1   **small package cherry
gelatin**
1   **(8 ounce) can crushed
pineapple, with juice**
1   **cup sugar**
1   **cup cold water**
1   **cup grated Longhorn
cheese**
1   **envelope whipped topping
(prepared)**
½   **cup chopped pecans
(optional)**

Heat pineapple (with juice) and sugar until dissolved. Add gelatin and pour into bowl. Chill until almost firm. Fold in cheese, whipped topping and nuts. Chill until firm.

Mrs. Kenneth R. Pruitt (Nevellyn)
Austin

Sour Cream Delight

2   **(11 ounce) cans mandarin
oranges, drained**
2   **cans Angel Flake coconut**
2   **(8 ounce) cans pineapple
tidbits, drained**
1   **cup chopped pecans**
2   **cups miniature
marshmallows**
2   **cups sour cream**

Combine all ingredients and toss gently. Chill several hours before serving.

Mrs. Manuel Daniel (Bertha)
San Antonio

In 1820 Texas was a very sparsely inhabited land. The total population was about 3,000. San Antonio de Bexar was the most populous with 1,814 souls. Bahia (present day Goliad) had 600. The remainder were scattered along the lower Rio Grande Valley.
     —*Juan Antonio Padilla, "Texas in 1820,"*
Southwestern Historical Quarterly, 23 (1919), 61.

Pineapple Cucumber Mold

Serves 8 to 10

1 cup crushed pineapple, drained
1 small package lemon gelatin
½ teaspoon salt
½ cup finely grated carrots
1 envelope unflavored gelatin
¼ cup cold water
1 cup mayonnaise
½ cup half and half cream (sour cream may be used)
1 tablespoon grated onion
½ cup finely chopped celery
½ cup grated cucumber, drained
½ teaspoon salt

Drain pineapple. Add enough water to syrup to make 1¾ cups liquid. Heat this to boiling and dissolve gelatin. Chill until slightly thickened. Add salt, carrots and pineapple. Turn into ring or mold. Chill until firm. Soften unflavored gelatin in cold water, then dissolve over hot water. Combine remaining ingredients, adding gelatin, and blend. If desired, tint a pale green with food coloring. Pour over pineapple layer in mold. Chill until firm. Unmold onto serving plate, garnishing with salad greens.

Mrs. Allan Shivers (Marialice)
Austin

Angel Salad

Serves 10

1 (8 ounce) package cream cheese
½ cup sugar
1 teaspoon vanilla
1 (16 ounce) can fruit cocktail, drained
1 (20 ounce) can crushed pineapple, well drained
1 envelope Dream Whip (prepared)
1 cup chopped nuts

Prepare Dream Whip according to directions. Blend cream cheese, sugar and vanilla. Add drained fruits and mix gently. Fold in Dream Whip. Sprinkle nuts on top. Chill at least 4 hours before serving.

Mrs. James H. Duran (Luella)
Red Rock

SALADS

Apricot Delight

Serves 12 to 14

2   small packages orange
    gelatin
2   cups boiling water
½   cup juice (apricot and
    pineapple)
1   (16 ounce) can apricots,
    drained and chopped
    (reserve juice)
1   (20 ounce) can crushed
    pineapple, drained
    (reserve juice)
1½ cups miniature
    marshmallows (more if
    preferred)
½   cup sugar
3   tablespoons flour
1   egg, beaten
1   cup fruit juice
2   tablespoons butter or
    margarine
1   cup whipping cream,
    whipped
¾   cup grated cheese

Dissolve gelatin in water, then add
½ cup fruit juice. Chill until frothy.
Fold in fruits and marshmallows.
Pour into dish and chill until firm.
Spread with topping. To prepare
topping, combine sugar and flour
in saucepan. Blend in egg and
gradually add 1 cup juice. Cook
over low heat until thick. Add butter. Cool thoroughly. Whip cream
and fold into cooled mixture.
Spread over salad. Sprinkle with
grated cheese. Chill thoroughly
before serving.

Mrs. Eugene A. Mees (Norma Blotter)
Austin

Mrs. John Blatsos (Aphrodite)
Manchester, New Hampshire

Frozen Banana Salad

Serves 10 to 14

1   cup sour cream
1   cup sugar
2   (12 ounce) cartons
    whipped topping
1   (20 ounce) can crushed
    pineapple, drained
1   (8 ounce) jar maraschino
    cherries, drained
5   bananas, mashed
1   cup chopped nuts
2½ teaspoons lemon juice

Blend sugar and sour cream, then
add other ingredients. Freeze. Let
stand about fifteen minutes
before serving. This salad can be
re-frozen over and over again.

Mrs. Rufus Spraberry (Doris)
Abilene

133

Blueberry Salad

Serves 8 to 10

1   large package blackberry or raspberry gelatin
2   cups boiling water
1   cup juice from fruits
1   (8 ounce) can crushed pineapple, drained (reserve juice)
1   (14 ounce) can blueberries, drained (save juice)
1   (8 ounce) package cream cheese
1   cup sour cream
½   cup sugar
1   teaspoon vanilla
½   cup chopped pecans

Mix gelatin with boiling water and 1 cup fruit juices. Add pineapple and blueberries. Refrigerate until completely firm. Combine cream cheese and sour cream with sugar and vanilla. Spread over congealed salad. Sprinkle nuts on top.

Mrs. Leonard Tallas (Jean)
Austin

Cherry Salad

Serves 12 to 14

2   (16 ounce) cans water-packed whole cherries, drained (reserve juice)
1   (20 ounce) can crushed pineapple, drained (reserve juice)
4   small boxes cherry gelatin
1   cup sugar
3   cups ginger ale
1   cup chopped pecans
½   cup coconut (optional)

Drain pineapple and cherries. Add enough water to juices to make 3 cups liquid. Heat with sugar. Pour into gelatin and mix well. Add fruits and chilled ginger ale. Chill until partially set, then add pecans and coconut. Chill until thoroughly set.

Mrs. Larry Yandell (Gayle)
Austin

Cranberry Salad

Serves 6 to 8

1   cup ground fresh
       cranberries
1   cup sugar
1   cup whipping cream,
       whipped
1   cup miniature
       marshmallows
½   cup walnuts, chopped

Grind cranberries, add sugar and let set overnight in refrigerator. Whip cream and fold in cranberries, marshmallows and nuts. Chill until served. (Salad can be prepared 2 to 4 hours before serving.)

Mrs. Joe Montgomery (Norma)
Austin

Cherry Party Salad

Serves 12

1   (9 ounce) carton whipped
       topping
1   can sweetened
       condensed milk (not
       evaporated)
1   (11 ounce) can mandarin
       oranges, diced and
       drained
1   can cherry pie filling
1   (20 ounce) can crushed
       pineapple with juice
2   cups miniature
       marshmallows
1   cup chopped nuts
       (optional)

Mix whipped topping and condensed milk. Add remaining ingredients and refrigerate until congealed (about 3 hours).

Mrs. Wilfred A. Martin (Cathy)
McQueeney

Creative Fruit Salad

Serves 8 to 10

1   can cherry pie filling
1   small box instant vanilla
     pudding mix
1   (20 ounce) can pineapple
     chunks (with juice)
2 to 3 cups fresh strawberries,
     sliced
1   medium banana, chopped

Combine all ingredients until well blended. Refrigerate until using. (Can be kept up to a week if tightly covered.)

Mrs. Darrel Baker (Linda)
Austin

Frozen Fruit Cups

Serves 32

1   (12 ounce) can frozen
     orange juice
     concentrate
1   (12 ounce) can water
1   (16 ounce) can pineapple
     tidbits, undrained
1   (17 ounce) can apricots,
     drained and diced
6   bananas, diced
1   cup miniature
     marshmallows (optional)
1   cup sugar
2   tablespoons lemon juice

Fold all ingredients together, gently. Place paper muffin liners in muffin pans. Fill liners with salad and freeze. When frozen, remove from muffin tin and store in freezer bags. Remove individual salads as needed, a few minutes before serving. Remove paper liner and serve.

Mrs. Charles M. Kiefner (Marilyn)
Perryville, Missouri

Heavenly Fruit Salad

Serves 8

1½ cups cold milk
3 tablespoons Triple Sec or any fruit liqueur
1 small package instant vanilla pudding mix
1 (8 ounce) carton whipped topping
1 (11 ounce) can mandarin oranges
2 bananas, sliced (dip in lemon juice to keep from turning dark)
4 cups fresh fruits in season (cantaloupe, strawberries, seedless grapes, apples, peaches, pears, pineapple, etc.)

Mix milk and Triple Sec or liqueur with pudding mix. Beat at low speed for 1 minute. Add whipped topping and beat for 1 minute. Mix fruit of your choice. Layer ½ fruit mixture, then half of pudding mixture. Layer remainder of fruit, and top with remaining pudding. Refrigerate.

Mrs. William L. Seals (Betty)
Austin

Holiday Fruit Salad

Serves 4 to 6

1 (3 ounce) package cream cheese, softened
1 (8 ounce) can pineapple chunks (drained)
24 maraschino cherries, quartered
1½ cups miniature marshmallows
¼ cup chopped pecans or other nuts

Mix cream cheese with a little cherry juice to soften. Combine all ingredients and chill for 4 hours before serving. (Salad may be frozen and kept for up to 2 months.)

This salad is a family favorite and a "must" with our Thanksgiving and Christmas dinners. It can easily be doubled.

Mrs. Stephen B. McElroy (Eleta)
Houston

Cooked Fruit Salad

Serves 12

2   **envelopes unflavored gelatin**
1   **cup cold water**
1   **cup sugar**
⅔   **cup vinegar**
½   **cup fruit juice**
2   **eggs, well beaten**
1   **(8 ounce) can crushed pineapple (reserve juice)**
1   **(16 ounce) can apricots, chopped (reserve juice)**
1   **cup whipping cream, whipped**
1   **(8 ounce) package Velveeta cheese, grated**

Dissolve gelatin in cold water and set aside. Combine sugar, vinegar, fruit juice and eggs in saucepan and cook for 5 minutes, stirring constantly. Remove from heat and add gelatin mixture. Add remaining ingredients and chill until firm.

Good served with ham!

Mrs. Thomas I. Gabbert (Jo Beth)
Ballinger

Orange Cream Fruit Salad

Serves 14 to 16

1   **(20 ounce) can pineapple chunks, drained well**
1   **(32 ounce) can peach slices, drained well**
2   **(11 ounce) cans mandarin oranges, drained well**
3   **medium bananas, sliced**
2   **medium apples, chopped (peel, if desired)**
1   **small package instant vanilla pudding mix**
½   **cup milk**
½   **(6 ounce) can undiluted frozen orange juice**
1   **cup sour cream**

Mix all drained fruits in large bowl and add bananas and apples. Cover and chill. Blend together the pudding mix, milk and orange juice. Beat in sour cream until well mixed. Chill until ready to serve. Combine fruits and pudding mixture when ready to serve. (Do not combine before serving as it does not keep well.)

Mrs. Lewis King (Pat)
Austin

Mrs. Morgan's Green Salad

Serves 12 to 16

1 small package lime gelatin
1 small package lemon
  gelatin
4 cups boiling water
12 to 18 large marshmallows,
  chopped (or 2 cups
  miniatures)
1 cup crushed pineapple,
  drained (use juice as
  part of liquid)
½ cup chopped pecans
1 cup whipping cream,
  whipped (or 1 envelope
  whipped topping,
  prepared)
1 (3 ounce) package cream
  cheese

Combine gelatins, marshmallows and boiling water, stirring until completely dissolved. Chill until slightly thickened. Combine pineapple, pecans, cream cheese and whipped cream and fold into gelatin mixture. Chill until firm.

Instead of dissolving marshmallows, they may be placed on top of chilled salad as topping.

Mrs. Milton Ray Ooley
Colorado Springs, Colorado

Nutty Green Salad

Serves 8 to 10

2 small packages lime
  gelatin
1 cup boiling water
1 (20 ounce) can crushed
  pineapple, with juice
1 (13 ounce) can evaporated
  milk
1 cup chopped pecans

Combine gelatin and water. Mix well. Allow to cool to room temperature. Add milk, pineapple and pecans. Pour into mold and chill until firm.

Mrs. Joe Gregory (Gloria)
San Antonio

Strawberry Delight

Serves 12

1	large package strawberry gelatin
1	cup boiling water
2	(10 ounce) packages frozen, sliced strawberries (thawed)
1	(20 ounce) can crushed pineapple, drained
3	medium bananas, mashed
1	cup chopped nuts
1	(8 ounce) package cream cheese
1	cup sour cream

Combine gelatin and water and stir until dissolved. Add strawberries, pineapple, bananas and nuts. Pour one-half into a 12x8-inch dish and refrigerate until firm. Soften cream cheese and blend with sour cream. Spread evenly over chilled salad. Gently spoon on remaining half of strawberry mixture. Chill. (Whipped topping may be substituted for cream cheese, if desired.)

Mrs. Harold Loftis (Billie)
Austin

Green Gage Plum Salad

Serves 6

1	small package lemon gelatin
1	cup boiling water
1	(3 ounce) package cream cheese
1	(16 ounce) can green gage plums, drained and diced (reserve juice)
1	cup liquid (plum juice and water)
2	teaspoons vinegar

Dissolve gelatin in boiling water. Add cream cheese, vinegar, plums and liquid. Chill until firm, stirring occasionally. Serve with Curried Salad Dressing (see index).

Mrs. Leonard Tallas (Jean)
Austin

Cucumber Dressing

½   cup mayonnaise
¼   cup minced cucumber
1   tablespoon minced Bell
      pepper
1   teaspoon tarragon vinegar
¼   teaspoon salt
⅛   teaspoon cayenne pepper

Combine all ingredients and mix well.

Delicious served over Congealed Shrimp Salad.

Curried Salad Dressing

2   cups mayonnaise
Juice of 1 lemon
1   teaspoon curry powder
4   tablespoons orange
      marmalade
½   cup slivered almonds,
      toasted

Combine all ingredients and re-frigerate several hours before serving.

Especially good with Green Gage Plum Salad.

Mrs. Leonard Tallas (Jean)
Austin

Honey Dressing

Yields approximately 1 pint

⅔   cups sugar
5   tablespoons vinegar
1   teaspoon celery seed
1   teaspoon salt
1   teaspoon dry mustard
1   tablespoon grated onion
Juice of two lemons
1   cup oil
⅔   cup honey

Heat sugar and vinegar in saucepan until sugar is melted. Allow to cool completely before adding other ingredients. Mix all ingredients and refrigerate. Serve as dressing over varied fruits (banana slices, pineapple chunks, peach slices, cantaloupe balls, strawberries, seedless grapes, etc.).

Mrs. Willie L. Scott (Billie)
Austin

141

Mountain Top Dressing

2	cups mayonnaise
1	(12 ounce) bottle chili sauce
4	hard-boiled eggs, chopped
2	Bell peppers, finely chopped
½	bunch parsley, chopped
1	small jar chopped pimientos
1	small onion, finely chopped

Mix all ingredients and chill. Stir before serving.

Mrs. Walter J. Dingler (Gayle)
Austin

Poppy Seed Dressing

1	cup salad oil
⅓	cup vinegar
½	cup sugar
1	tablespoon dry mustard
1	teaspoon salt
½	tablespoon poppyseeds
1	small onion, chopped
⅛	teaspoon cayenne pepper

Mix all dry ingredients in blender jar. Add vinegar and small amount of oil. Blend a few seconds, then add remaining oil very slowly, while continuing to blend.

Mrs. Leonard Tallas (Jean)
Austin

Ranch Dressing Mix

¾	cup buttermilk powder
3	tablespoons instant minced onion
2	teaspoons garlic chips *or* 1 teaspoon garlic powder
3	tablespoons parsley flakes
½	cup water
1	cup mayonnaise

Mix buttermilk powder, minced onion, garlic chips and parsley flakes. Store, tightly covered, in refrigerator.

Mix ¼ cup mix with water and mayonnaise. Blend until smooth and chill for two hours before using.

The Cookbook Committee

Secret Salad Dressing

1   cup mayonnaise
¼   teaspoon salt
1   teaspoon Beau Monde
         seasoning
1   tablespoon grated onion
1   tablespoon chopped
         chives
½   teaspoon Worcestershire
         sauce
¼   teaspoon paprika
½   teaspoon lemon juice
1   teaspoon parsley flakes
1   clove garlic, crushed
⅛   teaspoon curry powder
½   cup sour cream

Blend all ingredients well, then fold in sour cream. Keep refrigerated.

This dressing is good over salad greens, but is equally good as a sandwich spread or sauce for seafood.

Mrs. John Bottoms (Diane)
Austin

Green Pastures' Strawberry Dressing

2   tablespoons powdered
         sugar
1   cup freshly crushed
         strawberries
2   tablespoons fresh lemon
         juice
1   cup sour cream
1   cup mayonnaise

Mix all ingredients. Chill well and serve over fresh fruit.

Sweet & Sour Salad Dressing

1   cup vegetable oil
⅓   cup catsup
¼   cup cider vinegar
1   teaspoon onion flakes
1   teaspoon Worcestershire
         sauce
⅛   teaspoon ground cloves
⅓   cup sugar

Blend all ingredients and refrigerate.

This dressing is equally good on salad greens or assorted fruits.

Mrs. William L. Byrd (Maxine)
Round Rock

Migas (Corn Tortillas With Eggs)

Serves 4

6 slices bacon, diced
8 to 10 corn tortillas, diced
½ medium onion, sliced
4 eggs, well beaten
Salt and pepper
1 fresh tomato, diced
2 to 3 tablespoons picante sauce

Cook bacon until crisp. Dice tortillas and add to bacon and fry until crisp. Add sliced onion, salt and pepper and simmer 3 to 5 minutes. Drain excess grease. Add eggs and cook until almost done. Blend in diced tomato and picante sauce just until heated. Serve with slices of avocado and steaming hot refried beans.

This is an "anytime" dish you can serve for breakfast, lunch, dinner or midnight snack. In the essence of time you may wish to use Fritos in place of corn tortillas, but omit the salt and add the Fritos with the tomatoes and picante sauce.

Mrs. Ruben Torres (Olga)
Alice

Philly Eggs

Serves 6

1 tablespoon chopped green onions
1 tablespoon margarine
1 (8 ounce) package cream cheese, crumbled
¾ cup milk
3 hard-boiled eggs, sliced
1 teaspoon lemon juice
Salt and pepper
3 English muffins
6 thin slices ham or Canadian bacon, cooked
Paprika

In saucepan sauté onion in melted margarine. Add cheese and milk. Over low heat stir until sauce is smooth. Add eggs, juice and seasonings. Butter English muffin halves and toast lightly under broiler. Top each half with slice of meat and spoon egg mixture over top. Sprinkle with paprika and serve immediately.

Artichoke Frittata

Bake at 350° for 1 hour
Serves 4 to 6

1 **(14 ounce) can artichokes**
  or **1 package frozen**
6 **green onions**
2 **tablespoons olive oil**
4 **eggs, beaten**
1 **teaspoon salt**
¼ **teaspoon cayenne pepper**
¼ **teaspoon garlic powder**
2 **tablespoons grated**
  Romano or Parmesan
  cheese
1 **cup grated Cheddar**
  cheese
1 **tablespoon chopped**
  parsley
¼ **cup fine dry Italian**
  Seasoned bread
  crumbs
Paprika

Chop artichokes and green onions. Mix all ingredients. Sprinkle bread crumbs in bottom of 7x9-inch baking dish and pour ingredients over bread crumbs. Sprinkle with paprika. Bake for 1 hour or until set. Microwave 8 minutes 30 seconds covered with wax paper.

May be cut into squares and served as an hors d'oeuvre and broccoli can be substituted for artichokes.

Mrs. Vernon Andrews (Grace)
Lansing, Michigan

Ham and Broccoli Quiche

Bake at 400° for 15 minutes;
300° for 25 to 30 minutes
Serves 4 to 6

1 **cup minced ham**
1 **(10 ounce) package frozen**
  chopped broccoli
1 **cup grated Swiss cheese**
⅓ **cup chopped onion**
1 **9-inch pie shell, unbaked**
3 **eggs, beaten**
1¾ **cups milk**
½ **teaspoon salt**
⅛ **teaspoon pepper**

Sprinkle ham, broccoli, cheese and onion in pie shell. Combine eggs, milk, salt and pepper and pour into pie shell. Bake until custard is set. Allow to stand 10 minutes before serving.

Mrs. W. David Counts (Mary)
Knox City

145

Broccoli-Carrot Frittata

Serves 6 to 8

1½	cups chopped broccoli
½	cup medium diced carrots (about 1 medium)
¼	cup water
8	eggs
½	cup milk
1	tablespoon instant minced onion
2	teaspoons prepared mustard
1	teaspoon seasoned salt
⅛	teaspoon pepper
¾	cup grated Cheddar cheese
1	tablespoon butter

Place broccoli, carrot and water in a 10-inch skillet with ovenproof handle. Cover and cook over medium-high heat until carrot is crisp tender, about 5 to 10 minutes. Drain well and set aside. Beat together eggs, milk and seasonings. Stir in cheese and drained broccoli and carrot. Melt butter in same pan over medium heat. Pour egg-vegetable mixture into pan. Cook over low-medium heat until eggs are almost set, 8 to 10 minutes.

Cover pan, remove from heat and let stand 8 to 10 minutes or broil about 6 inches from heat until eggs are completely set, 2 to 3 minutes. Cut into wedges and serve from pan or invert onto serving platter.

This is a lazy-man's omelet.

Brunch Casserole

Bake at 350° for 40 minutes
Serves 8 to 10

6	slices buttered bread, crusts removed
1	pound "hot" breakfast sausage, browned and drained
6	eggs, slightly beaten
1	teaspoon salt
1	pound Cheddar cheese, grated
2	cups half and half cream
1	teaspoon dry mustard

Grease 9x13-inch baking dish. Layer bread on bottom. Add sausage, then cheese. Combine eggs, cream, salt and mustard. Pour over cheese. Refrigerate overnight. Bake until firm and lightly browned.

Mrs. Victor Byrd (Jean)
Mrs. R. Bruce Harris (Georgia)
Austin

Crouton Casserole

Bake at 325° for 55 minutes

2   cups croutons, plain or
       flavored
1   cup grated Cheddar
       cheese
4   eggs, beaten
1   cup minus 2 tablespoons
       half and half cream
1   cup minus 2 tablespoons
       milk
4   tablespoons sherry
1   teaspoon salt
1   teaspoon pepper
½   teaspoon dry mustard
⅛   teaspoon Accent
⅛   teaspoon garlic salt
4   slices bacon, fried crisp,
       drained and crumbled

Butter casserole dish and spread croutons evenly. Cover with cheese. Combine eggs, half and half, milk, sherry, salt, pepper, mustard, Accent and garlic salt and pour over cheese. Sprinkle bacon on top. Leftovers can be frozen and reheated in foil.

Mrs. J. Travis Blakeslee (Gladys)
Austin

Mexican Quiche

Bake at 425° for 15 minutes,
350° for 20 to 25 minutes
Serves 6 to 8

1   (4 ounce) can chopped
       green chilies
6   slices bacon, cooked and
       crumbled
1   cup grated Swiss cheese
1   9-inch deep dish pie shell,
       unbaked
3   eggs
1   cup half and half cream
¼   teaspoon salt
Dash ground nutmeg

Fry bacon, drain and crumble. Mix with green chilies. Sprinkle cheese over pie shell, then add bacon and chilies. Mix eggs, cream, salt and nutmeg. Pour over cheese mixture. Preheat oven and cookie sheet. Bake quiche on cookie sheet to prevent spills. Bake until knife inserted in center comes out clean. Allow to set 10 to 15 minutes before serving.

Mrs. Jackie Shaw (Marlene)
Pampa

Egg-Cheese Casserole

Bake at 350° for 30 minutes
Serves 12

8   slices bread, crusts
     removed
6   tablespoons butter, melted
Prepared mustard
6   eggs (at room
     temperature)
3   cups milk
1   pound *sharp* Cheddar
     cheese, grated
1   teaspoon salt
½   teaspoon Tabasco sauce
½   cup fresh mushrooms,
     sliced
Cooked sausage, bacon or ham,
     optional

Brush one side of bread with melted butter. Cover lightly with mustard. Cut each slice into 9 little squares. Grease 9x12-inch baking pan and line with bread squares, butter side up. Beat eggs and add milk, cheese, salt, Tabasco sauce, and mushrooms. Add meat, if desired. Mix and pour over bread squares. Distribute evenly. Cover and refrigerate overnight. Uncover and put into a cold oven. Turn to 350° and bake 30 minutes or until done. Let stand a few minutes before serving.

I especially like this recipe to serve for brunch.

Mrs. Jack Redmond (Sue)
Houston

Mexican Breakfast

6   eggs, well beaten
Salt and pepper to taste
10 to 12 tortillas (corn or flour),
     heated
Picante sauce
Optionals:
2   green onions (chopped)
Diced green chilies
Sausage, cooked and drained
Potatoes, cooked and chopped
Refried beans
Grated cheese

Combine eggs and your choice of optional ingredients (one or more). Scramble in oiled skillet. Lightly butter a hot tortilla, add 2 tablespoons egg mixture and hot sauce to taste. Roll up and enjoy!

Mrs. O. W. McClure (Louise)
Friendswood

148

Cheese Enchiladas

Bake at 350° for 20 to 30 minutes
Serves 12

2	cups finely chopped onion
4	cloves garlic, chopped
¼	cup oil
2	cups chicken broth
1	(16 ounce) can tomatoes
½	can Rotel tomatoes and chilies
¼	cup chili powder
2	teaspoons salt
2	teaspoons cumin
2	teaspoons oregano
¼	teaspoon pepper
24	corn tortillas
6	cups grated Cheddar or Monterey Jack cheese

Sauté onion and garlic in oil till tender. Drain excess oil. Add broth, tomatoes, chili powder and seasonings. Heat to boiling. Simmer 20 minutes. Dip tortillas in sauce to soften slightly. Place about 2 tablespoons cheese on each tortilla and roll up. Place seam side down in baking dish. Pour remaining sauce over enchiladas and sprinkle with remaining cheese. (Use two 9x13x2-inch baking dishes.)
Optional: add sour cream to sauce depending on taste.

Mrs. Don Daniel (Gerry)
Portland

Mrs. Charles Holland (Judy)
Fort Worth

Rice-A-Roni Quiche

Bake at 375° for 35 to 40 minutes
Serves 6 to 8

1	(8 ounce) package chicken-flavored Rice-A-Roni
1½	cups grated cheese (Swiss, Cheddar or Monterey Jack)
1	cup milk
¼	cup oil
3	eggs, beaten
¼	cup thinly sliced green onions
¼	teaspoon salt
⅛	teaspoon pepper
6	slices bacon, cooked and crumbled

Cook Rice-A-Roni in 2½ cups water following directions on box. Cool and press into a 9 or 10-inch pie plate to form crust. Combine cheese, milk, oil, eggs, green onions, salt and pepper and pour into shell. Crumble bacon pieces on top. Bake until firm. Allow to set 5 minutes before serving. ½ cup sausage or ham may be substituted for bacon.

Mrs. John Byrns (Helen)
Garland

Never-Fail Cheese Soufflé

Bake at 450° for 5 minutes;
325° for 50 to 60 minutes
Serves 10 to 12

12 to 14 slices bread
1½ cups grated Old English
      sharp cheese
1   cup unsalted butter,
      melted
5   eggs
2½ cups half and half cream
Salt and pepper to taste

Remove crusts from bread. Cube bread. Grease 2-quart casserole; line bottom with bread cubes, then alternate layers of bread and cheese, ending with bread. Sprinkle with salt and pepper. Beat eggs until light, combine with butter, then milk. Pour over bread and cheese. Cover and allow to stand in refrigerator 8 to 10 hours. Place, uncovered, in shallow pan with hot water.

Mrs. Robert M. Cavett (Dorothy)
Austin

Easy Quiche

Bake at 425° for 20 to 25 minutes
Serves 6 to 8

1   can crescent rolls
2   cups grated cheese
      (Cheddar or Monterey
      Jack)
4   eggs
¾   cup milk
½   tablespoon minced onion
½   medium Bell pepper, finely
      chopped
Salt and pepper, to taste
Meat: 12 to 16 ounces brown
      and serve sausages, *or*
1   cup chopped ham, *or*
1   pound pan sausage,
      browned and drained

Line 9x13-inch baking dish with crescent rolls. Layer meat over rolls, then sprinkle cheese. Combine remaining ingredients and pour over cheese.

An easy main dish for a ladies luncheon!

Mrs. Thomas Stone (Claudette)
Temple

Vegetable Medley Quiche

Bake at 375° for 20 to 25 minutes.
Serves 4

2	cups cooked vegetables (cauliflower, broccoli, yellow squash, etc.)
1	cup grated Cheddar cheese
½	cup chopped onion
1	cup milk
4	eggs
4	tablespoons flour
1	teaspoon baking powder
1	teaspoon salt
⅛	teaspoon pepper
4	teaspoons oil

Lightly grease 10-inch pie pan or quiche pan. Sprinkle vegetables on the bottom, then cheese and onion. Mix the remaining ingredients in the blender and pour over vegetables and cheese. Bake until golden brown or knife inserted comes out clean. Let stand a few minutes before serving.

Vary cheeses and vegetables for a completely different taste. Too good to be "low calorie".

**Mrs. Stephen Tomac (Bonnie)
Richardson**

Zucchini Quiche

Bake at 375° for 18 to 20 minutes
Serves 6 to 8

4	cups zucchini, thinly sliced
1	cup chopped onion
½	cup margarine
2	tablespoons parsley flakes
½	teaspoon salt
½	teaspoon pepper
¼	teaspoon garlic powder
¼	teaspoon sweet basil leaves
¼	teaspoon oregano
2	eggs, beaten
1	cup grated mozzarella cheese
1	teaspoon prepared mustard
1	10-inch pie shell, unbaked

Sauté zucchini and onion in margarine (may be microwaved, if desired) until tender. Add parsley flakes, salt, pepper, garlic powder, basil and oregano. Blend eggs and cheese and add to zucchini mixture. Spread mustard on pie shell. Pour in the squash mixture. After baking, allow to stand 5 to 10 minutes before serving.

**Mrs. Clarence Lucas (Thelma)
Austin**

Roast Filét of Beef

Bake at 425° 20 to 30 minutes
Serves 8

1	(4 pound) filét of beef, trimmed

3 or 4 cloves garlic
1   teaspoon salt
1   teaspoon freshly ground pepper
½   teaspoon Tabasco sauce
1   cup soy sauce
½   cup olive oil
1   cup port wine
1   teaspoon rosemary
1   bay leaf
Bacon strips

Make small gashes in roast and fill with slivers of garlic. Rub well with salt, pepper and Tabasco. Marinate for several hours in soy sauce, olive oil, port wine, and herbs. (Marinade may be made the day before.) Turn meat several times. Place on a rack in a shallow roasting pan, top with bacon strips, and roast at 425° for 25 to 30 minutes. Baste with marinade several times.

Mrs. Carl D. Wallace (Yvonne)
Lebanon, Tennessee

Roast Beef

Bake at 325° to desired taste

4 to 6 pound sirloin tip roast
Garlic salt
Lemon-pepper

Sprinkle roast generously with garlic salt and lemon-pepper. Place roast, fat side up, on a rack in an open roasting pan. Insert meat thermometer so bulb is centered in the thickest part, being sure bulb does not rest in fat. Do not add water. Do not cover. Roast in a slow oven to desired taste. Remove from oven to set for 20 minutes for easy carving.

Internal temperature of roast:
140° - rare
160° - medium
170° - well done

Mrs. Willie L. Scott (Billie)
Austin

152

Party Tenderloin

Bake at 400° for 35 minutes
Serves 8

4	pound beef tenderloin
½	teaspoon Lawry's seasoning
½	teaspoon garlic salt
½	teaspoon coarse black pepper
½	teaspoon salt
3	green onions, diced
2	slices bacon, cut in 4 pieces each (optional)

Rub meat with all seasonings and press into meat. Place in shallow roasting pan and broil on both sides until brown and crispy. Arrange bacon pieces on top of meat. Press diced green onions on top of tenderloin and bake for 35 minutes for rare. (Place slices of meat under broiler for a few minutes for those who prefer medium doneness.) Remove meat to serving platter and lightly cover to keep warm. Add small amount of water to pan drippings for *au jus* and season to taste.

Mrs. J. W. Small (Polly)
Austin

Gourmet Pot Roast

Serves 6

3 to 4	pound beef pot roast
1	tablespoon olive oil
3	(4-inch) pieces of celery
1	large carrot, cut in chunks
1	large onion, quartered
½	teaspoon rosemary
½	teaspoon thyme
1	slice bacon, cut in 5 or 6 pieces
⅓	cup Burgundy wine
½	cup water
2	bay leaves
1½	teaspoons salt
¼	teaspoon pepper
1	teaspoon flour

In Dutch oven, brown roast in oil. In skillet or saucepan cook celery, carrot, onion, rosemary, thyme and bacon pieces, stirring constantly and until onion is golden. Add to meat. Add wine, water, bay leaves, salt and pepper. Cover and simmer 2½ hours. Thicken liquid with flour blended with a little cold water or wine. Cook 30 minutes longer. Strain liquid, discarding vegetables and bay leaves. Serve gravy with sliced roast.

Mrs. Lewis King (Pat)
Austin

Sauerbraten

4	pound pot roast
Salt	
1	cup wine vinegar
1	cup boiling water
1	large onion, thinly sliced
2	bay leaves
10	whole cloves
6	whole peppercorns
2	tablespoons sugar
3	tablespoons oil
6	gingersnaps, rolled to fine crumbs

Place roast in deep bowl and sprinkle generously with salt. Pour in vinegar and boiling water and add onions, bay leaves, cloves, peppercorns and sugar. Cover and refrigerate for 24 to 36 hours, turning several times. Remove meat, reserving marinade. Pat roast dry and brown in oil in heavy skillet. Place browned roast in slow cooker, pour in 1 cup of marinade, cover and cook on low for 7 to 8 hours or until meat is tender. Remove meat, strain juices and return juice to cooker. Cook on high and add gingersnap crumbs, stirring constantly till gravy is of desired consistency.

Serve with boiled red cabbage and new potatoes. If you have leftover meat, you may make Tyrolean Beef Tips (see index).

Mrs. Gaston Barmore (Camille)
Houston

Brisket of Beef

Bake at 225° for 8 hours

4 to 5 pound brisket
Celery salt
Seasoning salt
Garlic salt
Meat tenderizer
| 4 | tablespoons Worcestershire sauce |
| 1 | (5 ounce) bottle liquid smoke |

Sprinkle brisket with spices and tenderizer and place in container for marinating. Combine Worcestershire sauce and liquid smoke and pour over meat. Cover and marinate for 24 hours for best results. Place brisket with marinade in baking pan and bake for 8 hours. Slice and serve.

Mrs. Don McLain (Shirley)
Mesquite

Captain's Choice Swiss Steak

Bake at 350° for 1½ hours
Serves 4

Flour
Pepper
Salt
2   pounds tenderized beef
       round steak
Shortening
2   cups carrots, sliced
4   cups stewed tomatoes
1   medium onion, chopped
1½   cups chopped celery

Mix flour, salt and pepper and pound into steak. Cut meat into serving size pieces and brown in shortening. Use a large covered casserole dish and layer remaining items and meat. Cover and bake at 350° for 1½ hours.

Serve with whipped potatoes, blackeyed peas, cornbread and cold fresh tea for a meal guaranteed to please.

Mrs. Cortis McGuire (Neta)
Austin

Gourmet Beef Stroganoff

Serves 6

2   pounds sirloin steak
       (venison may be
       substituted)
4   tablespoons butter
1   cup chopped green onions
1   clove garlic, minced
1   pound fresh mushrooms,
       sliced
3   tablespoons flour
2   teaspoons meat extract
       paste (or use Kitchen
       Bouquet)
1   tablespoon catsup
½   teaspoon salt
¼   teaspoon pepper
1   (10 ounce) can beef
       bouillon
½   cup dry white wine
½   teaspoon dry dill weed
1½   cups sour cream
4   cups cooked rice

Trim fat from meat and cut in small serving size pieces. Melt butter in heavy skillet and add just enough meat to cover bottom and cook over high heat; sear quickly. Remove and continue with rest of meat. Set aside. In same skillet, melt 3 tablespoons butter; sauté onions, garlic, mushrooms. Remove from heat. Add flour, meat extract, catsup, salt and pepper; stir until smooth. Gradually add bouillon; bring to a boil, stirring. Reduce heat. Add wine, dill and meat and simmer about 1 hour or until meat is tender. Stir in sour cream just until heated. DO NOT BOIL. Serve over egg noodles or rice.

Mrs. Leigh Spray (Patsy)
Round Rock

Oriental Beef

Serves 6 to 8

2	pounds flank steak
2	tablespoons sherry
2	tablespoons soy sauce
1	tablespoon cornstarch
½	teaspoon salt
2	tablespoons peanut oil
2	(10 ounce) packages frozen peas, thawed only until they can be separated
1	(6 ounce) package frozen mushrooms in butter sauce
1	slice fresh ginger root *or*
½	teaspoon ground ginger
1	(5 ounce) can water chestnuts, thinly sliced

Cut beef across the grain into slices about 2 inches long and ¼ inch thick, removing fat. In a large bowl, blend together sherry, soy sauce, cornstarch and salt; pour over meat. Refrigerate for 30 minutes or longer. When ready to cook, heat oil in Chinese wok or large skillet. Add ginger and meat. Cook, stirring over high heat until browned, about 2 minutes. Remove beef and reduce heat. Add peas and frozen mushrooms. Cook, stirring, until vegetables are thawed and tender. Add beef, water chestnuts, and marinade; simmer, covered, 5 minutes or until heated. Serve immediately with cooked rice.

Mrs. Otto Scherz (Gwen)
San Angelo

Tyrolean Beef Tips

Serves 4

Oil to cover bottom of skillet	
2	large potatoes, boiled, peeled and diced
1	large onion, diced
Salt and pepper to taste	
2	eggs, beaten
1	cup leftover Sauerbraten (see index), cut into small pieces

Heat oil in skillet. Stir in potatoes, onion, salt, pepper, eggs and sauerbraten. Stir until onions are tender and eggs are set.

Mrs. Gaston Barmore (Camille)
Houston

Oven Barbecued Steaks

Bake at 350° for 2 hours
Serves 10

3   **pounds beef round steak,**
      ¾-inch thick
2   **tablespoons salad oil**
3   **tablespoons instant**
      chopped onion
¾   **cup catsup**
¾   **cup water**
½   **cup vinegar**
1   **tablespoon brown sugar**
1   **tablespoon prepared**
      mustard
1   **tablespoon Worcestershire**
      sauce
½   **teaspoon salt**
⅛   **teaspoon pepper**

Cut meat into 10 serving pieces. In large skillet, brown meat in oil over medium heat; remove meat to Dutch oven. Add remaining ingredients to skillet; simmer 5 minutes. Cover and bake at 350° for 2 hours or until meat is tender.

Mrs. Don Woolsey (Vicky)
Arlington

Meatball Stroganoff

Serves 12 to 15

3   **pounds ground round**
1   **cup bread crumbs**
3   **eggs, beaten**
2   **cups water or stock**
2   **teaspoons prepared**
      mustard
4   **teaspoons salt**
Freshly ground pepper
¼   **cup seasoned flour (with**
      salt and pepper)
3   **tablespoons oil**
½   **pound fresh mushrooms,**
      sliced
1   **(10 ounce) can onion soup**
½   **cup sherry**
1   **cup sour cream**
2   **teaspoons chives for**
      garnish

Mix meat, bread crumbs, eggs, water, mustard, salt and pepper and form into balls. Roll in flour and sauté balls a few at a time in oil. Set aside. Sauté mushrooms, then add onion soup and sherry, scraping bottom of pan to form sauce. Return meatballs to pan and simmer 20 minutes. Add sour cream lightly stirring around meatballs to blend into sauce. DO NOT BOIL. Serve over noodles or rice.

Mrs. Eugene A. Mees (Norma Blotter)
Austin

Reikchen's Rouladen

Serves 6 to 8

10	(3x8x¼-inch) slices sirloin or round steak

Salt and pepper to taste
Mustard

5	slices bacon, cut in half
1	large onion, thinly sliced
10	pieces dill pickle, little longer than width of meat strips

Flour
Shortening
Water

⅛	teaspoon sugar

Trim meat of fat and gristle and cut into desired slices, lay on flat surface. On one side sprinkle salt and pepper, spread mustard and place a slice of bacon, piece of onion and a piece of pickle. Roll up and fasten with toothpick or tie with string. Cover rolls well with flour, shake off excess and brown in shortening. Drain any excess grease and add enough hot water to cover meat halfway. Sprinkle with sugar and more salt and pepper, if desired. Simmer, covered, approximately 1 hour or until tender. Remove string or toothpicks. Serve rouladen on platter of noodles with gravy poured over it.

This recipe has been passed down through 5 generations (my paternal great-great grandmother who was born in Dusseldorf, Germany). It has been changed occasionally to suit different tastes; such as leaving out the pickle and mustard, but this is the original Rouladen and very delicious. I named it Reikchen's Rouladen after my great grandmother.

Mrs. Michael Small (Lisa)
Austin

Teriyaki Steak

½	cup soy sauce
½	teaspoon garlic salt
2	tablespoons brown sugar
½	teaspoon ground ginger
2	tablespoons Worcestershire sauce
1	flank steak

In a plastic bag or pyrex dish, combine all the ingredients and put the steak in the sauce. Refrigerate for 12 to 24 hours, turning steak several times. Broil or grill over very hot coals for seven minutes to a side. Warm marinade and use as sauce.

Mrs. Walter J. Dingler (Gayle)
Austin

Pepper Steak

Boiling water
4	cups green peppers, thinly sliced
3	tablespoons salad oil
3	cups onions, thinly sliced
¾	teaspoon salt
2	garlic cloves, chopped
5	scallions, thinly sliced
1½	pounds sirloin, cut in small pieces
2	teaspoons Accent
1½	teaspoons sugar
⅛	teaspoon pepper
⅓	cup cooking sherry
1½	teaspoons ginger
1	(10 ounce) can consommé
3	tablespoons cornstarch
2	tablespoons soy sauce
Cooked rice or noodles

Place sliced green peppers in boiling water for three minutes, then rinse in cold water. Heat oil in skillet, adding green pepper slices, onions, salt, sliced garlic and scallions and stir on high for 3 minutes. Add meat, cooking and stirring on high for two minutes. Add Accent, sugar, pepper, sherry and ginger and stir for one minute. Add consommé and bring to a boil. In a small bowl, combine cornstarch, soy sauce and ¾ cup of COLD water. Mix and add in skillet cooking and stirring until the sauce is thick and translucent. Serve immediately. If you have any left over, add a little water before you reheat it.

Served with fresh, warm rolls and a tossed salad, this meal is great for everyday dining or for special guests.

Cindy Smith
Bryan

Beef Tips

Serves 8 to 10

5	pounds beef cubes (1-inch)
1	teaspoon salt
1	teaspoon pepper
1	medium onion, chopped
Garlic to taste
⅛	teaspoon Accent
⅛	teaspoon sweet basil
⅛	teaspoon dried parsley

In slow cooker, combine all ingredients and cook for 8 hours. No need to add liquid. Thicken with potato starch or flour when meat is tender. Serve over rice, noodles or spaghetti.

Mrs. D. J. Willis (Grace)
Weatherford

Moussaka Camille

Bake at 350° for 45 minutes
Serves 8 to 10

3	pounds ground beef
½	cup chopped onion
2	(12 ounce) cans tomato paste
2	teaspoons salt
½	teaspoon pepper
1	teaspoon garlic powder
1	teaspoon oregano, crushed
1	teaspoon sweet basil, crushed
4	cups water
¼	cup butter or oleo
¼	cup flour
½	teaspoon salt
2	cups milk
1	(15 ounce) carton ricotta cheese
½	teaspoon ground cinnamon
3	eggs
1	large eggplant, peeled and sliced ⅜-inch thick
1	pound durum lasagna noodles (or enough for 2 layers)
½	cup grated Parmesan cheese

Enough oil to fry eggplants

Brown beef, add onion and cook 5 minutes. Add tomato paste, salt, pepper, garlic powder, oregano and basil. Stir in water and simmer uncovered 1 hour. In medium saucepan melt butter, add flour and ½ teaspoon salt to make a paste. Stir milk in slowly and cook, stirring constantly, until white sauce is thick and smooth. In small bowl, combine white sauce, ricotta cheese, cinnamon and eggs. Fry eggplant lightly in oil. Cook lasagna in boiling, salted water until not quite tender, about 12 minutes. Rinse with cold water, drain. Pat off excess moisture. Cover bottom of 15x10-inch pan with ⅓ of the meat mixture, half of the eggplant, ⅓ of the ricotta cheese mixture and ½ of the noodles. Repeat layers. Dot top with remaining ricotta cheese mixture. Ladle meat mixture around dots of ricotta mixture. Swirl together with a spoon. Sprinkle Parmesan cheese over top. Bake in preheated oven for 45 minutes. Allow to set about 10 minutes. Cut in squares and serve with a Greek salad. DO NOT LEAVE OUT THE CINNAMON — THAT IS WHAT MAKES THE DISH.

Mrs. Gaston Barmore (Camille)
Houston

Captain Brown's Flag of the Bloody Sword

Captain Brown's flag is one whose origins have several versions. However, the weight of the evidence indicates that the flag was designed by Captain William Brown and constructed by him during his brief stay in Goliad following the capture of San Antonio in December 1835. The flag was raised at the fort of Goliad on December 20, 1835, on the occasion of the adoption by the garrison of the Goliad Declaration of Independence. Later, the flag was taken by Captain Brown to Velasco where it flew from the flagstaff atop the American Hotel to welcome the volunteers from the United States. On January 8, 1836, it was flown with the Troutman Flag to celebrate the arrival of the Georgia Battalion at Velasco.

FLAG OF THE GOLIAD DECLARATION OF INDEPENDENCE
"Captain Brown's Flag of the Bloody Sword"

FLAG OF THE GEORGIA VOLUNTEERS
The Johanna Troutman Flag

The Flag of the Georgia Volunteers

With high enthusiasm for the Texan cause, William A. Ward raised a company of 120 men in Macon, Georgia. They became known as the Georgia Battalion. Miss Johanna Troutman of Knoxville, Georgia, designed a beautiful flag of white silk and embroidered upon it in blue, a large lone star. The lettering "Liberty or Death" was embroidered on one side and, in Latin, on the other side the slogan "Where liberty dwells, there is my country." The flag was first unfurled on Texas soil on January 8, 1836 at Velasco. Later, when the battalion was assigned to Fannin's command, the Troutman flag flew over Fort Defiance at Goliad. Shortly before the garrision evacuated the fort the beautiful flag was caught in the halyards and destroyed by the wind.

Spaghetti Sauce With Meatballs

Serves 4

2	cloves garlic, minced
1	medium onion, minced
4	tablespoons Worcestershire sauce
1	teaspoon chili powder
1	cup water, or more
1	teaspoon salt
½	teaspoon oregano
1	(16 ounce) can tomatoes
2 to 3	(16 ounce) cans water
1	(6 ounce) can tomato paste
1¼	pounds ground round
1	egg
½	teaspoon salt
½	teaspoon pepper
1	tablespoon Worcestershire sauce

In large saucepan combine garlic, onion, 4 tablespoons Worcestershire sauce, chili powder, 1 cup water, salt and oregano and simmer until onions and garlic are tender. Add tomatoes and 2 to 3 cans water and simmer, covered, about 2 hours. Stir occasionally and add more water, if needed. Add tomato paste 30 minutes before adding meatballs. To prepare meatballs, mix all remaining ingredients with hands and form into meatballs. Drop into sauce and simmer 30 to 45 minutes. Meatballs should be cooked, covered in sauce, at least 30 minutes.

Mrs. Jimmie F. Johnson (Judy)
Corpus Christi

Swedish Meatballs

2	pounds ground beef
¼	cup dried onion soup mix
½	cup milk
2	(3 ounce) packages cream cheese, softened
½	teaspoon salt
2	cups soft bread crumbs
Oil	
2	tablespoons flour
2	cups milk

Mix ground beef, onion soup mix, milk, cream cheese, salt and bread crumbs together, thoroughly but lightly. Form into meatballs of desired size and slightly brown in enough oil to cover bottom of skillet. Cover skillet and cook 20 to 25 minutes or until done. Remove meatballs. Mix flour into milk until blended and pour into skillet, stirring to make gravy. Return meat balls and simmer till thoroughly heated.

Mrs. Cliff Bachle (Linda)
Houston

Italian-Style Lasagna

Bake at 350° for 20 to 30 minutes

1   **(8 ounce) box wide lasagna noodles**
½   **pound Mozzarella cheese**

MEAT SAUCE

1½   **pounds ground round**
1   **medium onion, diced**
1½   **teaspoons salt**
½   **teaspoon pepper**
¼   **teaspoon oregano**
1   **tablespoon parsley flakes**
1   **(6 ounce) can tomato pureé**
1   **(15 ounce) can tomato sauce**

WHITE SAUCE

2   **tablespoons butter**
2   **tablespoons flour**
¼   **teaspoon salt**
⅛   **teaspoon pepper**
1   **cup milk**

Cook lasagna noodles according to directions on box. Drain and set aside to cool. Brown meat, add onion and simmer until onion is soft. Add spices, tomato pureé and tomato sauce. Simmer on low for a minimum of 30 minutes. Set aside. To prepare white sauce, melt butter over low heat and blend in flour and seasonings. Stir in milk. Simmer and stir constantly until mixture thickens. Remove from heat. Place cooled noodles in large casserole in layers with sauces and cheese in the following order — noodles, meat sauce, white sauce and cheese. Repeat, ending with cheese. Bake for 20 to 30 minutes or until bubbly.

We got this recipe while living in Italy.

Mrs. Gene Anderson (Becky)
Fort Worth

Beef Curry

1   **clove garlic, pounded**
1   **cup grated onion, pounded**
2-inch ginger root, pounded
2   **tablespoons curry powder**
⅛   **teaspoon salt**
1   **pound cubed beef**
Milk from 1 coconut
2   **medium cooked potatoes, cubed**

Fry pounded ingredients in salad oil until aromatic. Add curry powder and salt. Mix well, add beef. Slowly add coconut milk. Simmer for 1 hour. Add potatoes when ready to serve. Also good served with noodles or rice.

This recipe was very popular in Indonesia.

Mrs. Joe Hopson (Kay Faubion)
Austin

Mexican Hamburger Cornbread

Bake at 350° for 45 minutes

1	pound ground beef
1	large onion, chopped
1	teaspoon pepper
½	cup oil
1	cup cornmeal
2	eggs
1	cup milk
½	teaspoon soda
¾	teaspoon salt
1	(17 ounce) can cream style corn
1	(8 ounce) package Cheddar cheese, grated

Brown ground beef with onions and pepper in oil. Drain and set aside. Mix together cornmeal, eggs, milk, soda, salt and corn and mix until blended. In casserole dish layer part of cornbread batter, then meat mixture, cheese and top with remainder of cornbread batter. Bake.

Variation: Add 1 (3 ounce) can chopped green chilies on top of meat mixture when layering.

Mrs. C. D. Whitehead (Ginny)
Leander

Mrs. Doyle Wood (Brenda)
Wichita Falls

Sour Cream Enchilada Casserole

Bake at 350° for 15 to 20 minutes
Serves 6 to 8

1	pound ground meat
1	large onion, chopped
1	(16 ounce) can tomatoes (do not drain)
1	package Chili Seasoning Mix
1	(8 ounce) can tomato sauce
¼	teaspoon pepper
1½	cups grated longhorn style cheese
1	package corn tortillas, cut in half
¼	cup chopped black olives
1 to 2 tablespoons sliced jalapeño peppers
1	(8 ounce) carton sour cream

Brown ground meat, chopped onion and drain well. Add tomatoes with juice, chili seasoning, tomato sauce and pepper. Simmer 10 minutes. Grease an 8x12-inch baking dish or pan. Spread ¼ cup of meat sauce over bottom of dish. Cover with layer of tortillas then half the meat sauce and half the grated cheese. Use the remaining tortillas, meat sauce and cheese. Sprinkle chopped olives and jalapeño peppers on top. Bake 15 to 20 minutes or until bubbly. Let set 5 minutes before serving. Spoon dollops of sour cream on each serving.

Mrs. Arthur G. Coley (Susie)
San Antonio

Tamale Pie

Bake at 325° for 1½ hours

6	cups boiling water
2	cups corn meal
½	teaspoon salt
2	tablespoons shortening
1	medium Bell pepper, diced
1	large onion, minced
1½	pounds ground meat
¼	teaspoon pepper
1	tablespoon chili powder
1	(6 ounce) can tomato pureé
1½	cups water or meat stock (broth)
¾	cup grated Cheddar cheese

Sift corn meal and salt into boiling water. Cook, stirring constantly, until very thick. Set aside. Melt shortening in a skillet. Add green pepper and onion. Sauté till tender. Add ground meat, seasonings, tomato pureé, and water or meat stock. Simmer about 30 minutes. Grease 12x8-inch casserole. Spread ⅓ cornmeal mixture over bottom and sides of casserole. Fill with chili mixture. Spread remaining cornmeal mixture over chili and sprinkle with grated cheese. Bake.

Mrs. T. F. Hahn (LaVelle)
Austin

Cormier Covered Casserole

Bake at 350° for 1 hour

1	pound ground beef
	Garlic and pepper to taste, no salt
1	(10 ounce) can cream of mushroom soup
1	can mushroom steak sauce
1	(10 ounce) can onion soup
1	beef bouillon cube
1	cup rice, uncooked
½	cup chopped celery
⅓	cup chopped parsley
½	cup chopped Bell pepper
⅓	cup chopped green onion tops

Brown meat in skillet and drain. Season with garlic and pepper. Melt bouillon cube in onion soup and combine remaining ingredients, including meat. Pour into a casserole that can be covered very tightly. Bake.

Mrs. Horace Cormier (Marie)
Orange

Stuffed Bell Peppers

6	large Bell peppers
1½	pounds ground chuck
2	medium onions, chopped
4	cloves garlic, chopped
2	slices white bread (moistened and squeezed)
½	cup Progresso bread crumbs
2	tablespoons grated Romano cheese
3	eggs, slightly beaten

Salt and pepper

6	small red potatoes, peeled and cut in half
2	tablespoons oil
1	(16 ounce) can tomatoes, chopped
1	(16 ounce) can water

Cut off tops of peppers, wash, remove seeds and membrane and parboil 5 minutes; drain and set aside. In large skillet, brown meat with 1 chopped onion and 2 chopped cloves of garlic; drain excess grease off and set aside to cool. Mix crumbs with cheese, eggs, salt and pepper; add to meat mixture and mix thoroughly. Stuff peppers and replace tops. Place upright in large pot with potatoes. Add 2 tablespoons oil to skillet. Sauté the other chopped onion. Add the remaining 2 cloves of chopped garlic and can of tomatoes and water. Pour over peppers and potatoes and cover. Bring to boil; simmer slowly till potatoes are tender. Add more water if necessary.

Mrs. Jake F. Messina (Dorothy)
Port Arthur

Leesa's Casserole

Bake at 350° for 45 minutes
Serves 6 to 8

1	pound ground beef
1	medium onion, chopped
1	(8 ounce) package tortilla chips, crushed
1	(10 ounce) can cream of mushroom soup
1	(16 ounce) can Ranch Style beans, drained
1	(10 ounce) can Rotel tomatoes and chilies
2	cups grated Cheddar cheese

Brown beef and onion; drain. In a 9x13-inch casserole layer ½ of crushed tortilla chips, meat and onion, soup, beans, tomatoes and chilies, and remainder of tortilla chips. Bake. Add grated cheese and return to oven just until cheese melts.

Mrs. James S. Froncek (Leesa)
Austin

Rubion Steak Au Poivre (Pepper)

Serves 2

10   ounces ground round
1   teaspoon pepper
Salt
1   teaspoon minced chives
2   teaspoons minced parsley
½   cup Paul Masson Rubion,
        Gallo Hearty Burgundy,
        or any red Bordeaux
1   teaspoon fresh lemon
        juice
Cheese

Shape beef in 4 patties. Top 2 of the patties with cheese of your choice (bleu, Swiss, jalapeño, Cheddar have been tried and are equally good) and then top with second meat patty. Seal edges well to keep cheese from melting out. Shape patties to about 1-inch thick. Sprinkle with pepper, press into meat and let stand 30 minutes. Place heavy frying pan over high flame and let heat until piping hot. Sprinkle pan with salt, add patties, quickly sear and brown on one side. Reduce flame to medium, turn patties and cook to desired doneness. (4 minutes rare, 6 minutes medium, 8 minutes well done.) Remove patties to warm platter and sprinkle with chives and parsley. Add wine to frying pan, stirring to loosen drippings and boil until liquid is reduced to half. Stir in lemon juice and pour sauce on meat. Serve with green beans and big glasses of red wine.

Quick and easy favorite.

Mrs. Leigh Spray (Patsy)
Round Rock

166

Avocado-Taco Pie

Bake at 375° for 20 to 25 minutes
Serves 6 to 8

1	pound ground meat
½	medium onion, chopped
1	(8 ounce) can tomato sauce
1	package taco seasoning mix
⅓	cup sliced pitted ripe olives
1	can quick crescent dinner rolls
2	cups crushed corn chips
1	cup sour cream
1	cup grated Cheddar cheese

Shredded lettuce
Tomato slices
1   avocado, sliced

In large fry pan, brown ground beef and onion. Drain fat. Stir in tomato sauce, taco seasoning mix and olives. Separate crescent dough into 8 triangles. Place triangles in ungreased 9- or 10-inch pie pan, pressing to form a crust. Sprinkle 1 cup corn chips over bottom of crust. Spoon meat mixture over crust and corn chips. Spread sour cream over meat mixture, cover with cheese. Sprinkle on remaining corn chips. Bake until crust is golden. Serve in wedges topped with shredded lettuce, tomato and avocado slices. If desired, leftover pie can be reheated. Pie may also be frozen.

Mrs. Billy B. Pope (Vanessa)
Greenville

Hamburger Corn-Pone Pie

Bake at 425° for 20 minutes

1	pound ground beef
⅓	cup onion, chopped
1	tablespoon shortening
2	teaspoons chili powder
¾	teaspoon salt
1	teaspoon Worcestershire sauce
1	cup canned tomatoes
1	cup drained beans (use either cooked pinto beans or canned Ranch Style)
1	cup corn bread batter (½ recipe)

Brown meat and chopped onion in melted shortening. Add seasonings and tomatoes. Cover and simmer over low heat for 15 minutes, then add beans. Pour meat mixture into a greased 1 or 1½-quart casserole. Top with corn bread batter, spreading carefully with a wet knife. Bake at 425° for 20 minutes, or until corn bread is done.

Mrs. Arthur Birdwell (Becky)
Austin

Martabak

Serves 8

1 pound ground beef
1 medium onion, chopped
2 teaspoons chopped garlic
1 pound carrots, grated
2 teaspoons salt
3 teaspoons pepper
1 package eggroll wrappers
Peanut oil for frying
4 eggs
1 jar La Choy sweet and
   sour sauce

Brown meat, garlic and onion together in large skillet. Add grated carrots and cook until onions are clear, about 5 minutes. Add salt and pepper and set aside to cool. To ¼ of the cooled mixture, add 1 egg and blend. Put 3 tablespoons mixture in center of one eggroll wrapper (keep other wrappers covered to prevent drying out) and fold one corner to center over meat mixture. Take left and right corners to center. Roll toward last corner and stick corner together with a little egg white. Deep fry in peanut oil until wrapper is light brown and crispy. Continue in the same manner by adding an egg to another ¼ of meat mixture, rolling and frying. Serve with sweet and sour sauce. You may also make small ones for appetizers.

The men in your family will love you for this!

Mrs. Gerald Richardson (Sheila)
Grand Prairie

Quickie Beef and Potatoes

Serves 4

1 pound ground chuck
½ medium onion, chopped
½ teaspoon garlic powder
1 (16 ounce) can tomatoes,
   mashed
¼ cup Teriyaki Sauce
Salt and pepper to taste
2 large potatoes, diced

Brown meat in large skillet, drain. Add all ingredients except potatoes and simmer for 5 minutes. Add potatoes, cover and simmer for 25 minutes. Add water if needed for thinning.

Mrs. Danny L. Golden (Evelyn)
Irving

Oralia's Casserole

Bake at 400° for 15 minutes
Serves 8

1   pound hamburger meat
1   (16 ounce) can Ranch
     Style beans
1   (10 ounce) can cream of
     chicken soup
1   (14½ ounce) can yellow
     hominy, drained
2   tablespoons chiliquick
½   cup water
Salt and pepper
1½   cup grated Cheddar
     cheese

Brown meat in skillet, drain, add all ingredients except cheese. Stir together and simmer about 15 minutes. Place half of mixture in greased 12x8-inch casserole and add half the cheese, then pour in another layer of meat mixture and top with remaining cheese. Place in hot oven and bake until hot and bubbly.

Mrs. Charles Kone (Minda)
La Pryor

Otto's Dumb-Ass Surprise

Serves 4 to 6

1   pound ground beef
⅓   pound pork sausage
2   yellow squash, sliced
3   ribs celery, chopped
⅔   can water chestnuts,
     sliced and drained
1   (10 ounce) can cream of
     celery soup
½   teaspoon dry mustard
Salt and pepper to taste
½   cup cracker crumbs
⅔   cup grated cheese

Cook meat on high in covered dish in microwave, turning and stirring occasionally. Pour off excess grease. Add sliced squash, chopped celery, water chestnuts, soup, salt, pepper and mustard. Cook for 9 minutes on high, stirring once. Top with cracker crumbs and cheese, and put under browner for 5 minutes.

Otto Scherz
San Angelo

169

Texas Hash

Bake at 400° for 15 minutes
Serves 10 to 12

2 pounds ground beef
1 large onion, chopped
1 clove garlic, minced
1 (16 ounce) can tomatoes
1 (10 ounce) can tomato
  soup
1 (8 ounce) can tomato
  sauce
1 (17 ounce) can whole
  kernel corn, drained
1 (3¼ ounce) can ripe pitted
  olives, sliced
1 small jar sliced
  mushrooms
Salt and pepper to taste
1 (12 ounce) package egg
  noodles, cooked
1 tablespoon margarine
¼ teaspoon cayenne
1 cup grated Cheddar
  cheese

In large skillet brown meat and add onion and garlic. Drain. In saucepan mix tomatoes, soup, tomato sauce, corn, olives, mushrooms, salt and pepper. Heat. Cook noodles, drain, add margarine and cayenne. Mix noodles, soup mixture and meat mixture together and pour into 9x13-inch greased casserole. Sprinkle cheese over top. Bake until hot and bubbly. Can be made the day before, adding cheese just before baking.

Mrs. Samuel H. Wilds (Betty)
Temple

J-B Ranch Casserole

Bake at 350°

2 pounds ground meat
2 cloves garlic, minced
Salt and pepper to taste
½ medium onion, chopped
½ medium Bell pepper,
  chopped
2 tablespoons barbecue
  sauce
1 tablespoon Worcestershire
  sauce
1 (16 ounce) can Ranch
  Style beans
⅓ cup cooked white rice
½ cup grated Velveeta
  cheese

Add garlic, salt and pepper to meat and mix well. In large skillet, cook meat with onions and Bell pepper until done. Add barbecue sauce, Worcestershire sauce and beans. Simmer about 5 minutes. Stir in cooked rice and top with grated cheese. Bake until bubbly and cheese is melted.

Mrs. Bill Leon (Jeanette)
Austin

Veal Parmesan

Bake at 350° for 30 minutes

1 (8 ounce) can tomato
sauce
¼ cup catsup
½ teaspoon pepper
1 teaspoon garlic salt
1 teaspoon chili powder
½ teaspoon oregano
⅛ teaspoon horseradish
1 pound veal cutlets
Flour
Salt and pepper to taste
Mozzarella cheese, sliced,
2 for each cutlet
Parmesan cheese, grated

In saucepan, combine tomato sauce, catsup, pepper, garlic salt, chili powder, oregano and horse-radish and simmer. Flour cutlets, salt and pepper and brown in a frying pan, on both sides. Remove to baking dish and place slice of mozzarella on each cutlet. Cover with ⅔ sauce and parmesan cheese. Bake for 30 minutes. Place another slice of mozzarella on each cutlet and the remainder of sauce over this and sprinkle again with Parmesan cheese. Bake an additional 5 minutes.

Mrs. Bill Abernathy (Mary Helen)
Fort Worth

Veal Scaloppine, Marsala

Serves 4

1 pound veal, in small
flattened pieces
1 cup flour
Salt and pepper to taste
4 tablespoons butter
½ cup Marsala wine
¼ cup meat gravy

Place veal in flour and sprinkle with salt and pepper. In pan, melt butter and brown veal on both sides. As veal is turned, sprinkle with Marsala wine and let evaporate. Remove veal from pan. Add a little Marsala, butter, meat gravy, salt and pepper to pan. Cook for a few minutes. When sauce thickens, serve.

Chef's recipe on a Sun Princess cruise.

Mrs. William Green (Irene)
Houston

Summer Sausage

Bake at 160° for 9 hours
Yields 2 rolls

2   **pounds ground meat**
2   **tablespoons Morton's Quick Tender Salt**
1   **tablespoon whole black peppers**
1   **tablespoon mustard seed**
1   **teaspoon garlic powder**
1   **teaspoon onion powder**
1   **tablespoon liquid smoke**
1   **cup water**

Mix all ingredients in water and then add to meat. Mix as you would a meat loaf, mixing thoroughly. Cover and refrigerate from 2 to 4 days, mixing well every 24 hours. Form into 5 rolls and roll in foil and let stand overnight. Remove foil and bake on broiler rack. Slice thin and serve with cheese and crackers.

Mrs. Dennis Migl (Sandra)
San Antonio

Mrs. Stephen B. McElroy (Eleta)
Houston

SOS

1   **(2½ ounce) jar dried beef, cut in small pieces**
Oil
1½   **teaspoons pepper**
½   **cup flour**
Milk

In heavy skillet pour a little oil and add all of cut up dried beef. Stir and fry lightly. Add pepper, flour and stir till slightly browned. Gradually add milk, stirring constantly till desired consistency for gravy. Serve over hot buttered cornbread with pinto beans.

What would a cookbook, such as this, be without SOS??? Try it, you will love it!

Cookbook Committee

On February 24, 1836, the commander of the Alamo, William Barrett Travis, sent a letter through the lines addressed "To the People of Texas and all the Americans in the World." The letter contains a postscript explaining the rations available: "We have since [taking up defense of the Alamo] found in deserted houses 80 to 90 bushels [of corn] and got into the walls 20 to 30 head of Beeves."
—Manuscript, Travis letter "To the People of Texas,"
Archives, Texas State Library

Watermelon Ham

Bake at 450° for 1 hour;
350° for 4 hours

1   large red-meat watermelon, room temperature
1   (8 ounce) can sliced pineapple
1   (6 to 8 pound) boneless ham

Slice watermelon in half longways. Scoop out melon meat, leaving at least 2-inches of red meat on all sides of both halves of melon. (Use melon meat to make a salad or fruit plate) Place ham in half of melon and garnish with pineapple slices. Place top of melon over ham and pineapple. Place melon with ham in baking pan at least 4-inches deep. Bake in oven at 450° for 1 hour. Reduce heat to 350° for 4 hours. Remove from oven, discard melon shells and the ham is ready to serve.

Delicious!! It will melt in your mouth.

Thom Cartmell
Fort Worth

Pork Stir-Fry with Linguini

1   pound pork roast (partly freeze to slice thin)
1   tablespoon oil
1   clove garlic, minced
1   (6 ounce) package frozen pea pods
½   cup milk
1   teaspoon basil
⅛   teaspoon nutmeg
⅓   cup grated Swiss cheese
1   (4 ounce) can sliced mushrooms
1   (4 ounce) package linguini or spaghetti, cooked

In skillet or wok add oil, garlic and pea pods, stir and cook 2 minutes. Remove pea pods and add pork strips, stir fry. Add small amount of oil if necessary. Remove pork. In same skillet add milk, basil, nutmeg and cheese. Stir until cheese melts. Add pea pods, pork, mushrooms and toss and heat. Serve over linguini.

Stuffed Pork Chops

Serves 2

2   pork chops, 1¼-1½-
     inches thick
1   tart apple, sliced (1-2
     slices per chop)
1   clove, (head only) crushed
2   small slivers orange rind
     (no white)
¼   cup raisins, soaked in
     brandy
1   sliver fresh ginger *or*
2   slivers candied ginger
Salt and pepper
Oil

Cut pockets in each chop, or ask your butcher to. Mix apples, crushed clove, rind, raisins, ginger, salt and pepper; stuff each chop and close opening with toothpicks. Sauté in a little oil 40-60 minutes or until cooked and brown, turning often but do not cover. Add small amount of water, if necessary. Remove toothpicks when chops are done and serve.

Mexican Corn/Sausage Casserole

Bake at 400° for 45 minutes
Serves 8

1   cup yellow corn meal
1   (17 ounce) can cream
     style corn
2   eggs
¾   cup milk
1   teaspoon salt
½   teaspoon soda
½   cup oil
1   medium onion, grated
1   (2 ounce) can pimientos,
     chopped
1   (3 ounce) can green
     chilies, chopped
1½   cup grated Cheddar
     cheese
1   link of pork sausage
     (cooked) (cut sausage
     in 1-inch slices, use
     more if desired)

Mix all ingredients, except sausage and half of cheese. Pour into greased 10x6x1½-inch baking dish (1½ quart). Layer sausage slices in middle of mixture and sprinkle remaining ½ of cheese over top. Bake.

Mrs. Zack Swenson (Carolyn)
Austin

Pork Chops in Honey Sauce

Bake at 350° for 90 minutes
Serves 4

4	**double loin pork chops**
1	**(8½ ounce) can sliced pineapple (reserve juice)**
½	**cup honey**
¼	**cup pineapple juice**
¼	**cup orange juice**
1	**tablespoon lemon juice**
1	**tablespoon prepared mustard**
	Maraschino cherries

Cut pocket in each chop and insert ½ slice drained pineapple. Combine honey, all juice and mustard and spoon a little over each chop. Bake for 90 minutes, drizzling honey sauce over chops frequently. Remove chops from oven, topping each with ½ slice pineapple and cherry. Return to oven for couple of minutes to warm fruit. Heat any remaining honey sauce and serve with chops.

Mrs. Robert L. Stockton (Sylvia)
Waco

Pork Chop Casserole

Bake at 350° for 1 hour

2	**cups grated potatoes**
2	**tablespoons minced onion**
2	**tablespoons flour**
1½	**cups milk**
1	**teaspoon salt**
¼	**teaspoon pepper**
4	**(1-inch thick) pork chops**

Mix together potatoes, onion, flour, milk, salt and pepper and place in ovenproof baking dish. Brown the chops and place on top of potato mixture. Cover with aluminum foil and bake at 350° for 1 hour.

Joe Baitz
Austin

Masa, *the fine ground Mexican style corn meal, is the basic ingredient of* tortillas *and all the dishes made from them such as* tacos *and* enchiladas. *It is also a basic ingredient in* tamales *and, in modern times, some well known Texas* chile con carne *recipes.*

Colcanon - Traditional Irish

Bake at 325° for 25 minutes
Serves 4 to 6

2½ cups shredded cabbage
2½ cups chopped, cooked
potatoes
½ cup onion, finely diced
½ cup Bell pepper, finely
diced
1½ teaspoons salt
1½ teaspoons pepper
2 tablespoons butter or
margarine
½ to ¾ cup milk
1 cup Cheddar cheese,
grated
½ cup bread crumbs (any
type)
1 to 2 cups cooked meat
(optional)

Sauté cabbage just till transparent. Combine cabbage, cooked potatoes, onions, Bell pepper, salt, pepper and butter. Gently fold in milk just to a "gravy" consistency. Add cheese and stir. (Add meat at this time if desired.) Pour into lightly greased casserole dish and top with bread crumbs. Bake at 325° for 20 to 25 minutes, or until a light brown crust appears. Leftovers may be served as fried patties, much like hash browns.

Colcanon (pronounced KOL-KAY-NON) is a traditional Irish recipe, served primarily at Lent. It originally was designed as a meatless dish, but I have adapted it as a main course casserole. Although any type of cooked meat may be included, I particularly recommend bacon, hot sausage, crumbled, or smoked sausage cut into bite-size chunks.

Mrs. Gary Voelker (Pat)
Garland

Hawaiian Pork Chops

1½ cups soy sauce
1½ cups water
1 teaspoon ginger
½ cup dry vermouth
¼ teaspoon garlic powder
6 to 8 thick-cut pork chops

Mix all ingredients in shallow long pan and marinate pork chops for approximately 12 hours; turn pork chops several times to marinate evenly. Remove pork chops and cook on charcoal grill until well done, depending on thickness of chops. Marinade can be used to baste chops while grilling.

Mrs. Richard E. Harrison (Nancy)
Austin

Kaanapali Pork

Bake at 425° for 20 minutes
325° for 30 minutes per pound

1   cup soy sauce
½   cup honey
¼   cup dry sherry
2   tablespoons salad oil
⅛   teaspoon Tabasco sauce
1   tablespoon ground ginger
1   double loin of pork (8 to
       10 pounds)

In mixing bowl combine all ingredients and coat pork; refrigerate at least 6 hours. Place on spit to cook or put on rack in oven over a pan of water and bake. Brush with marinade while cooking. Bake at 425° for 20 minutes then reduce heat and bake at 325° for 30 minutes *per pound.*

Dilled Lamb Shanks

Serves 4

6   small lamb shanks or 3
       large ones
3   tablespoons butter
1   large onion, finely
       chopped
1½   cups dry white wine
½   cup bouillon
2   tablespoons flour
3   tablespoons water
3   tablespoons dill (dried)
1   pint sour cream
Salt and pepper to taste

Brown lamb shanks in butter over medium high heat. Add onion, leaving some of it on top of the shanks; add wine and bouillon. Cover and simmer about 1½ hours or until shanks are tender (almost falling off the bone). Remove shanks. Mix flour and water and *slowly* add to the hot gravy, stirring constantly with a French whisk (this is the only tricky part). Add dill and sour cream and stir until smooth with the whisk. Return shanks and spoon gravy over them and keep on low heat for about 15 minutes. You can make these ahead of time and then slowly reheat before serving.

Good served over noodles with fresh English peas.

Mrs. Alec Rhodes (Charlotte)
Dripping Springs

177

Buttermilk Baked Chicken

Bake at 425° for 1 hour
Serves 4

1	fryer chicken, cut in serving pieces
¾	cup flour
1½	teaspoons salt
¼	teaspoon pepper
¼	cup butter or margarine
1½	cups buttermilk
1	(10 ounce) can cream of chicken soup

Dip chicken in ½ cup of the buttermilk. Roll in flour seasoned with salt and pepper. Melt butter in 13x9x2-inch casserole. Place chicken in butter, skin side down, and bake at 425° for 30 minutes. Turn chicken over and bake 15 minutes more. Blend remaining buttermilk and soup; pour around chicken. Bake an additional 15 minutes or until drumstick is completely done.

Mrs. John Bottoms (Diane)
Austin

Chicken Cacciatore

Serves 4 to 6

3	tablespoons butter
3	tablespoons olive oil
8	pieces of chicken
1	large onion, chopped
1	cup chopped celery
1	clove garlic, minced
⅓	cup dry red wine
1	bay leaf
½	teaspoon basil
⅛	teaspoon rosemary
2	tablespoons dry mushrooms, cooked in ¼ cup hot water
1½	cups tomatoes
¼	cup black olives

Heat butter and oil in a large skillet. Brown chicken and set aside. Sauté onion and celery until softened; add garlic and cook another 2 minutes. Stir in wine and simmer for 2 minutes. Add remaining ingredients and bring to a simmer. Add chicken and lower heat to a very gentle simmer. Cover pan and cook 45 minutes to 1 hour, or until chicken is tender. Serve with boiled potatoes or pasta.

This dish reheats beautifully . . . actually, it is better the second day.

Mrs. John L. France (Carole)
Aurora, Colorado

Microwave Chicken and Rice

Serves 4 to 6

1¼ cups uncooked long-grain rice
1 small onion, thinly sliced
1 (10 ounce) can cream of mushroom soup
1 (10 ounce) soup can water
1 Bell pepper, cut in ¼-inch pieces
2 - 3 pound fryer chicken, cut in serving pieces
1 teaspoon salt
2 tablespoons butter
½ teaspoon paprika

In 3-quart casserole, blend rice, onion, soup, water and Bell pepper. Melt butter and add salt. Arrange chicken pieces on top of rice with large ends of chicken around edges of casserole and small pieces in center. Pour small amount of butter over each piece of chicken. Sprinkle with paprika. Cover casserole with wax paper and cook 30 minutes, rotating ¼ turn halfway through cooking time. Rest 10 minutes then check for doneness. Add a few minutes cooking time if needed.

Mrs. Gary Sharp (Sandra)
Fort Worth

Oven-Fried Chicken Parmesan

Bake at 350° for 1 hour

½ cup grated Parmesan cheese
¼ cup flour
1 teaspoon paprika
½ teaspoon salt
⅛ teaspoon pepper
2½ to 3 pound fryer chicken, cleaned
1 egg, slightly beaten
1 tablespoon milk
¼ cup melted butter or margarine

Combine cheese, flour and seasonings. Cut up chicken in serving pieces and dip in combined egg and milk; coat with cheese mixture. Place in flat baking dish; pour margarine over chicken. Bake at 350° for 1 hour or until tender.

Mrs. Bill Leon (Jeanette)
Austin

179

Chicken Cordon Bleu

Serves 6

6	chicken breasts (whole)skinned and boned
1	(8 ounce) package Swiss cheese slices
1	(8 ounce) package sliced cooked ham
3	tablespoons flour
1	teaspoon paprika
6	tablespoons butter or margarine
1	chicken bouillon cube
½	cup dry white wine
1	cup whipping cream
1	teaspoon cornstarch

Pound and spread chicken breasts to flatten. Fold one cheese slice and one ham slice to fit on top of chicken. Fold breasts to cover ham and cheese and fasten with toothpicks, tucking in edges. On wax paper mix flour and paprika; use mixture to coat chicken. In a large skillet over medium heat, melt butter and brown chicken on all sides. Do not burn butter. Add wine and bouillon cube and stir to mix. Reduce heat to low, cover and simmer 30 minutes or until fork-tender. Remove chicken breasts. In cup, blend cornstarch and cream until smooth. Gradually stir into skillet. Cook, stirring constantly, until thickened. Remove toothpicks and serve chicken with sauce.

Mrs. Eugene A. Mees (Norma Blotter)
Austin

Easy Microwave Chicken

Chicken pieces (legs, thighs, breasts)
Garlic salt
Onion salt
Paprika
Pepper
Parsley flakes
Tarragon
½ cup stuffed green olives, sliced
Worcestershire Sauce

Rinse chicken and pat dry. Season on both sides with first four ingredients. Arrange chicken in a single layer in a microwave proof dish and sprinkle with next four ingredients. Cover dish with well fitting lid. Cook on high for 8 minutes per pound of chicken. Let stand 5 to 10 minutes. Check to see if chicken is tender.

This is a good drill weekend dish; since it can be prepared ahead of time, stored in the refrigerator, and popped into the microwave when your soldier walks through the door!

Mrs. Terry Mathews (Candy)
Commerce

Chicken Dawn

Bake at 350° for 20 minutes
Serves 4

2	(10 ounce) packages frozen broccoli spears
¼	cup margarine
6	tablespoons flour
½	teaspoon salt
⅛	teaspoon white pepper
2	cups chicken broth
½	cup whipping cream
3	tablespoons dry white wine
3	whole or 4 halves chicken breasts, skinned and boned
Margarine	
¼	cup Parmesan cheese, grated

Cook broccoli according to package directions and drain. In saucepan melt margarine; stir in flour, salt and pepper. Gradually add chicken broth. Cook and stir until mixture is bubbly and thickens. Remove from heat. Stir in cream and wine and set aside. In skillet, sauté chicken breasts in margarine over low heat till brown and partially cooked. Place cooked broccoli crosswise in 12x7-inch baking dish. Pour half of sauce in dish. Place chicken breasts in sauce, top with Parmesan cheese and spoon remainder of sauce over chicken. Sprinkle with some additional Parmesan. Bake for 20 minutes or until chicken is tender. Place under broiler for approximately 5 minutes or until sauce is golden.

Mrs. Thomas N. Fuller (Dorothy)
Austin

Easy Chicken Breasts

Bake at 300° for 3 hours
Serves 6

6	thin ham slices (or Canadian bacon)
6	boned chicken breast halves
6	slices bacon
1	can cream of mushroom soup
1	(8 ounce) carton sour cream
Season to taste	

Place ham in a 9x13-inch casserole. Lay chicken pieces over ham. Combine soup and sour cream. Season chicken and pour soup mixture over chicken. Top with uncooked bacon slices. Bake uncovered for 3 hours.

Mrs. Jim Daniel (Julia Ann)
Little Rock, Arkansas

181

Chicken Nicolse

Serves 6

6   chicken breast halves, with bone
2   tablespoons butter
3 to 4 tablespoons olive oil
1½   teaspoons tumeric
3   cloves garlic, cut in half
1   teaspoon dried tarragon
1   teaspoon dried thyme
½   teaspoon dried sage
2   bay leaves
Salt and pepper to taste
1   (16 ounce) can tomatoes
1   (3¼ ounce) can pitted ripe olives
1   (7 ounce) jar Spanish olives
1¼   cups dry white wine
1¼   cups chicken stock or bouillon

Brown chicken in olive oil and butter. Turn the heat to low and sprinkle chicken with the spices. Add garlic and bay leaves. Chop tomatoes coarsely and add them with the juice. Add olives, wine and bouillon. Cook slowly, covered, for about 1 hour or until the chicken is done. Remove bay leaves. Serve over noodles. This dish may be made 3-4 days ahead and reheated. It also freezes well.

Men go crazy over this particular dish.

Mrs. Alec Rhodes (Charlotte)
Dripping Springs

Tex-Mex Chicken Casserole

Bake at 350° for 45 minutes
Serves 8 to 10

1   medium onion, chopped
1   stick margarine
6   chicken breasts, boned, skin removed and cooked
3   (10 ounce) cans cream of chicken soup
1½   cups chicken broth
2   (3 ounce) cans chopped green chilies
1   large package Doritos
1   cup grated Cheddar or Monterey Jack cheese

Sauté onion in margarine. Cut chicken in bite size pieces and mix with soup, broth, chilies and add onions. Mix well. Line buttered flat 9x12-inch casserole with Doritos. Pour in the chicken mixture; top with additional Doritos. Sprinkle top with cheese and bake at 350° for about 45 minutes or till bubbly.

Mrs. Jay Matthews (Babs)
Austin

Chicken No-Name

Bake at 350° for 45 minutes
Serves 6

6 half chicken breasts, boned and skinned
2 sticks margarine
1½ cups water
1½ cups dry white wine or dry vermouth
½ teaspoon cayenne, or to taste
½ pound fresh asparagus, cut in 1-inch pieces
½ pound fresh green beans, cut in 1-inch pieces
½ cup chopped celery
1 pound fresh mushrooms, sliced
1 large onion, chopped
4 garlic cloves, minced
4 chicken bouillon cubes
Salt and pepper to taste
2 tablespoons cornstarch

Cut chicken into 1-inch pieces. Using a heavy skillet, melt margarine and brown chicken pieces on all sides, a handful at a time, until all are browned, and place them into a large casserole. Add 1½ cups water to skillet, scrape bottom and pour water and scrapings into casserole with the chicken. Add remaining ingredients to casserole, except cornstarch, making sure chicken is covered with liquid. Bake covered at 350° for 45 minutes or till chicken is tender. Remove from oven and thicken with cornstarch to desired thickness. Serve over linguini or rice.

Mrs. John F. Gore (Georgia)
East Lyme, Connecticut

Curried Chicken Spaghetti

1 large chicken fryer
1 stick margarine
1 large green Bell pepper, chopped
2 medium onions, chopped
1½ cups chopped celery
2 (16 ounce) cans tomatoes
2 teaspoons curry powder
1 (16 ounce) package spaghetti
Grated Parmesan cheese
Salt
Pepper

Boil chicken in 6 to 8 cups salted water until very tender. Remove chicken from broth, reserving broth. Bone chicken and cut into bite-size pieces. Melt margarine and sauté green pepper, onion and celery. Add chopped canned tomatoes, salt, pepper and curry powder. Add chicken and heat thoroughly for seasonings to blend. Cook spaghetti in reserved chicken broth. Drain. Add chicken mixture and serve with grated cheese. Freezes well.

Mrs. Leonard Tallas (Jean)
Austin

Paprika Artichoke Chicken

Bake at 375° for 40 minutes
Serves 4 to 6

4 to 6 chicken breast halves,
    boned and skinned
4 to 6 teaspoons paprika
6   tablespoons butter
1   (16 ounce) can artichoke
    hearts, drained
¼   pound fresh mushrooms,
    sliced
3   tablespoons chopped
    green onion
2   tablespoons flour
⅔   cup chicken broth
¼   cup sherry
½   teaspoon crushed
    rosemary

Season chicken breasts with paprika. In skillet melt about half of butter over moderately high heat. Brown chicken breasts on both sides. Transfer chicken to a 2-quart casserole and arrange artichoke hearts between chicken breasts. Add other half of butter to drippings in skillet, scraping bottom of skillet to loosen stuck pieces. Add mushrooms and green onions and sauté till tender. Sprinkle the flour over the mushrooms and onions. Stir in chicken broth, sherry and rosemary. Cook the mixture stirring constantly for 3 to 5 minutes. Pour the sauce over the chicken and bake approximately 40 minutes or until chicken is real tender. You can use a whole cut-up chicken in place of chicken breasts.

This sauce is delicious served separately in individual cups to use as a "dunk" for French bread.

Mrs. Lewis King (Pat)
Austin

Mandarin Chicken

Bake at 350° for 50 minutes
Serves 4 to 6

⅓	cup butter
1	teaspoon salt
½	teaspoon mace
6	split chicken breasts, bone in and skinned
1	(10 ounce) jar orange marmalade
1	(11 ounce) can Mandarin oranges, drained
1	cup seedless green grapes

In 13x9-inch baking pan melt butter in oven. Add salt and mace; stir to blend. Dip chicken pieces into melted butter, turning to cover both sides. Place chicken in same baking pan. Bake until chicken is fork tender. Meanwhile in small bowl combine marmalade, oranges and grapes. Spoon mixture over and around chicken. Return to oven and continue baking for 15 to 17 minutes or until sauce is clear and heated through.

Chicken Tamayo

Bake at 350° for 1 hour

3	whole chicken breasts, skinned and boned
1	teaspoon salt
1	small onion stuck with cloves and peppercorns
3	ribs celery
Several sprigs of parsley	
6	medium tamales
1 or 2	(4 ounce) cans chopped green chilies
1	cup tomato sauce
1	cup sliced ripe olives
½	cup seedless raisins
2	teaspoons chili powder
1	cup beef bouillon
3	ounces dry sherry
¾	cup sour cream

Simmer chicken breasts with salt, onion stuck with cloves and peppercorns, celery and parsley. Cool in broth. Cut tamales crosswise and line in square casserole dish. Cut chicken in strips. Top tamales with alternate layers of green chilies and chicken strips. Mix tomato sauce, olives, raisins, chili powder, bouillon and sherry and pour over chicken. Bake at 350° for 30 minutes or until bubbly. Remove from oven and spread sour cream over mixture and return to oven just long enough to heat sour cream.

Do not leave out the raisins . . . they make the dish.

Mrs. W. R. Morrison (Mavis)
Las Vegas, Nevada

185

Chicken a la King - a la Tallas

1	large fryer chicken
1	stick margarine, melted
¼	cup flour
1½	cups chicken broth
1½	cups evaporated milk
3	large carrots, sliced
1	(10 ounce) package frozen English peas
1	stick margarine
1	cup chopped celery
½	pound fresh mushrooms, sliced
½	(2 ounce) jar pimientos

Simmer fryer in seasoned water (salt, pepper and some celery) until very tender. Bone chicken and cut into small pieces. Strain broth, discarding celery. (This should be done day before using.) Melt margarine (1 stick) and add flour, stirring until smooth. Add 1½ cups broth and about ½ of the chicken fat which rose to the top on the broth. Add evaporated milk and stir until smooth and slightly thickened. Add cut up chicken and set aside. Parboil carrots and peas. Drain. Melt remaining 1 stick margarine in large saucepan and add celery. Sauté until transparent and then add mushrooms and pimientos. Add vegetables to creamed chicken mixture. Adjust seasonings for salt and pepper. Add more cream or broth as needed, if too thick. If too thin, add a little sauce to 1 to 2 tablespoons cornstarch, mix and return to saucepan. Serve over pastry shells. This is also good over noodles or biscuits. For chicken pie, pour thin mixture into shallow container and top with thin biscuits. Bake at 375° until biscuits are brown.

Mrs. Leonard Tallas (Jean)
Austin

Chicken Bundles

Bake at 375° for 20 minutes
Serves 5 to 6

2	(3 ounce) packages cream cheese with chives
4	tablespoons butter, softened
⅛	teaspoon pepper
½	cup chopped nuts (optional)
6	tablespoons butter, melted
2	cups cooked, cubed chicken
⅔	cup chopped mushrooms
2	cans Pillsbury Crescent Rolls
1½	cups Pepperidge Farm Stuffing Mix (used dry)

Mix cream cheese, soft butter and pepper together. Add chicken and ½ cup stuffing mix, mushrooms and nuts. Flatten crescent rolls into separate triangles and place about ¼ cup of mixture onto each piece of dough. Roll and tuck ends under. Roll in melted butter and then roll in dry stuffing mix. Place on baking sheet and bake at 375° for 20 minutes. May be frozen before baking or after. Serve as they are or with a chicken gravy.

Mrs. Barry Ottley (Sandra)
Austin

Chicken Sopa

Bake at 325° for 30 minutes
Serves 6

1	(10 ounce) can cream of chicken soup
2	chicken bouillon cubes
1	(10 ounce) soup can water
1	(10 ounce) can cream of mushroom soup
½	cup finely diced onion
1	(3 to 4 ounce) can chopped chilies
1	(1 dozen) package corn tortillas (torn in strips)
1	cooked chicken, boned and cut into small pieces
1	pound Monterey Jack cheese, grated

Dissolve bouillon cubes in water. Mix cream of chicken soup, mushroom soup, bouillon water, chilies and onions together. In a greased large shallow casserole, layer half soup mix, tortillas, chicken and top with other half soup mix. Top with grated cheese. Bake at 325° about 30 minutes or until bubbly.

Mrs. James C. Harvie (Peggie)
Houston

Upper Crust Chicken

Bake at 375° for 30 minutes
Serves 8

10	white bread slices (day-old)
2	cups cooked chicken, in chunks
1	cup sliced celery
2	cups grated Cheddar cheese
1	cup mayonnaise
2	eggs, slightly beaten
½	teaspoon salt
½	teaspoon poultry seasoning
1½	cups milk

Trim crusts from bread, reserving crust. Cut bread slices diagonally into quarters. Cut reserved crusts into cubes. Combine bread cubes, chicken, celery and 1¾ cups cheese; mix well. Spoon into 11x7-inch buttered baking dish. Arrange bread quarters over chicken mixture in four rows. Combine mayonnaise, eggs and seasonings. Mix well. Gradually add milk, mixing until blended. Pour over bread and sprinkle with remaining cheese. Cover. Refrigerate several hours or overnight. Bake uncovered at 375° for 30 minutes or until bubbly.

Mrs. Robert M. Cavett (Dorothy)
Austin

Party Chicken

Bake at 275° for 3 hours
Serves 8

8	large chicken breast halves, skinned and boned
8	slices bacon
1	(2½ ounce) jar dried beef
1	(10 ounce) can cream of mushroom soup
1	(8 ounce) carton sour cream

Cut dried beef in pieces and lay in bottom of greased 9x13-inch casserole. Wrap each chicken piece with bacon and lay on top of dried beef. Mix soup and sour cream and pour over chicken. Can be refrigerated overnight. Bake at 275° for 3 hours. Very good served with rice.

Chicken Broccoli Puff

Bake at 400° for 25 minutes
Serves 4 to 6

2	(10 ounce) packages frozen broccoli spears, cooked and well drained
1	(10 ounce) can cream of chicken soup
¼	teaspoon nutmeg
1	teaspoon Worcestershire sauce
1	cup grated Parmesan cheese
1	chicken, cooked, boned and cut in chunks
½	cup whipping cream, whipped
¾	cup mayonnaise

Place broccoli in 2-quart baking dish (however, this really looks prettier on an *ovenproof* platter). Combine soup, nutmeg and Worcestershire sauce; pour half of this mixture over broccoli and top with ⅓ cup Parmesan cheese. Layer chicken and pour remainder of soup mixture and ⅓ cup of cheese over chicken. Bake for 25 minutes. Remove from oven. Whip cream until stiff peaks form, blend in mayonnaise and spread over the top. Sprinkle remaining ⅓ cup cheese and broil until brown and puffy. Serve atop saffron rice or rice with yellow food coloring in it.

Serve with salad and rolls to complete your meal.

Mrs. Jim Daniel (Julia Ann)
Little Rock, Arkansas

Hawaiian Chicken

Bake at 350° for 1½ hours
Serves 12

12	chicken breast halves, skinned
1	package Lipton onion soup mix
1	(8 ounce) bottle Catalina dressing
1	(10 ounce) jar apricot preserves

Combine soup mix, dressing and preserves in large mixing bowl. Add chicken and coat each piece (you may marinate chicken overnight). Place chicken on large pan, bake at 350° for 1½ hours, basting occasionally with excess marinade.

Mrs. Don Daniel (Gerry)
Portland

Chicken Enchiladas

Bake at 350° for 30 minutes
Yields 2 dozen

FILLING

1	fryer chicken, boiled and boned
1	cup chopped onion
½	cup minced green onion
3	cloves garlic, minced
1	pound grated Monterey Jack cheese
1	pint sour cream
¼	teaspoon cayenne pepper
½	teaspoon ground comino
½	teaspoon salt

SAUCE

4	tablespoons butter
4	tablespoons flour
¼	teaspoon salt
⅛	teaspoon pepper
1	cup milk
1	cup chicken broth
24	corn tortillas

Bone chicken and chop. In large mixing bowl, combine chicken, onion, garlic, ⅔ pint sour cream, ½ pound cheese, pepper, salt and comino. Mix well. Gently heat tortillas (one at a time) in vegetable oil until soft (approximately 30 seconds). Fill tortillas with filling (approximately 1 heaping tablespoon per tortilla). Roll up and place in oblong glass baking dish. Cover with remaining cheese and pour sauce over. To prepare sauce: Make basic white sauce with butter, flour and seasonings, adding milk/broth liquid last. Stir until thick. Remove from heat and add remaining ⅓ pint sour cream. Bake at 350°, 30 minutes, covered with foil.

John Bottoms
Austin

Chicken and Mushroom Bake

Bake at 350° for 1 hour
Serves 6

3	chicken breasts, split and skinned (boned if preferred)
1	(10 ounce) can cream of mushroom soup
8	ounces sour cream
½	pound fresh mushrooms or small jar of sliced mushrooms
½	cup dry white wine

Place chicken in a 9x13-inch pan, mix remaining ingredients together and pour over chicken. Bake for at least 1 hour at 350°. Serve with rice or noodles.

Mrs. Joe W. Montgomery (Norma)
Austin

Chicken Crepes

Bake at 375° for 15 to 20 minutes
Serves 10 to 12

CREPES

2	eggs
1	tablespoon melted butter
¼	teaspoon sugar
¼	teaspoon salt
⅓	cup unsifted flour
⅔	cup milk

Beat eggs, add butter, sugar, salt and flour. Beat until smooth. Add milk and mix well. Grease 6-inch skillet lightly (or use crepe pan) and pour ⅛ cup of batter to cover bottom of pan. Tip the pan until batter is evenly spread. Cook until golden. Repeat for 12 crepes. Stack crepes.

FILLING

3	tablespoons butter
½	cup chopped fresh mushrooms
3	tablespoons flour
½	teaspoon salt
¼	teaspoon pepper
½	teaspoon celery salt
1	teaspoon curry powder
1	cup chicken broth
1	cup half and half cream
2	egg yolks, beaten
2	cups chopped chicken
½	cup grated Cheddar cheese

Melt butter and sauté mushrooms. Add flour and stir. Add seasonings and broth and simmer for five minutes. Gradually add cream mixed with beaten egg yolks; add chicken. Heat and thicken, but DO NOT BOIL. Spoon 2 tablespoons of mixture on each crepe, roll and place seam side down in ungreased 12x8-inch pan. Cover with white sauce and sprinkle with grated cheese. Bake in 375° oven for 15 to 20 minutes or till hot and cheese melts. *See index for white sauce recipe.*

Mrs. Darrel Baker (Linda)
Austin

191

Hot Chicken Salad Casserole

Bake at 400° for 15 to 20 minutes
Serves 6 to 8

1½   cups cooked, diced chicken
2   tablespoons finely chopped onion
½   cup slivered almonds
1½   cups cooked rice
1   (10 ounce) can cream of chicken soup
1½   teaspoons salt
1   cup chopped celery
½   teaspoon cayenne pepper
½   teaspoon pepper
1   tablespoon lemon juice
3   hard boiled eggs, coarsely chopped
¾   cup mayonnaise
Potato chips

Mix all ingredients together, except potato chips, and pour into a greased 9x12-inch baking dish. Top with crushed potato chips. Bake for 15 minutes or until bubbly.

Flavor is best when prepared the day before.

Mrs. James Roden (Charley)
Denton

Mrs. George Allen (Frances)
Austin

Chicken Superb

Bake at 350° for 35 minutes

1   large chicken, cooked
4   ounces egg noodles
6   tablespoons butter
6   tablespoons flour
1½   teaspoons salt
½   teaspoon pepper
½   teaspoon celery salt
¼   teaspoon marjoram
2   cups chicken broth
2   cups half and half cream, scalded
½   cup grated Cheddar cheese
⅛   cup chopped parsley
1   (8 ounce) can English peas, drained

Bone chicken and cut into bite-size pieces. Cook noodles and drain. Melt butter and add flour, seasonings and broth; stir constantly til mixture thickens. Blend in cream and cheese. Place chicken, parsley and peas in buttered casserole. Cover with cheese sauce. Bake uncovered for 35 minutes.

Mrs. Edgar Perry (Linda)
Austin

Asparagus-Turkey Mornay

Bake at 350° for 15 to 20 minutes

1   (10½ ounce) can
    asparagus, drained
½   pound thinly sliced turkey
    breast
1   green onion, minced
1   (10½ ounce) can cream
    mushroom soup
½   cup grated Parmesan
    cheese
½   cup grated Cheddar
    cheese
Salt and pepper to taste

Place asparagus in well buttered 8-inch square baking dish. Top with turkey slices. In saucepan (or microwave) mix soup, onion, Parmesan cheese, Cheddar cheese and salt and pepper. Heat just until cheese melts. Pour over asparagus and turkey. Bake at 350° for 15 to 20 minutes or until bubbly.

Impossible Turkey Pie

Bake at 400° for 30 to 35 minutes
Serves 6 to 8

2   cups cut up cooked and
    boned turkey
1   (4½ ounce) jar sliced
    mushrooms, drained
1   (2 ounce) jar pimiento
    pieces
½   cup sliced green onions
½   teaspoon salt
1   cup grated natural Swiss
    cheese
1½ cups milk
¾   cup Bisquick baking mix
3   eggs

Grease 10-inch pie plate. Sprinkle turkey, mushrooms, pimientos, onions, salt and cheese in pie plate. Beat baking mix with milk and eggs until smooth, 15 seconds in blender on high or 1 minute with hand beater. Heat oven to 400°. Pour egg mixture over turkey mixture in plate. Bake 30 to 35 minutes until knife inserted in center comes out clean. Cut in wedges to serve.

Mrs. Robert Owen (Jodie)
Elgin

Courtbouillon (Koó bee yon)

1 cup flour
1 cup oil
1 large onion, finely chopped
1 Bell pepper, finely chopped
3 ribs celery, finely chopped
3 cups water
3 tablespoons lemon juice
1 (15 ounce) can tomato sauce
1 (12 ounce) can tomato paste
3 tablespoons Worcestershire sauce
⅛ teaspoon chili powder
3 quarts water
3 pounds fish or shrimp, raw

In an iron pot make a roux of the flour and oil. Stir flour into hot oil and keep stirring until roux starts browning. Turn heat down low and cook until dark brown in color. Add onions, peppers and celery and sauté. Add 3 cups water and bring to a boil. Pour into a large pot and add remainder of ingredients. Add salt and pepper to taste. Turn heat low, cover and cook for 4 hours. Add water as needed. Serve over hot rice. If you like it spicier and hotter, chop up 3-4 jalapeños in it.

This is a delicious South Louisiana Acadian dish.

Mrs. Johnye L. Slaughter (Tommie)
Angleton

Stuffed Crabs

Bake at 350° for 25 minutes
Yields 12 shells

1 pound crab meat
7 to 8 slices of bread, soaked in water
3 tablespoons margarine
½ cup chopped onion
¼ cup chopped Bell pepper
⅓ cup chopped celery
2 tablespoons pimiento
2 cloves garlic, halved *or* ½ teaspoon garlic juice
1 teaspoon Tabasco sauce
1 teaspoon salt
½ teaspoon pepper

Sauté onion, celery, peppers and garlic halves in margarine. Remove garlic and discard. Squeeze water from bread. Combine all ingredients. Place in crab-shaped tins and bake at 350° for 25 minutes. May also be used to stuff flounder.

Mrs. Cliff Bachle (Linda)
Houston

Microwave Five Fish Casserole

Serves 6 to 8

½	**pound sole**
½	**pound scallops**
½	**pound trout**
½	**pound shrimp**
½	**pound crab (from legs)**
2	**tablespoons butter**
1	**cup chicken stock**
2	**tablespoons flour**
1	**cup evaporated milk**
1	**green onion, sliced very fine**
⅛	**teaspoon dried thyme**
Salt and pepper to taste	
¼	**teaspoon parsley**
¼	**cup white wine or vermouth**
¾	**cup almonds, sliced**
2	**teaspoons butter**
Buttered bread crumbs	
Parmesan cheese	
Paprika	
4	**whole mushrooms**

Cook crab legs until pink, approximately 3 to 4 minutes on medium high. Parboil shrimp 3 minutes to shell. Drain. Cut sole, trout and crab meat into bite sized chunks. Place sole, trout and scallops into pie pan; cover and cook on medium for 6 to 7 minutes. Drain, saving fish stock for chowder. Prepare sauce by combining butter, chicken stock, flour, and evaporated milk in microwave-proof container. Bring to a boil. Add green pepper, thyme, salt and pepper and parsley. Return to microwave and let bubble up. Remove and add ¼ cup white wine or vermouth. Toast sliced almonds in butter on high 2 to 3 minutes. To assemble casserole, layer all fish except shrimp. Gently pour sauce over, then top with shrimp. Sprinkle with buttered bread crumbs, Parmesan cheese, paprika, almonds and mushrooms. Return to microwave and bake until sauce is gently bubbling — 6 to 7 minutes.

Serve with wild or brown rice and tiny green peas. It's a real party casserole.

Mrs. Eugene A. Mees (Norma Blotter)
Austin

Crab Imperial

Bake at 350° for 15 minutes
Serves 4

1	pound lump crabmeat
⅛	teaspoon white pepper
⅛	teaspoon celery seed
⅛	teaspoon Accent
¼	teaspoon dry mustard
1	small jar pimientos, chopped (reserve some for garnish)
3	tablespoons chopped Bell pepper
½	tablespoon butter or margarine
1	egg, beaten
½	cup mayonnaise (reserve small amount for garnish)

Sauté Bell pepper in butter until tender. Combine all ingredients and mix gently. Spoon mixture into 4 buttered ramekins, or entire amount into a buttered, one-quart casserole. Top with mayonnaise and garnish with a few pimiento strips. Bake at 350° for 15 minutes. (If you bake in crab shells, place these on cookie sheet for baking.)

Mrs. Rufus G. Martin (Dee)
Alexandria, Virginia

Mussels In Wine and Garlic Sauce

4	dozen mussels in their shells
4	tablespoons butter
¾	cup finely chopped onion
1	tablespoon finely diced garlic
¼	teaspoon thyme
2	tablespoons chopped parsley
2	cups dry white wine
2	cups water

Scrub mussels thoroughly under cold running water with a stiff brush and soapless scouring pad. Cut or pull hairlike tufts (beards) from shells. In 6 to 8-quart pot, melt butter. Add onions and garlic and cook for five minutes. Add thyme, parsley, wine and water. Drop in mussels and bring to a boil. Cover, reduce heat to low and steam for 10 minutes, turning the mussels once or twice. After 10 minutes all shells should be open. Discard any mussels that remain shut. Serve over linguine.

Robert Preston
Indian Mills, New Jersey

Barbecued Shrimp

1   dozen shrimp (jumbo size)
½   cup flour
1   egg
1   cup sweet milk
Salt and pepper to taste
1   cup fine cracker crumbs
1   quart cooking oil
1   pint Hickory House Smoke
       Sauce

Peel and devein shrimp, leaving shell on tails. Wash and clean thoroughly. Dust shrimp with flour. Break egg in bowl, beat well. Add milk, salt and pepper to taste. Dip shrimp in egg and milk mixture, then roll in fine ground cracker crumbs. Pour oil in deep saucepan and heat to 350°. Drop in shrimp and fry for 4 minutes to seal moisture in shrimp. Remove from deep fat and saturate in Hickory Smoke Sauce. Put in shallow pan and place under broiler or in oven for 5 minutes or until shell and tails become brown and crisp. Shrimp are ready to serve. Serve a mild, tasty barbecue sauce with shrimp.

Mrs. William Green (Irene)
Houston

Shrimp Creole

Serves 4

2   tablespoons Wesson oil
1   cup chopped onion
1   cup chopped Bell pepper
1   clove garlic, minced
1   (16 ounce) can tomatoes
1   (8 ounce) can tomato
       sauce
1   cup white wine
1   teaspoon salt
¼   teaspoon chili powder
1   pound cooked shrimp
2   cups cooked rice

Cook vegetables and garlic in oil. Mix in tomatoes, tomato sauce, wine and seasonings. Simmer 45 minutes. Add shrimp and heat thoroughly. Serve over cooked rice.

Mrs. Bernard Butler (Bonnie)
San Antonio

Mrs. John C. L. Scribner (Edna)
Austin

Seafood Casserole

Bake at 350° for 20 to 30 minutes
Serves 8

2   pounds shrimp, cooked,
        peeled and deveined
1   cup chopped onion
1½   cups chopped celery
½   cup chopped Bell pepper
1   pound backfin crab meat
Juice of ½ lemon
1   cup Durkee's dressing
1   cup mayonnaise
1   teaspoon salt
2   teaspoons Lea and
        Perrins Sauce
⅛   teaspoon Tabasco sauce
Red pepper to taste

Mix shrimp, onion, celery, and Bell pepper and spoon in 9x13x2-inch baking dish. Put crabmeat on top of this mixture. Mix remaining ingredients and spoon over top, covering completely. Bake in 350° oven about 20 to 30 minutes or until hot and bubbly. It is important to use *Durkee's* dressing. This casserole may be prepared the day before. You may sprinkle bread crumbs on top before baking, if desired.

Leftovers are good on English muffin halves!

Mrs. William E. Ingram (Betty)
Raleigh, North Carolina

Shrimp Étouffée

Serves 4 to 6

6   tablespoons butter
3   tablespoons flour
1   cup chopped onion
6   green onions and tops,
        chopped
½   cup chopped Bell pepper
½   cup chopped celery
2   cups chicken broth
3   pounds shrimp, peeled
        and deveined
¼   cup chopped parsley
1   small bay leaf
Salt and red pepper to taste

In a skillet, melt butter and stir in flour. Cook, stirring constantly until a rich, dark brown in color. Stir in broth, vegetables, shrimp, parsley and seasonings. Simmer uncovered for 20 minutes or until shrimp are done. (Boiled, peeled, deveined shrimp may be used. Stir cooked shrimp in after combining all other ingredients and heat until bubbly, then serve.) Remove bay leaf. Serve over hot rice.

Mrs. Bobby W. Hodges (Lu)
Arlington

Coconut Shrimp With Marmalade Sauce

Serves 6

SAUCE

½   cup orange marmalade
2   tablespoons medium dry
    sherry
1   tablespoon horseradish
Hot pepper sauce

Process marmalade in blender till smooth. Pour into small saucepan. Stir in sherry, horseradish and hot sauce and blend well. Warm gently over low heat, stirring frequently.

CREPE BATTER

1   egg
¼   cup milk
¼   cup water
½   cup flour
⅛   teaspoon salt
1   tablespoon butter, melted

Beat egg with whisk. Add liquids a little at a time, beating well after each addition. Stir in flour, salt and blend until smooth. Stir in butter. Cover and refrigerate until thickened; or overnight if possible.

SHRIMP

Vegetable oil
1½   pounds cooked medium
     shrimp, peeled and
     deveined
Crepe batter
Shredded or flaked unsweetened
    coconut

Heat about 1-inch oil in heavy skillet. Coat shrimp with crepe batter and roll in coconut. Fry in batches until golden about 2 to 3 minutes. Remove with slotted spoon and drain on paper towel.

Place sauce in bowl and surround with shrimp.

Mrs. Fred Kaiser (Suzan Balagia)
Kerrville

199

Shrimp Gumbo

Serves 6

1	pound raw shrimp, peeled and deveined (or any combination of seafood)
6	slices bacon
¼	pound salt pork
½	cup flour
1	cup chopped onion
1	(10 ounce) package frozen sliced okra (or 2 cups fresh okra, sliced)
½	cup Worcestershire sauce
½	teaspoon sweet basil
½	teaspoon thyme
1	teaspoon pepper
1	medium onion, chopped
½	cup chopped Bell pepper
½	cup chopped parsley
2	cloves garlic, chopped
1	(1 pound) can Italian style tomatoes, undrained, cut up
1	(13 ounce) can chicken broth
1	teaspoon monosodium glutamate
2	bay leaves
4	drops liquid hot pepper sauce
¼	teaspoon gumbo filé

Hot cooked rice

In large stew pot, cook bacon and salt pork until bacon is crisp. Crumble bacon and set aside. Remove salt pork. To make roux, add flour gradually and stir until mixture is medium brown. Add remaining ingredients except shrimp, filé and rice. Cook for 20 minutes. Add shrimp, cover and simmer for 15 minutes. Remove bay leaf. Just before serving, stir in filé. Serve over hot fluffy rice.

Mrs. L. James Starr, Jr. (Jo Ann)
Austin

200

Jambalaya a la John

Serves 12

1 pound smoked sausage, sliced
1 cup chopped Bell pepper
1 cup chopped onion
3 cloves garlic, crushed
1 tablespoon oil
2 tablespoons flour
1 (28 ounce) can tomatoes, undrained
1 bay leaf
2½ cups water
2 tablespoons chopped fresh parsley
2 cups uncooked regular rice
2 tablespoons Worcestershire sauce
2 teaspoons salt
½ teaspoon dried whole thyme
½ teaspoon red pepper
Black pepper to taste
1 cooked and boned chicken, cut in bite-size pieces
1½ pounds shrimp, peeled and deveined

Cook sausage until browned in large Dutch oven. Drain off ½ pan drippings. Add Bell peppers, onions and garlic; cook until tender. Add flour and stir until well blended. Stir in tomatoes, water and parsley and bring to a boil. Add remaining ingredients, except shrimp, and return to a boil. Reduce heat and simmer, covered, 20 minutes. Add shrimp, cover and cook 10 more minutes.

John Bottoms
Austin

Popolo Salmon Patties

Serves 4

1 (16 ounce) can red Sockeye salmon
1 egg, well beaten
⅓ cup sour cream
1 cup crushed potato chips
1 small onion, grated

Remove all skin and bone from salmon. Add beaten egg, sour cream and grated onion and mix well. Fold in crushed potato chips and shape into patties. Pan fry slowly in shortening. Brown on both sides.

Lynn Hosny
Austin

Spanish Paella

Serves 5 to 10

¼	cup flour
1	teaspoon salt
⅛	teaspoon pepper
1	2½ to 3 pound chicken, cut up
¼	cup olive oil
2	carrots, pared and sliced lengthwise
1	clove garlic, crushed
¼	cup diced pimiento
¼	teaspoon salt
¼	teaspoon ground oregano
¼	teaspoon ground saffron
⅔	cup long grain rice, uncooked
2	(14½ ounce) cans chicken broth
1	(9 ounce) package frozen artichoke hearts, thawed
¾	pound shelled raw shrimp
12	small clams in shell

Combine flour, 1 teaspoon salt and ⅛ teaspoon pepper in plastic or paper bag. Add a few chicken pieces at a time; shake to coat. In heavy skillet, brown chicken in hot oil about 20 minutes. Transfer to large kettle and add carrots, garlic, pimiento, ¼ teaspoon salt, oregano, saffron, rice and broth. Simmer, covered, 30 minutes. Add artichoke hearts, shrimp and clams in shells. Cook, covered, 15 to 20 minutes longer.

Mrs. Manuel Daniel (Bertha)
San Antonio

Tuna Patties

Bake at 350° for 25 minutes
Serves 6

2	eggs
2	(6½ ounce) cans chunk light tuna in water, well drained and flaked
⅛	teaspoon pepper
⅓	cup milk
1	teaspoon lemon juice
2	tablespoons pickle relish
1	cup Kellogg's 40% Bran Flakes cereal

Cheese sauce (see index)
Snipped fresh parsley

Beat eggs slightly. Add remaining ingredients and mix well. Shape into 6 patties and place on lightly greased baking sheet. Bake at 350° for 25 minutes, turning patties after 15 minutes. Serve warm with cheese sauce and parsley, if desired.

Mrs. Jay Hodgson (Barbara)
Cedar Creek

Shrimp Seashell Supper

Serves 6

2	cups small shell macaroni, cooked (1 cup uncooked)
¼	cup butter
1	(12 ounce) package frozen 1½-inch shrimp, thawed and drained
¼	cup butter
¼	cup flour
2	cups milk
1	tablespoon dried parsley flakes
1½	teaspoon marjoram leaves
1	teaspoon garlic salt
Salt and pepper	
¼	teaspoon paprika
¼	teaspoon Tabasco sauce
1	(17 ounce) can whole kernel corn
1	(10 ounce) package frozen peas, thawed and drained

Have ready, cooked shell macaroni; set aside. In heavy 3-quart saucepan melt ¼ cup butter, add shrimp and stir. Cook over medium heat about 5 minutes. Pour into small bowl and set aside. In same saucepan melt ¼ cup butter, add remaining ingredients except macaroni, shrimp, corn and peas. Stir to blend. Continue cooking, stirring occasionally until sauce is thickened, 6 to 8 minutes. Add remaining ingredients and cook over medium heat, stirring until mixture is heated through.

Poached Flounder in Galliano Butter

⅔	cup slivered blanched almonds
⅔	cup butter (not margarine)
¼	cup Galliano
¼	cup lemon juice
Salt	
Pepper, freshly ground	
2	pounds flounder fillets

In large skillet or chafing dish sauté almonds in butter until lightly toasted. Allow butter to lightly brown then stir in Galliano, lemon juice and seasonings. Add flounder fillets. Cover and cook over medium heat 7 to 10 minutes or until fish flakes easily with fork.

Lynn Hosny
Austin

203

Shanghai Sweet and Sour Shrimp

Serves 4 to 6

1	medium onion, quartered
1	cup celery, diagonally sliced
2	tablespoons oil
⅔	cup firmly packed brown sugar
2	tablespoons cornstarch
½	teaspoon salt
¼	teaspoon ginger
⅓	cup vinegar
3	tablespoons soy sauce
1	(6 ounce) can pineapple juice
1¼	cups water
2	cups pineapple chunks
1	pound cleaned, uncooked shrimp
1	Bell pepper, cut in 1-inch pieces
Hot cooked rice	

Sauté onion and celery in hot oil. In small mixing bowl combine sugar, cornstarch, salt and ginger; stir in vinegar and soy sauce. Add vinegar mixture, pineapple juice and water to onions and celery, cooking and stirring constantly until thickened and clear. Add pineapple, shrimp and Bell pepper. Cover and continue cooking 5 minutes, or just until shrimp are done.

This makes a pretty addition to a buffet table alongside the bowl of rice.

Pheasant Bavarian

Bake at 350° for 1 hour 15 minutes

2	pheasants, cleaned and quartered
¼	cup butter
2	cups coarsely chopped tart apples, not peeled
½	cup Calvados brandy
2	cups whipping cream
¼	cup fresh lemon juice
2	teaspoons salt
½	teaspoon pepper
1	tablespoon cornstarch
1	tablespoon cold water

In heavy skillet, melt butter and sauté birds till brown but DO NOT BURN butter. Remove birds and sauté apples in same skillet. Place apples in 2-quart casserole, then birds. Pour brandy in same skillet, stir and pour over birds. Cover tightly and bake 45 minutes. Add cream, juice, salt and pepper and bake uncovered for 30 more minutes. Remove birds. Mix cornstarch and water and pour into casserole drippings to make gravy.

Smothered Deer Steak

Serves 5

1½ to 2 pounds deer steak
Salt and pepper to taste
Flour for coating
Small amount of shortening
¼ cup flour
1 (10 ounce) can tomato soup

Tenderize steak, season with salt and pepper and coat with flour. Brown in small amount of shortening and drain meat. Reserve 3 tablespoons shortening in skillet and add ¼ cup flour, mix and cook till bubbly. Mix in tomato soup thoroughly and add 1½ cans water. Bring to a boil, return steak to sauce and simmer until tender (about 1 hour).

Mrs. Theophil Krienke (Sharon)
Round Rock

205

Venison Sauerbraten

Serves 10

1 pint cider vinegar
1 pint red wine
½ cup olive oil
1 quart water
1 large lemon, thinly sliced
½ teaspoon ground allspice
½ teaspoon ground cloves
3 whole peppercorns
1 large clove garlic, crushed
2 medium onions, sliced
¼ cup brown sugar, or to
   taste
6 to 7 pound venison roast
½ pint sour cream

In large marinating bowl, mix all ingredients except meat and sour cream. Add meat that has been trimmed of all fat and sinewy tissue to sauce, marinate at least 12 hours, turning occasionally. Drain off sauce and reserve. In Dutch oven, brown meat on all sides in bacon grease. Add 1 cup of marinade and cook until tender, either on top of stove or in oven. Add additional marinade as needed for basting. When meat is tender (1½ to 2 hours) remove from pan. Add about ½ cup flour to pan drippings and additional marinade to make a thick gravy. Stir in sour cream before serving.

Mrs. Roger Greenwood (Heidi)
Lodi, Wisconsin

Mexicali Pot Roast of Venison

Slow Cooker on low for 8 hours;
on high for 3 hours

1 roast of venison, about 4
   pounds
Salt, pepper and garlic powder
   to taste
1 tablespoon oil
1 teaspoon dried parsley
2 envelopes dried onion
   soup mix
1 (28 ounce) can green chili
   salsa
1 cup dry red wine

Season venison with salt, pepper and garlic powder. Pour oil into cooker on high and brown roast. Mix parsley, onion soup mix with salsa and wine and pour over roast. Cover and cook.

Venison Roll Ups

Bake at 350° for 1 to 1½ hours
Yields 6 rolls

1	pound venison round steak, ½-inch thick
½	teaspoon salt
½	teaspoon pepper
1	tablespoon mustard
3	slices bacon, halved
3	medium dill pickles, halved
1	large onion, sliced into 6 slices
¼	cup fat
2	cups water
1	bouillon cube
3 to 5	peppercorns

Pound steak to ¼-inch thickness, remove any fat or sinewy tissue. Cut into 4 to 6-inch pieces. Sprinkle with salt and pepper. Cover with a thin layer of mustard. Place strips of bacon, pickle and onion on each roll. Roll and tie each with string. Brown in hot fat (I prefer bacon drippings). Add water, bouillon cube and peppercorns. Cook on top of stove, medium-low heat about 1½ hours, or bake at 350° covered for 1½ hours. Make gravy out of liquid left from cooking by adding a little corn starch for thickening.

Mrs. Roger Greenwood (Heidi)
Lodi, Wisconsin

Venison Roast

Bake at 325° for 1 to 1¼ hours
Serves 6 to 8

4	pound roast of venison
½	cup burgundy wine
½	cup chili sauce
¼	cup salad oil
3	tablespoons wine vinegar
Salt and pepper to taste	
1	clove garlic
1	tablespoon chopped onion
1	tablespoon Worcestershire sauce
1	bay leaf

Trim off all fat and sinewy tissue. Prick meat all over with roasting forks. Combine remaining ingredients and place roast in marinade for 24 hours to 3 days, turning meat and basting with marinade several times each day. Place in uncovered roasting pan in 325° oven and roast 20 to 25 minutes per pound. Baste often with remaining marinade.

Mrs. Roger Greenwood (Heidi)
Lodi, Wisconsin

Grilled Duck Breasts

Clean wild ducks and bone out the breasts. Place breasts in bowl and cover with French dressing. Marinate about 12 hours. Drain, but do not dry. Charcoal broil on hibachi or grill in fireplace for 3 to 6 minutes on each side. Slice very thinly cross grain. Serve on thin toast points.

Delicious as hors d'oeuvres on a cold night around the fireplace.

William Roy Morrison
Las Vegas, Nevada

Roast Wild Duck With Beer Sauce

Bake at 350° for 20 minutes per pound

BEER SAUCE

¼	**cup roast duck drippings**
¾	**cup beer**
2	**cups Claret wine**
⅓	**cup chopped onion**
2	**tablespoons chopped parsley**
¾	**teaspoon salt**
¼	**teaspoon pepper**
½	**pound fresh mushrooms, sliced**
2	**tablespoons flour**

Clean ducks and dry. Stuff with your favorite dressing. Fold wings back after placing ducks on a rack in an open roaster. Place strips of bacon across the breast. Roast in moderate oven about 20 minutes per pound of each duck. During last 30 minutes, baste with beer sauce.

Pour ¼ cup drippings from roasting pan and combine with all other ingredients, except flour. Use this mixture for basting ducks. Mix flour with small amount of water and blend in remaining sauce. Heat, stirring to thicken and serve with ducks.

Beets in Orange Sauce

Bake at 350° for 15 to 20 minutes

2 cups sliced cooked beets, drained, reserving ½ cup juice
2 tablespoons margarine
1 tablespoon sugar
1 tablespoon cornstarch
½ teaspoon salt
⅛ teaspoon paprika
½ cup beet juice
½ cup orange juice
1 teaspoon lemon juice

Place beets in a 1-quart casserole. Melt margarine in saucepan. Remove from heat and stir in sugar, cornstarch, salt and paprika. Cook over low heat until mixture bubbles. Remove from heat and gradually stir in beet juice. Cook rapidly, stirring constantly until mixture thickens. Blend in orange and lemon juice. Pour over beets and bake.

Marinated Green Beans

Serves 8

2 (16 ounce) cans whole green beans, drained
½ cup sugar
½ cup vinegar
¼ cup water
2 tablespoons salad oil
½ teaspoon Accent
1 large onion, sliced
Salt and pepper to taste

In saucepan combine green beans, sugar, vinegar and water and bring to a boil. Add oil, Accent, onion, salt and pepper. Chill in refrigerator.

This recipe came from Mrs. Jeffrey's Tearoom in Mission sometime in the '40s. It was a popular place for teas, luncheons, receptions, etc.

Mrs. Sherwood Stuart (Vivian)
McAllen

209

Ritzy Broccoli Casserole

Bake at 350° for 25 to 30 minutes
Serves 6

2   (10 ounce) packages
      frozen chopped broccoli
½   pound Velveeta cheese,
      cubed
½   box (small size) Ritz
      crackers, crushed
1   stick margarine
Salt and pepper to taste

Cook broccoli according to package directions and drain. Place in casserole and top with cheese. Combine margarine and crackers and sprinkle over top. Bake at 350° until hot and browned on top - approximately 20 to 30 minutes.

For parties, buffets, etc., the casserole may be prepared in a crock pot. Place ingredients in pot in the above order. After arriving at the party, plug in the pot and cook on high setting.

Mrs. Mike McKinney (Judy)
Arlington

Cheese Broccoli Supreme

Bake at 350° for 35 minutes

1½ cups water
¼   cup butter
1   (6 ounce) package
      cornbread stuffing mix
2   (10 ounce) packages
      frozen broccoli spears,
      thawed and drained
½   cup bacon bits or fried
      bacon, crumbled
Salt and pepper, to taste
2   tablespoons butter
2   tablespoons flour
1   teaspoon chicken flavored
      bouillon granules
¾   cup milk
1   (3 ounce) package cream
      cheese, softened
¼   teaspoon salt
1   cup grated Cheddar
      cheese
4   green onions, chopped

Combine water, butter and stuffing mix. Line a 13x9-inch buttered baking dish with mixture. Drain broccoli and place over mixture in dish. Sprinkle with bacon and salt and pepper to taste. In medium saucepan melt 2 tablespoons butter and add flour stirring until smooth. Add bouillon granules and gradually add milk stirring until smooth and thickened. Add cream cheese and salt, stirring constantly, until cheese is melted. Spoon over broccoli and sprinkle with grated cheese and onions. Cover with foil and bake 35 minutes; uncover and bake another 10 minutes.

Mrs. J. W. Small (Polly)
Austin

St. Reta's Bake

Bake at 350° for 30 minutes
Serves 10 to 12

3	(10 ounce) packages frozen chopped broccoli
3	tablespoons chopped onion
3	tablespoons chopped celery
1½	sticks butter or margarine
3	cups herb stuffing mix
3	(17 ounce) cans cream style corn
3	eggs, well beaten
1	teaspoon salt
4	strips bacon, cooked, drained and crumbled

Cook broccoli according to package directions, drain. Sauté onion and celery in butter, then add to *dry* stuffing mix. Mix well and add to broccoli. Blend in corn, eggs and salt and mix thoroughly. Pour into 2 buttered square baking pans or 1 long baking pan. Sprinkle top with crumbled bacon and bake.

Green Bean-Broccoli Casserole

Bake at 350° for 30 minutes
Serves 8 to 10

2	(10 ounce) packages frozen chopped broccoli, drained
1	(16 ounce) can cut green beans, drained
1	cup Miracle Whip salad dressing
1	teaspoon salt
½	teaspoon pepper
1	(10 ounce) can cream of mushroom soup
1	cup grated Cheddar cheese
1	medium onion, chopped

Cook broccoli according to directions. Drain well. Mix salad dressing, salt, pepper, soup and cheese and heat. Pour half of drained broccoli into greased casserole. Pour in can of green beans, then half of the sauce. Add remaining broccoli, then remaining sauce. Sprinkle additional grated cheese on top. Bake for 30 minutes at 350°.

I serve this when I'm having a large group for dinner.

Mrs. Sherman L. Vinyard (Naomi E.)
Austin

211

Swedish Baked Beans

Bake at 325° for 1½ hours
Serves 8 to 10

2	pounds (4⅔ cups) pinto beans
12	cups water
½	teaspoon soda
4	teaspoons salt
4	tablespoons cooking oil or butter
8	slices bacon, cut in 1-inch pieces
¼	cup diced onion
1	medium clove garlic, sliced
¼	teaspoon coarse-grind black pepper
¼	cup light molasses
1	cup catsup
1	teaspoon Worcestershire sauce
1½	cups light brown sugar
½	cup cider vinegar
¼	teaspoon dry mustard
3	tablespoons cornstarch, mixed with
¼	cup cold water

2 to 3 drops Tabasco sauce

Place washed beans in large kettle, add water. Bring to boiling point. Boil 2 minutes only. Remove from heat, add soda to cut down cooking time. Cover and let stand 1 hour. (Or soak beans with soda in measured amount of water overnight.) To cook, put kettle of beans with soaking water on high heat. Add salt and oil or butter to keep down the foam. When boiling, reduce heat to simmer. Cover tightly and cook 2 hours or until tender. This may be done the day before. In fact, the entire recipe may be made ahead, to be reheated as needed. It's a good freezer idea. But do make two recipes instead of doubling up! Mix together bacon, onion, garlic, black pepper, molasses, catsup, Worcestershire sauce, brown sugar, vinegar, mustard, cornstarch, water and Tabasco sauce and add to the cooked beans, stirring carefully with a wooden spoon to avoid breaking beans. Cook slowly, covered, on surface unit of range for about 1 hour, or place in 325° oven for 1½ hours. Serve hot.

This recipe is really improved by standing and reheating.

Mrs. James E. Gravier (Donnie)
Austin

VEGETABLES

Quick Spinach Casserole

Serves 6 to 8

2 (10 ounce) packages frozen chopped spinach
1 (8 ounce) carton sour cream
½ package Lipton's dried onion soup mix
1 cup grated Longhorn or Cheddar cheese

Cook spinach as directed, but cook down thoroughly dry. Add remaining ingredients, stirring gently over low heat. DO NOT BOIL.

Quick and delicious.

Mrs. Joe W. Montgomery (Norma)
Austin

Cabbage Supreme

1 head cabbage, cut up
1 Bell pepper, diced
1 large onion, diced
3 ribs celery, diced
1 (16 ounce) can tomatoes
2 tablespoons vinegar
2 tablespoons margarine
1 quart water
⅛ teaspoon sugar
Salt and pepper

Place all ingredients in a large pan. Bring to a boil and simmer for 1 hour. Add salt and pepper to taste.

Mrs. Johnye L. Slaughter (Tommie)
Angleton

Sinful Potatoes

Bake at 350° 40 to 45 minutes
Serves 12

1 (32 ounce) package frozen hash-brown potatoes
1 pint Hellman's mayonnaise
1 pound Velveeta cheese, grated
2 tablespoons chopped onion
2 tablespoons Bacos
2 tablespoons parsley flakes

Thaw potatoes. Add remaining ingredients and mix thoroughly. Pour into 9x11-inch baking dish and sprinkle more Bacos over top. Bake 40 to 45 minutes at 350°.

Mrs. John Wooldridge (Pally)
Terrell

213

Nopalitos (Cactus)

Serves 4

1   **dozen medium size cactus or three (8 ounce) jars**
3   **tablespoons cooking oil**
½   **teaspoon cominos, crushed (or cumin)**
½   **teaspoon whole black peppers, crushed**
1   **large clove garlic, crushed**
3   **teaspoons chili powder**
¼   **cup water**
1   **egg**
Salt and pepper to taste
Diced onion (optional)
Diced fresh tomato (optional)

Clean cactus of all thorns, rinse, then dice. Boil diced cactus for about 20 minutes. Pour in colander and rinse thoroughly again. In skillet, put 3 tablespoons oil and pour drained cactus in skillet. Sauté for about 3 minutes. Meanwhile, mix all spices together with about ¼ cup water. Add spices in the middle of skillet and mix, then add the egg. Mix all together until egg is cooked. Optional: Add diced onion when you sauté cactus and diced fresh tomato after egg is cooked. Serve with fresh cooked pinto beans and flour tortillas.

If you buy the cactus in jars, just rinse and omit the boiling procedure. If you use fresh cactus, to test for freshness, break a piece off. If it snaps when broken, it is fresh.

Mrs. Ruben Torres (Olga)
Alice

Quickie Chinatown Vegetables

Serves 4

½   **cup pitted ripe olives**
2   **tablespoons salad oil**
1½   **cups diagonally sliced ¼-inch thick carrots**
1½   **cups diagonally sliced celery**
1   **tablespoon instant minced onion**
1   **tablespoon butter or margarine**
Salt to taste

Cut olives in half. Heat oil in skillet. Toss carrots and celery to coat with oil. Sprinkle onion on top. Cover and steam on high for 3 minutes. Add butter, olives and salt and stir just til mixed. If using electric skillet set at 375°.

Mrs. Clay Kruckemeyer (Rosie)
Arlington

Curried Baked Cauliflower

Bake at 350°
Serves 8 to 10

1	large head cauliflower
½	teaspoon salt
1	(10 ounce) can cream of chicken soup
1	cup grated Cheddar cheese
1	cup mayonnaise
1	teaspoon curry powder
¼	cup dried bread crumbs
2	tablespoons butter or margarine, melted

One hour before serving, break cauliflower into flowerets. Cook in large covered saucepan over medium heat with 1-inch water and salt. Cook for 10 minutes. Drain well. In saucepan, mix soup, cheese, mayonnaise and curry powder. Add cauliflower to sauce and stir gently. Spoon into 2-quart casserole. Mix bread crumbs and melted butter and sprinkle over top of cauliflower. Bake until bubbly. To freeze, mix all items, but do not bake. Thaw overnight. Bake until bubbly.

Mrs. John Byrns (Helen)
Garland

Tangy Mustard Cauliflower

Serves 6

1	medium head cauliflower
¼	cup water
½	cup mayonnaise
1	teaspoon finely chopped onion
1	teaspoon prepared mustard
¼	teaspoon salt
½	cup grated Cheddar cheese

Place cauliflower and water in 1½-quart glass casserole dish with glass lid. Place in microwave oven for 9 minutes on High setting, or boil until barely tender on burner. Drain. Combine mayonnaise, onion, mustard and salt in small mixing bowl. Spoon mustard sauce on top of cauliflower. Sprinkle with cheese. Microwave for 1½ to 2 minutes on Roast to heat topping and melt cheese. Let stand 2 minutes before serving.

Mrs. J. Travis Blakeslee (Gladys)
Austin

Cheesy Baked Celery

Bake at 350° for 20 minutes

4   cups celery, thinly sliced
¼   cup butter, melted
3   tablespoons flour
1   teaspoon salt
1   cup milk
1   (4 ounce) can chopped
     mushrooms, drained
2   tablespoons chopped Bell
     pepper
2   tablespoons chopped
     pimiento
1   cup grated sharp Cheddar
     cheese
1   cup soft bread crumbs
2   tablespoons butter, melted

In large skillet sauté celery in ¼ cup butter until crisp-tender. Push celery aside and stir in flour and salt until smooth. Add milk and stir to blend. Cook until smooth and thick. Add mushrooms, Bell pepper, pimiento and cheese to celery mixture and stir until cheese melts. Spoon mixture into greased 2-quart shallow dish. Combine bread crumbs and butter, toss well and sprinkle over celery. Bake at 350° for 20 minutes.

Corn Casserole

Bake at 400° for 1 hour
Serves 12

1   (17 ounce) can creamed
     corn
1   (17 ounce) can whole
     kernel corn, drained
1   cup grated sharp Cheddar
     cheese
1   cup cracker crumbs
½   cup grated onion
1   (2 ounce) jar pimiento
1   egg
⅔   cup evaporated milk
½   cup butter or margarine,
     melted
1   teaspoon salt
1½   teaspoons pepper
1   tablespoon sugar
½   teaspoon cayenne
½   cup chopped Bell pepper
Paprika

Mix all ingredients together, except paprika, in order given, stirring well. Pour into slightly oiled casserole, sprinkle with paprika and bake approximately 1 hour.

Mrs. Delmer Nichols (Mary Ann)
Taylor

Mrs. Charles Black (Jo)
Fort Worth

216

Mexican Corn

Bake at 350° for 30 to 35 minutes

1 (17 ounce) can cream
    style corn
1 egg
½ cup cornmeal
½ stick margarine, melted
Salt and pepper to taste
1 (4 ounce) can green
    chilies
Grated cheese

Butter an 8x8-inch baking dish. Mix corn, egg, cornmeal, melted margarine, salt and pepper. Put a thin layer of corn mixture in dish, add a layer of grated cheese and a layer of green chilies, ending with corn on top. Bake at 350° for 30 to 35 minutes.

Mrs. James Hamilton ('Cille)
Austin

Fried Cucumbers

1 egg
Cornmeal
Cucumbers

Beat egg thoroughly with fork. Peel and slice cucumbers lengthwise approximately ¼-inch thick. Dip cucumbers into the egg, then into the cornmeal. Fry in hot oil until golden brown. Drain on paper towels.

Squash may be fried the same way.

Mrs. Cliff Bachle (Linda)
Houston

In the winter of 1825-1826 Choctaw and Tahuacano Indians ranged into the lands of the Austin Colony. In the summer of 1826, Stephen F. Austin called a consultation of the six militia district representatives to develop a plan to guard against Indian incursions. An arrangement was adopted to keep ". . . from twenty to thirty mounted rangers in service all the time." The Texas Rangers have been a force to be reckoned with ever since.
—*Eugene C. Barker,* Life of Stephen F. Austin, *p. 165, as quoted in Walter Prescott Webb,* The Great Plains, *p.164.*

Old-Timey Southern Cornbread Dressing

Bake at 425° for 45 minutes

1 cup diced celery
1 cup chopped onion
¼ cup margarine
3 to 4 cups chicken or turkey broth
1 tablespoon sage
1 teaspoon poultry seasoning
1 teaspoon pepper
3 eggs, slightly beaten
5 cups finely crumbled cornbread
4 cups day-old bread crumbs
Salt to taste

In saucepan, sauté celery and onion in margarine just until clear. Pour in one cup of broth, add sage, poultry seasoning and pepper and let simmer. In large bowl beat eggs, add all of crumbs and stir well. Add broth mixture and stir until well mixed. Add remaining 3 cups broth or just until mixture is mushy. Add salt to taste. Pour into a well greased 9x13 baking pan. Bake for 45 minutes or until set.

Camille's Eggplant Casserole

Bake at 350° for 1 hour
Serves 8 to 10

2 large eggplants
1 medium onion, chopped
1 Bell pepper, chopped
3 tablespoons bacon drippings
½ pound hot country style sausage
1½ cups cooked rice
1 (10 ounce) can Cheddar cheese soup
Lawry Seasoning Salt

Peel, dice and cook eggplants in salted water until tender. Drain and set aside. Sauté chopped onion and Bell pepper in bacon drippings. Cook sausage until well done. Cook rice according to directions. Mix all ingredients lightly and spoon into a 2-quart casserole. Sprinkle with Lawry Seasoning Salt. Bake at 350° for 1 hour. If a less spicy dish is desired, use regular sausage.

Mrs. Gaston Barmore (Camille)
Houston

Scalloped Eggplant

Bake at 350° for 30 minutes
Serves 8

1   **(1½ to 2 pound) eggplant**
1   **large onion, chopped**
1   **(10 ounce) can tomatoes
     with juice**
¼   **cup cracker crumbs**
¼   **cup grated Cheddar
     cheese**

Peel eggplant. Cut into 1-inch pieces. Boil in salted water until tender. Brown onions in bacon grease. Add tomatoes with juice and simmer. Drain eggplant and stir into tomato mixture. Pour into shallow casserole and bake at 350° for 30 minutes. Remove from oven and add cracker crumbs and cheese. Return to oven and bake until cheese melts and browns.

Squash may be used with eggplant. May be prepared ahead of time and frozen without crumbs and cheese.

Mrs. Watson Arnold (Mary Beck)
Austin

Eggplant Soufflé

Bake at 375° for 45 minutes

1   **medium eggplant**
2   **tablespoons butter or
     margarine**
2   **tablespoons flour**
1   **cup milk**
1   **cup grated Cheddar
     cheese**
2   **eggs, separated**
¼   **cup soft bread crumbs**
2   **teaspoons grated onion**
2   **tablespoons catsup**
Salt and pepper to taste

Peel and dice eggplant. Boil in salted water until tender. Make white sauce of butter, flour and milk. Add cheese, egg yolks, bread crumbs, onion, catsup, salt and pepper. Mash eggplant and add to white sauce. Beat egg whites until stiff and fold into mixture. Bake in greased baking dish for 45 minutes.

Mrs. E. H. "Mickey" Walker, Jr. (Tuta)
Washington, D. C.

Ratatouille

Bake at 350° for 45 minutes
Serves 8

1	**medium eggplant**
4	**medium zucchini**
1	**medium Bell pepper**
1	**medium onion, sliced thin**
2	**medium tomatoes, cut into eighths**
⅓	**cup oil**
2	**tablespoons vinegar**
2	**cloves garlic, crushed**
2	**teaspoons salt**
2	**tablespoons sugar**
1	**teaspoon oregano**
1	**teaspoon basil**

Peel and cut eggplant in ⅜-inch slices and then into 3x1-inch strips. Slice zucchini lengthwise in ¼-inch slices and then cut into 1½-inch sticks. Half Bell pepper and then cut into ¼-inch strips lengthwise. Mix oil, vinegar, garlic and salt and sprinkle over eggplant, zucchini and pepper in flat baking dish. Bake, *covered tightly* with foil, for 45 minutes. Uncover. Add onions and tomatoes. Sprinkle with a mixture of sugar, oregano and basil. Return to oven. Bake for 15 minutes, uncovered.

This may be served cold as an appetizer.

Mrs. J. Fred Fairchild (A.M.)
Perryville, Missouri

The Mexican government decided to encourage immigration to Texas in the 1820's by contracting with individuals to settle large grants of land with colonists. These contractors were called "empresarios." The most famous and successful of these was Stephen F. Austin, the "Father of Texas." By 1828 the population of the Austin Colony had risen to over 2,000, in 1830 to over 4,000, and in 1831 to 5,665. These settlers were for the most part farmers from Tennessee, Missouri and Kentucky.
—*Eugene C. Barker,* The Life of Stephen F. Austin

Potatoes Romanoff

Bake at 350° for 40 to 45 minutes
Serves 8 to 10

1 (32 ounce) package frozen hash brown potatoes *or*
5 cups cooked potatoes, diced
2 teaspoons salt
2 cups creamed cottage cheese
1 cup sour cream
¼ cup minced green onions
1 small clove garlic, crushed
½ cup grated American cheese
Paprika

Sprinkle diced cooked potatoes with 1 teaspoon salt. Combine cottage cheese, sour cream, onion and garlic with remaining salt. Fold into potato cubes. Pour into a buttered 1½-quart (oblong) baking dish and bake at 350° for 40 to 45 minutes. Top with American cheese and sprinkle lightly with paprika. Return to oven until cheese melts.

This is even better when made the day before, and is a wonderful dish to "take away from home" - church dinners, etc. It also freezes well.

Mrs. John Henry (Rosalie)
San Angelo

Orange-Glazed Sweet Potatoes

Serves 12

12 medium sweet potatoes
1½ cups boiling water
2 teaspoons salt
6 tablespoons butter or margarine
1 tablespoon grated orange peel
2 tablespoons orange juice
1½ cups dark corn syrup
½ cup brown sugar
6 or 8 orange slices, cut in half

Pare and halve sweet potatoes. Add boiling water and salt. Simmer in covered skillet until tender, about 15 minutes. Drain off all but ½ cup of liquid. Dot potatoes with butter. Combine orange peel, juice, syrup, sugar and orange slices and pour over potatoes. Cook approximately 15 minutes, uncovered, over low heat, or until glazed. Baste frequently, turning potatoes once.

Mrs. Charles Black (Jo)
Fort Worth

221

Pecan-Topped Sweet Potatoes

Bake at 375° for 1 hour
Serves 10 to 12

2	(29 ounce) cans sweet potatoes, drained, but reserve juice
1	stick butter
1/8	teaspoon allspice
4	teaspoons nutmeg
1	teaspoon cinnamon
4	teaspoons vanilla
1/2	cup sugar
1	cup chopped pecans (more if desired)

Drain sweet potatoes (reserving juice). Mash, melt butter and add to sweet potatoes with enough juice to whip to consistency of mashed potatoes. Add seasonings and sugar; mix well. Spread in lightly greased 6-quart baking dish and top with chopped pecans. Bake, covered, for 1 hour. Remove cover for 5 minutes to lightly brown. Miniature marshmallows may be added during browning period, if desired.

Mrs. Charles Black (Jo)
Fort Worth

Sherried Sweet Potatoes

Bake at 350° for 30 minutes
Serves 6 to 8

6	sweet potatoes, boiled, peeled and mashed
1	stick butter, melted
2	eggs, well beaten
1/2	cup brown sugar
1/2	cup dry sherry
1/4	teaspoon salt
1/2	cup chopped walnuts

In a mixing bowl beat the hot potatoes with all ingredients until smooth. Spoon into a buttered baking dish and bake at 350° for 30 minutes.

Mrs. Sherwood Stuart (Vivian)
McAllen

Hoppin' John

Serves 5 or 6

1	(10½ ounce) can condensed onion soup
1	(10½ ounce) can water
¼	teaspoon salt
½	teaspoon Tabasco sauce
1	(10 ounce) package frozen black-eyed peas
1½	cups cooked ham strips
2	tablespoons salad oil
1½	cups water
1½	cups packaged pre-cooked rice

In a medium saucepan combine onion soup, water, salt and Tabasco and bring to a boil. Add black-eyed peas. Cover and simmer 40 to 45 minutes, or until peas are tender. Sauté ham in oil. Add 1½ cups water, rice and ham strips to pea mixture. Continue to simmer about 5 minutes until rice is tender and water absorbed.

Happy Hoppin' John appeared in a New Year Greeting ad from Frost Brothers many years ago!

Mrs. Sherwood Stuart (Vivian)
McAllen

Pot-Luck Peas

½	pound bacon
2	cups finely chopped celery
2	cups finely chopped onion
2	cups finely chopped Bell pepper
1	(16 ounce) can stewed tomatoes, undrained
1	(16 ounce) can tomatoes, undrained
3-4	(16 ounce) cans Ranch Style black-eyed peas, drained

Salt and pepper, to taste

Fry bacon in skillet; remove, drain, crumble and set aside. In a small amount of the bacon grease sauté celery, onion and Bell pepper until tender. Add all tomatoes and cook together 15 to 20 minutes on low heat. Add drained peas, salt and pepper. Cook 10 more minutes on low heat. Add crumbled bacon just before serving.

Cornbread is a must with Pot-Luck Peas!!

Mrs. John Bottoms (Diane)
Austin

Okra Gumbo

3	slices bacon, cut into small pieces
½	onion, chopped
1	(20 ounce) package cut okra, fresh or frozen (if frozen, do not thaw)
1	(16 ounce) can stewed tomatoes

Salt and pepper to taste
Water as needed
Cooking oil as needed

Brown bacon in heavy skillet or saucepan; add cooking oil if necessary to prevent sticking. Add chopped onion and sauté until tender. Add okra and sauté until dry and slightly browned. Stir frequently during cooking time and add oil if necessary to prevent sticking. When okra has cooked dry, add tomatoes and juice. Since some cans of tomatoes have more juice than others, add water as necessary to create a liquid that nearly covers okra. Add salt and pepper to taste and cover. Simmer over low heat, stirring occasionally. This dish can simmer from 30 minutes to an hour depending upon how tender you want the okra.

The secret to "slime free" gumbo is not adding any liquid until the "slime" has cooked out of the okra.

Mrs. Edmond Komandosky (Susan)
Taylor

Fried Okra

Serves 2 to 4

2	cups okra, cut in 1-inch slices
Salt	
½	cup buttermilk
½	teaspoon baking powder
½	cup flour
½	cup cornmeal

Slice okra, sprinkle with salt, cover with buttermilk and soak for 15 minutes. Drain well; mix baking powder, flour and cornmeal and coat lightly. Fry in deep hot fat 4 to 5 minutes till golden brown. Drain well and serve immediately.

This is a great way to serve your home-grown okra!

Mrs. Vernon Scofield (Audrey)
Austin

The Flag of the Alabama Volunteers

Dr. John Shackleford of Courtland, Alabama, raised a company of 70 volunteers who became known as the "Red Rovers." The unit uniformed themselves in red jeans cut after the fashion of the U.S. uniforms of the day. They adopted a solid red square of cloth as the banner of the company. After journeying to Texas, the company was accepted for Texas service on February 3, 1836, and moved to Goliad where they became a unit in the Lafayette Battalion under Colonel James Fannin. The company fought in the Battle of Coleto and was surrendered by Colonel Fannin. Most met their tragic end in the massacre at Goliad.

THE FLAG OF THE ALABAMA VOLUNTEERS
The Red Rovers Flag

FLAG OF THE KENTUCKY VOLUNTEERS
The San Jacinto Flag

The San Jacinto Flag

Captain Sidney Sherman and the men of the State Militia Company of Newport, Kentucky, voted to go to the assistance of the Texans. As they trained and prepared for the trip to Texas, the ladies of Newport made a flag of white silk, fringed with gold colored braid on which was painted the figure of a woman holding in her hand a sword over which was draped a banner with the words "Liberty or Death." The flag was presented to the company at a ball given on the eve of their departure for Texas. James Sylvester obtained a favor from his lady—an evening glove which was attached to the staff of the flag—and carried it throughout the Texas campaign. The company joined Houston shortly after the fall of the Alamo and served throughout the campaign. The flag, flown in the attack at San Jacinto, became identified with that great event. The flag now hangs in the House of Representatives in the State Capitol at Austin.

Garden Vegetable Pie

Bake at 400° for 35 to 40 minutes
Serves 6 to 8

2	cups chopped fresh broccoli or sliced fresh cauliflowerets
½	cup chopped onion
½	cup chopped Bell pepper
1	cup grated Cheddar cheese
1½	cups milk
¾	cup Bisquick baking mix
1	teaspoon salt
¼	teaspoon pepper

Cook broccoli or cauliflowerets in 1-inch salted water until almost tender (about 5 minutes) and drain thoroughly. (If you use frozen broccoli or cauliflower, DO NOT COOK before mixing with onion, bell pepper and cheese. Just thaw and drain.) Mix broccoli, onion, Bell pepper and cheese and put in a 10-inch lightly greased pie plate. Beat remaining ingredients until smooth (15 seconds in blender on high speed or 1 minute with hand beater.) Pour into pie plate. Bake at 400° until golden brown and knife inserted halfway between center and edge comes out clean, about 35 to 40 minutes. Let stand for 5 minutes. Garnish if desired and serve. Refrigerate any remaining pie.

Mrs. John Byrns (Helen)
Garland

Spinach Royale

Bake at 350° for 30 minutes
Serves 6

2½	tablespoons margarine
2¼	tablespoons flour
1	(3 ounce) package cream cheese
½	cup grated blue cheese
1	cup milk
2	(10 ounce) packages frozen chopped spinach
8	Wheatstone crackers, crushed

Blend margarine, flour and cheeses. Add milk. Cook and stir until cheese melts and makes a smooth sauce. Cook spinach, drain well. Stir in milk and cheese mixture. Spoon into baking dish, top with cracker crumbs and bake for 30 minutes.

Mrs. Paul R. Day (Mary)
Portland, Maine

Spanish Hominy

Serves 6 to 8

1	large onion, chopped
½	stick margarine
1	heaping tablespoon flour
1	cup milk
2	cans yellow hominy, drained
½	pound Velveeta cheese
2	mild jalapeño peppers (may use canned), or to taste

In large saucepan, sauté onions and margarine until slightly browned. Blend in flour and milk and stir. Add hominy, cheese and pepper. Cook over low heat, stirring constantly until cheese has melted and is thick.

Serve with Mexican food - or great at a fish fry!

Mrs. Darrell Vinson (Anita)
Arlington

Artichoke and Spinach Casserole

Bake at 350°
Serves 6 to 8

1	(14 ounce) can artichoke hearts, drained
1	cup chopped onion
½	stick butter or margarine
2	(10 ounce) packages frozen chopped spinach
1	(8 ounce) carton sour cream
½	cup Parmesan cheese

Drain artichoke hearts and cut in pieces. Sauté onions in butter until golden. Steam spinach until done, drain well. Mix all ingredients. Pour into buttered casserole. Sprinkle more Parmesan cheese on top. Bake at 350° until heated through.

Mrs. William L. Seals (Betty)
Austin

Spinach and Cheese Casserole

Bake at 350° for 1 hour
Serves 8

1	(24 ounce) carton cottage cheese
6	eggs, lightly beaten
1	stick butter or margarine, cut in pieces
8	ounces Velveeta cheese, cubed
2	(10 ounce) packages frozen chopped spinach, thawed and drained
6	tablespoons flour

Combine cottage cheese, eggs, butter, cheese cubes, spinach and flour and stir until well mixed. Pour into 13x9x2-inch greased baking dish.

Very good to be so easy.

Mrs. Thomas Berry (Jo Ann)
Houston

Gourmet Baked Spinach

Bake at 375° for 20 minutes

1	pound fresh spinach or
2	(10 ounce) packages frozen chopped spinach
2	tablespoons minced onion
3	tablespoons margarine, melted
3	tablespoons flour
2	cups milk
¼	teaspoon nutmeg
3	hard-boiled eggs, chopped

Salt and pepper to taste
| ½ | cup grated American cheese |
| ½ | cup buttered breadcrumbs |

Paprika

Wash spinach and cook in small amount of boiling salted water till tender. Drain and chop. (Or cook frozen spinach according to package directions.) Cook onion in margarine until transparent. Add flour and blend well; gradually add milk and cook , stirring until thick and smooth. Fold in spinach, nutmeg and boiled eggs. Season with salt and pepper. Spoon into a buttered shallow baking dish. Top with mixture of cheese and breadcrumbs and sprinkle with paprika.

Vegetarian Lasagne

Bake at 375° for 30 minutes
Serves 8

10   lasagne noodles
2   (10 ounce) packages frozen chopped spinach
½   cup chopped onion
1   tablespoon oil
1   cup grated raw carrots
2   cups sliced fresh mushrooms
1   (15 ounce) can tomato sauce
1   (6 ounce) can tomato paste
½   cup chopped pitted ripe olives
1½   teaspoon dried oregano
2   cups cream style cottage cheese
1   pound Monterey Jack cheese, sliced
¼   cup grated Parmesan cheese

Place noodles in pot of boiling, salted water and cook 8 to 10 minutes. Drain. Prepare spinach according to package directions (or simply defrost ahead of time). Meanwhile, sauté onion in oil until soft. Add carrots and mushrooms; cook until crisp-tender. Stir in tomato sauce, paste, olives and oregano. Butter or grease a 13x9x2-inch casserole dish. Layer in ½ each of noodles, cottage cheese, spinach and sauce mixture and ⅓ of the cheese slices. Repeat, placing remaining ⅓ of the cheese slices on top. Sprinkle with Parmesan cheese. Bake at 375° for 30 minutes.

Mrs. Edward D. Abrahamson (Trisha)
Round Rock

Barbecued Lima Beans

Bake at 400° for 30 minutes
Serves 4

2   slices bacon
1   medium onion, sliced
1   clove garlic
1   tablespoon flour
1   cup canned tomatoes
1½   teaspoons dry mustard
2   tablespoons sugar
2   tablespoons vinegar
1   (17 ounce) can lima beans.

Cut bacon slices in half and fry. Drain all bacon fat except 2 tablespoons. Add onions and garlic to fat and brown slowly. Stir in flour until well blended. Add tomatoes, mustard, sugar and vinegar. Remove garlic. Drain beans. Add to tomato sauce. Pour into 1½ quart casserole. Top with crisp bacon and bake in 400° oven for 30 minutes

Mrs. George Bowers (Jonnie)
Austin

Zucchini Bake

Bake at 350° for 40 minutes
Serves 6 to 8

1   **pound zucchini squash**
1   **(16 ounce) can tomatoes**
¼   **cup cooked bacon with grease**
½   **cup chopped onion**
½   **cup chopped Bell peppers**
1   **cup bread crumbs**
½   **cup grated Cheddar cheese**
2   **tablespoons melted butter**
Salt

Clean and cut squash in small chunks. In large saucepan, combine tomatoes, onion, bacon and Bell pepper and bring to a boil. Cook until vegetables are tender. Put squash in a 9x13-inch casserole dish, blend in tomato mixture and bake in 350 ° oven for about 40 minutes. Remove from oven. Combine crumbs, grated cheese and melted butter and sprinkle over top of casserole and return to oven to melt cheese and brown crumbs.

Mrs. Don Fiero (Pat)
Leander

Bobbie's Squash Casserole

Bake at 350° for 1 hour
Serves 8 to 10

8   **cups frozen or fresh squash**
1   **pound sausage, cooked, crumbled and drained**
3   **cups grated sharp Cheddar cheese**
1   **tablespoon chopped chives**
2   **eggs, beaten**
1¾   **cups sour cream**
1   **stick butter**
2   **cups bread crumbs**
Optional:
1   **(2 ounce) jar chopped pimientos, drained**
1   **(8 ounce) can sliced water chestnuts, drained**

Cook squash until tender in small amount of water, or microwave with no water. Drain *well* and set aside. In skillet, brown sausage and drain off excess grease. Add cheese, chives, beaten eggs and sour cream (and optional items, if desired) to sausage and mix well. Mix in squash and stir gently. In small saucepan melt butter and mix in bread crumbs, stirring constantly to brown crumbs. Spoon squash-sausage mixture into casserole dish and top with buttered crumbs. Bake at 350 ° for 1 hour.

Mrs. W. David Counts (Mary)
Knox City

Zucchini Casserole

Bake at 350° for 30 to 35 minutes
Serves 8 to 10

4	cups grated zucchini
1	cup Bisquick
½	cup chopped onion
½	cup grated Parmesan
½	teaspoon salt
½	teaspoon marjoram
½	cup cooking oil
4	eggs, slightly beaten

Pepper and garlic powder,
to taste

Combine ingredients and put into a greased 9x13-inch pan. Bake at 350° for 30 to 35 minutes. DO NOT OVERCOOK.

Mrs. Allen Black (Wanda)
Austin

Glazed Acorn Squash Rings

Bake at 350° for 15 minutes
Serves 6

2	medium acorn squash, unpeeled
½	cup orange juice
½	cup brown sugar
¼	cup light corn syrup
¼	cup butter
2	teaspoons grated lemon rind
⅛	teaspoon salt

Cut off ends of squash. Cut crosswise into slices and remove pulp and seeds. In large covered saucepan, cook squash rings in orange juice (add a little water if necessary). Cook just until slightly tender. Place rings in large shallow casserole. Combine any liquid left in saucepan and/or enough orange juice to make ⅓ cup, and brown sugar, syrup, butter, grated lemon rind and salt. Simmer for 5 minutes. Pour over squash rings and bake, uncovered, basting occasionally.

Greek-Style Stuffed Squash

Serves 4 to 6

12 to 14 zucchini squash
    (6-inches long or less)
1   cup raw rice
1   pound ground beef or
    ground lamb
½   teaspoon cinnamon
1   teaspoon salt
Pepper to taste
3   large tomatoes, chopped,
    or 1 (1 pound) can
    stewed tomatoes
2   teaspoons salt
1   teaspoon dried mint
1   clove garlic, chopped

Core zucchini with potato peeler or melon baller, leaving ½-inch walls (be careful not to pierce walls of squash). Rinse and drain. Mix rice, meat, cinnamon, 1 teaspoon salt, pepper and ½ the tomatoes. Stuff zucchini with mixture, stuffing ¾ full (rice expands). Arrange flat in saucepan and add the rest of the tomatoes. Barely cover with water and 2 teaspoons salt, dried mint, and garlic. Cook, covered, about 35 minutes, or until rice is done. Serve with sauce from pan.

Mrs. John R. Milne (Beverley)
Warren, Michigan

Jalapeño Squash Casserole

Bake at 350° for 40 minutes
Serves 6 to 8

1½   pounds yellow squash
1   medium onion, chopped
Salt and pepper to taste
1   (3 ounce) can chopped
    green chilies
2   eggs, well beaten
1   (8 ounce) jar plain or
    jalapeño Cheese Whiz
Bread crumbs

Cook squash and onions with salt and pepper until barely tender. Drain. Add green chilies and eggs and mix thoroughly. Spread cheese in shallow baking dish. Pour squash mixture over cheese and top with bread crumbs. Bake for 40 minutes or until bubbly.

Mrs. Kenneth R. Pruitt (Nevellyn)
Austin

Quick Sautéed Summer Squash

Serves 4 to 6

10 small, tender yellow
　　crookneck squash
½ stick margarine
1 small onion, diced
¼ teaspoon garlic salt
2 tablespoons sugar
Salt and pepper, to taste

Wash and slice, vertically, all squash, then set aside. Melt margarine on low heat in skillet. Add diced onions to margarine and simmer, on low heat, until soft. Place sliced squash in skillet with onions, add garlic salt, salt and pepper and sugar. Sauté over low heat; then cover and simmer until tender. Serve hot. Parmesan cheese tastes great sprinkled over the top just before serving.

DON'T FORGET THE SUGAR. This retards the natural bitterness of the squash.

Mrs. Richard Brito (Joanne)
San Antonio

Italian-Style Eggplant and Zucchini

Bake at 350° for 1 hour
Serves 10 to 12

⅔ cup flour
1 teaspoon salt
½ cup milk
1 medium eggplant, peeled
　　and cut into ¼-inch
　　slices
Vegetable oil, heated
2 medium zucchini, thinly
　　sliced
1 medium onion, chopped
⅛ teaspoon cayenne pepper
2 cups cottage cheese
2 eggs
½ cup dry bread crumbs
1 (8 ounce) package
　　mozzarella cheese,
　　sliced
1 (15½ ounce) jar spaghetti
　　sauce with mushrooms

Combine flour and salt. Dip eggplant slices in milk; dredge in flour mixture, then fry in hot oil until golden brown. Drain on paper towel and set aside. Reserve drippings in skillet. Add zucchini and onion to skillet. Sauté vegetables until barely tender. Stir in cayenne pepper. Combine cottage cheese, eggs and ½ teaspoon salt in a small bowl. Mix well and set aside. Arrange half of eggplant slices in lightly greased 13x9x2-inch baking dish. Spoon half of zucchini and onion mixture over eggplant. Top with half of bread crumbs, half of cottage cheese mixture, half of mozzarella cheese, and half of spaghetti sauce. Repeat layers. Bake at 350° for 1 hour or until bubbly.

Mrs. Darrel Baker (Linda)
Austin

Zucchini Stuffed With Hot Sausage

Bake at 350° for 30 minutes
Serves 10 to 12

6	medium zucchini, halved lengthwise
½	pound (or more) hot sausage
1	small onion, chopped
¼	cup Parmesan cheese
1	clove garlic, crushed
⅓	cup Italian bread crumbs (or more)
¼	pound mozzarella cheese, grated

Cook zucchini in boiling salted water in large skillet 10 minutes. Drain. Scoop pulp out, leaving ¼-inch shell. Mash pulp, drain well and place shells in shallow baking dish. Cook sausage, crumbling it as you cook it, add onion and garlic and sauté until tender. Mix mashed zucchini pulp, bread crumbs and Parmesan cheese. Spoon mixture into shells and sprinkle with grated mozzarella cheese. Bake in 350° oven 30 minutes or until hot. This can be prepared ahead and frozen. One-half zucchini per person is adequate.

Mrs. Harry Smith (Ginny)
Austin

Big John's Tomato Delight

Serves 4 to 6

2	tablespoons finely chopped purple onion
2	tablespoons finely chopped Bell pepper
1	tablespoon garlic flavored butter
1	(10 ounce) package frozen chopped broccoli
1¼	cups (5 ounces) grated Swiss cheese
4	large tomatoes

Sauté onions and Bell pepper in garlic butter. Let stand until needed. Cook broccoli according to package directions; drain. Add cheese and onion/pepper mixture, stirring well. Cut tomatoes into 1-inch slices and place on baking sheet. Spoon broccoli mixture onto each slice. Broil 3 to 5 inches from heat until bubbly and cheese is melted.

John (Cajun) Stegall
Ballinger

233

Easy Italian Baked Tomatoes

Bake at 325° for 20 minutes
Serves 4

4   medium tomatoes,
       unpeeled
1   teaspoon minced onion
4   tablespoons Caesar
       dressing
12 - 15 Sociable crackers,
       crumbled
2   tablespoons melted butter
Parmesan cheese (enough to
       sprinkle on top of each
       tomato)

Hollow out each tomato. Sprinkle hollow of each tomato with minced onion and spoon 1 tablespoon Caesar dressing in each. Mix cracker crumbs in butter and sauté. Fill each tomato with cracker crumbs and sprinkle top of each with Parmesan cheese. Bake in 350° oven for 20 minutes.

Mrs. Garry D. Patterson (Sharon)
Arlington

Poke Salad

Early in the spring, pick a mess (grocery bag stuffed full) of tender leaves from Poke Salad plant. (Before the berries appear.) In a large heavy pot, place all leaves, mashing them down to get them all in. Pour pot about ½ full of water and bring to a rolling boil. Let steam for about 15 minutes and after they are completely wilted, drain off *all* water. Add 1 (16 ounce) can drained spinach, salt and pepper to taste and a small piece of salt pork or bacon drippings. Continue to cook over medium heat until very tender. Slice hard boiled eggs over top and serve with hot cornbread.

An old East Texas tale is that you must have 3 messes of Poke Salad in the spring in order not to have fever and chills in the summer.

Kenneth P. Barton
Garrison (deep East Texas)

Improvised Rice

Serves 6

1 small onion, chopped
1 rib celery, chopped
1 carrot, chopped
1 small zucchini squash, chopped
1 yellow squash, chopped
2 tablespoons oil
½ pound fresh mushrooms
1 cup rice, uncooked
1½ cups chicken broth
1½ teaspoons salt

Cut first five ingredients into fairly small cubes. In large skillet, sauté in a small amount of oil. Add mushrooms, rice, broth and salt. Bring to a boil, cover, lower heat and simmer for 20 to 30 minutes or until rice is done. Most of the liquid should be absorbed.

Mrs. Walter J. Dingler (Gayle)
Austin

Wild Rice Casserole

Bake at 325° for 30 minutes
Serves 6

1 cup wild rice, uncooked
1 pound bulk sausage
8 ounces fresh mushrooms, sauteéd in butter
2 tablespoons butter
3 tablespoons flour
2 cups milk
Fresh sage
Cheese, grated

Cook rice according to package directions. Lightly brown sausage, drain and add cooked rice and sauteéd mushrooms. Make cream sauce of butter, flour and milk. Mix with rice mixture. Pour into shallow casserole dish. Crush sage over top and sprinkle with grated cheese. Bake 30 minutes. This is best made the night before serving.

Good for brunch with spinach salad and fried apples.

Mrs. John G. Castles (Towlesey)
Corbin, Virginia

235

Monterey Rice

Bake at 350° for 30 minutes
Serves 6

1   cup rice, uncooked
1   (8 ounce) carton sour
       cream
1   (4 ounce) can mild
       chopped jalapeño
       peppers *or*
1   (3 ounce) can chopped
       green chilies
1   (10 ounce) package
       Monterey Jack cheese,
       grated

In medium saucepan cook rice according to package directions. Mix in sour cream and peppers. In a 1-quart baking dish, place ½ of rice mixture and top with ½ grated cheese. Repeat. Bake at 350° 30 minutes or until cheese is melted. May be baked in a mold; spray mold with Pam.

Mrs. Harry Steel (Louisa)
San Antonio

Savory Rice

Bake at 400° for 1 hour
Serves 6 to 8

½   stick butter
1   medium onion, chopped
1   cup rice, uncooked
2   (10 ounce) cans beef
       bouillon
1   teaspoon ground oregano
1   (4 ounce) can sliced
       mushrooms and juice
1½   teaspoons salt

Sauté onions in butter until soft. Add rice and brown. Spoon into greased casserole. Mix bouillon, oregano, mushrooms and salt; pour over rice. Bake covered 1 hour.

Good with game or barbecued chicken.

Mrs. Lewis Stephens (Nancy)
Dallas

Onion Rice

Bake at 350° for 30 to 40 minutes

1   cup cooked Minute Rice
1   cup water
1   stick margarine, sliced in
       small pieces
1   can onion soup

Combine all ingredients in oven-proof dish and bake uncovered at 350° for 30 to 40 minutes. (Very good warmed up.)

Judy Duncan
Livingston

Jalapeño Hot Rice

Serves 4

1	medium onion, chopped
1	medium Bell pepper, chopped
2	jalapeño peppers, seeded and finely chopped
¾	cup butter or margarine, melted
1	(4 ounce) can mushroom stems and pieces, undrained
1	(10¾ ounce) can chicken broth, undiluted
1	cup uncooked rice

Sauté onion, Bell pepper and jalapeño in butter in a medium saucepan until tender. Add mushrooms, chicken broth and rice. Cover and simmer 15 to 20 minutes or until rice is tender.

Mrs. J. C. Kirschner (Judy)
Austin

Rice Dressing

Bake at 350° for 40 minutes

1	pound ground chuck
½	cup chopped onion
½	cup chopped Bell pepper
½	cup chopped celery
1	can (10 ounce) chicken noodle soup
1	can (10 ounce) cream of mushroom soup
¾	cup long grain rice, uncooked
¼	teaspoon salt
⅛	teaspoon pepper

Brown beef slowly in a large skillet until most of the pink disappears. Add onion, pepper and celery; mix well. Continue cooking 5 minutes longer, or until all pinkness disappears. Remove from heat; drain. Add undiluted cans of soup, rice, salt and pepper. Mix well. Spoon into 2-quart casserole. Cover and bake at 350° for 40 minutes. Stir once after cooking 20 minutes.

Mrs. Lane A. Duhe (Lois)
Port Arthur

Country Noodle Casserole

Bake at 350° for 30 to 40 minutes

½	pound sliced bacon
1	package (1 pound) very fine vermicelli noodles (DO NOT OVERCOOK)
3	cups cottage cheese
3	cups sour cream
2	cloves garlic, crushed
2	medium onions, minced
2	tablespoons Worcestershire sauce
⅛	teaspoon Tabasco sauce
4	teaspoons salt
5	tablespoons horseradish
1	cup grated Parmesan cheese

Fry bacon until crisp. Drain on paper towels and crumble. Cook noodles "al dente" according to package directions. Drain well. Mix all remaining ingredients, except Parmesan cheese. Add noodles and bacon and toss until well mixed. Put in deep buttered casserole. Cover and bake at 350° 30 to 40 minutes. Sprinkle with Parmesan cheese before serving.

Mrs. Mark White (Linda Gale)
Austin

Nasi Goreng (Fried Rice)

Serves 6 to 8

2	cups rice, uncooked
3½	cups chicken broth
½	cup oil
2	cups chopped onions
3	minced garlic cloves
2	cups julienne-cut, cooked chicken
1½	cups diced ham
1	cup diced cooked shrimp
½	teaspoon cumin
½	teaspoon dried, ground chili peppers
1	teaspoon ground coriander
2	tablespoons cashew nuts
4	tablespoons peanut butter

Combine the rice and broth in a saucepan; cover and bring to a boil and cook over low heat 20 minutes. Spread on a flat surface to cool and dry. If possible, refrigerate for 2 hours. Heat the oil in a deep skillet and sauté onions and garlic 10 minutes. Stir in the rice; sauté until browned, stirring frequently. Mix in chicken, ham, shrimp, cumin, chili peppers, coriander, cashew nuts and peanut butter. Cook over low heat 10 minutes, stirring occasionally.

This was a favorite dish of all Americans living in Jarkarta, Indonesia.

Mrs. Joe Hopson (Kay Faubion)
Austin

Grits Casserole

Bake at 325° for 45 minutes
Serves 10 to 12

1   cup instant grits
4   cups boiling water
    (Cook above ingredients
      as directed on grits
      box)
1   stick margarine
2   eggs, well beaten (add
      enough milk to beaten
      eggs to make 1 cup)
½   roll garlic cheese
      (squeezable type)

Blend cheese and butter in hot grits; add egg mixture. Pour into greased casserole dish. Bake at 325° about 45 minutes.

Good served for breakfast or brunch, especially with country ham and eggs.

Mrs. Billy G. Wellman (Betty)
Frankfort, Kentucky

Macaroni Casserole

Bake at 375° for 5 minutes
Serves 8 to 10

2   (7¼ ounce) packages
      macaroni cheese dinner
Boiling water
2   teaspoons salt
1   medium onion, sliced
1   cup grated cheese
½   stick butter or margarine
1   (16 ounce) can whole
      tomatoes, slightly
      mashed
Salt and pepper

Add macaroni and onion to 2½ quarts rapidly boiling salted water and stir. Cook 8 to 10 minutes or until tender; drain water. Add butter and ONE envelope cheese mix over macaroni; mix well. Then add tomatoes and mix again. Season to taste and pour into casserole dish. Sprinkle grated cheese over macaroni and bake at 375° for 5 minutes or until cheese is melted.

Mrs. Don Nash (Blanch)
San Antonio

239

Fettuccine Alfredo

Serves 4

1 (10 ounce) package
fettuccine noodles (or
medium egg noodles)
⅓ cup butter
1 (8 ounce) carton sour
cream
1 (8 ounce) carton whipping
cream, not whipped
½ cup grated fresh
Parmesan cheese
2 tablespoons chopped
chives
⅛ teaspoon nutmeg
Salt and pepper

Cook noodles according to package directions and strain. Set aside. Melt butter in large saucepan and add noodles. Blend in sour cream and simmer for 5 minutes. Add Parmesan cheese, cream, nutmeg and half of chives. Stir until cheese is melted. Do Not Boil. Sprinkle remaining chives on top.

Great accompaniment for beef, pork or chicken and also as an entreé, increase recipe.

Mrs. Robert Hefford (Valerie)
Austin

Macaroni and Cheese

Bake at 350° for 40 - 45 minutes
Serves 8

1 (7 ounce) package
macaroni, uncooked
1 pound sharp Cheddar
cheese, grated
2 cups milk
¼ cup butter
1 egg, beaten
1 teaspoon salt
Pepper
Paprika

Cook macaroni according to package directions, until tender and rinse with cold water. In a 2-quart casserole, alternate layers of macaroni and grated cheese, ending with cheese. Bring milk to a boil. Stir in butter, egg, salt and pepper. Pour over macaroni and cheese. Sprinkle paprika on top. Bake at 350° for 40 to 45 minutes.

Mrs. Thomas Berry (Jo Ann)
Houston

Baked Ziti

Bake at 350° for 15 to 20 minutes

1 **pound Ricotta cheese** **2 or 3 eggs** **Milk** **Salt** **Pepper** **Spaghetti sauce** **Tubular macaroni, parboiled** **Mozzarella cheese, grated**	Mix together Ricotta cheese and eggs. Whip together until smooth. Add some milk if necessary for smoothness. Add salt and pepper to taste. In small flat container, put a layer of spaghetti sauce, layer of macaroni, layer of Ricotta mixture, and end with a layer of macaroni. Sprinkle with grated Mozzarella. Bake at 350° for 15 to 20 minutes. Serve with a salad.

Mrs. Glenn Meadows (Martha)
Houston

The five-pointed single or Lone Star appeared first in 1819 on a flag made in Mississippi by Jane Wilkinson Long. It was embroidered on the silk of the wedding dress of Johanna Troutman and sent with the Georgia Volunteers in 1835. Sarah Dodson, who constructed a long banner for her husband's volunteer company in Harrisburg, was the first to employ the white star on a blue field. By 1835, as the movement for Texas independence gathered momentum, the Lone Star emerged as the almost-universal Texas symbol. The flag of the Republic became the flag of the state and Texas became known as the Lone Star State.

Noodles Romano

Serves 6

1 **(8 ounce) package fettuccine, thin noodles or spaghetti**
¼ **cup butter or margarine, softened**
2 **tablespoons dried parsley flakes**
1 **teaspoon dried basil, crushed**
1 **(8 ounce) package cream cheese, softened**
⅛ **teaspoon pepper**
⅔ **cup boiling water**
1 **clove garlic, minced**
¼ **cup butter or margarine**
¾ **cup grated Romano cheese or Parmesan cheese**

To make sauce, combine ¼ cup butter, parsley and basil; blend in cream cheese and pepper. Stir in ⅔ cup boiling water; blend mixture well. Keep warm over pan of hot water. Cook noodles according to directions on package, just till tender; drain. Cook garlic in ¼ cup butter 1 or 2 minutes. Pour over noodles, toss lightly and quickly to coat well. Sprinkle with ½ cup of the cheese; toss again. Pile noodles in a large serving bowl. Spoon the warm cream cheese sauce over and sprinkle with remaining ¼ cup cheese. Garnish with additional parsley.

Serve as a main dish, Italian style, or with fried chicken or beef ribs and tossed salad. Either way, noodles never tasted better.

Mrs. John Henry (Rosalie)
San Angelo

Raisin Granola

Bake at 300° for 1 hour
Yields 8 cups

2 **cups Old Fashioned oats**
1 **cup coconut**
½ **cup wheat germ**
1½ **cups coarsely chopped walnuts, almonds or pecans**
1 **teaspoon salt**
1 **cup sweetened condensed milk**
¼ **cup oil**
1½ **cups raisins**

Combine first 5 ingredients. Stir in milk and oil and mix thoroughly. Spread mixture on pan lined with waxed paper. Bake for 1 hour, stirring about every 15 minutes. Remove from oven and add raisins immediately. Cool and store in a tightly covered container.

Mrs. John Byrns (Helen)
Garland

Homemade Noodles

1 egg
2 tablespoons milk
1 teaspoon salt
1 cup flour

Beat egg, stir in milk, salt and flour. Mixture will be thick and doughy. Roll out thin on floured board. Let dry approximately 1 hour. Roll up and slice in desired width. Pull apart in 2 to 3-inch lengths and let dry again, turning and mixing noodles occasionally. Add to boiling chicken broth or beef broth. Cook noodles in broth until tender and then you are ready to serve.

This recipe is an old German recipe and one way it is served is ladled over mashed potatoes — try it, you'll love it!

Mrs. Jackson Kuhlman (Judy)
Austin

"Fit for a King" Granola

Bake at 250° for 50 to 60 minutes
Yields 10 cups

3 cups regular oats, uncooked
1 cup wheat germ
½ cup vegetable oil
½ cup honey
1 cup seedless raisins (dark or light)
1 cup chopped dried apricots
1 cup chopped dates
1 cup flaked coconut
1 cup chopped pecans, toasted, if desired

Combine oats, wheat germ, oil and honey and mix well. Spread mixture on lightly greased baking pan. Mixture should be in a thin layer. Bake for 50 to 60 minutes. Allow to cool and then break into bite-size pieces. While oat mixture is baking, cut up and mix fruit, coconut and pecans. Mix cooled oat pieces and fruit mixture and store in airtight container.

The toasted pecans give a very good flavor.

Lewis King
Austin

Shrimp Cocktail Sauce

Serves 6

1 (12 ounce) bottle chili
   sauce
8 tablespoons lemon juice
6 tablespoons horseradish
4 teaspoons Worcestershire
   sauce
1 teaspoon grated onion or
   juice
8 drops Tabasco sauce

Combine all ingredients and chill thoroughly to let the flavors blend. Serve with boiled shrimp.

Wonderful!

Orman Hot Sauce

Makes 3 to 4 cups

1 (15 ounce) can Hunt's
   tomato sauce
1 (3 to 4 ounce) can
   chopped green chilies,
   drained
½ medium onion, chopped
1 tablespoon Worcestershire
   sauce
¼ teaspoon garlic powder
½ teaspoon seasoned salt
⅛ teaspoon Accent

Mix all ingredients and chill before serving. Add Tabasco to taste.

Very good with eggs, Mexican food or on nachos, etc.

Mary Orman
Austin

Sinful Sauce

¼ cup milk
⅓ cup honey
2 tablespoons brown sugar
½ teaspoon grated lemon
   peel
¼ teaspoon vanilla
½ cup creamy peanut butter

Mix all together. Heat over medium heat stirring occasionally until sugar is dissolved. Serve over ice cream, pound cake, etc. Top with chopped peanuts if desired. Store in refrigerator, reheat to serve.

Ruthie's Barbecue Sauce

Yields 2 cups

1   tablespoon corn oil
1   cup finely chopped onion
½   cup Karo dark corn syrup
½   cup catsup
¼   cup cider vinegar
¼   cup prepared mustard
¼   cup Worcestershire sauce

In 1½-quart saucepan, heat corn oil over medium heat. Add onion and sauté, stirring. Cook 1 minute. Stir in remaining ingredients, stirring occasionally. Bring to a boil, reduce heat and simmer 15 minutes. Stir occasionally. Brush on chicken, beef or pork during last 15 to 20 minutes of grilling or broiling. Heat and serve any remaining sauce.

Variations: Western Chili Sauce — follow basic recipe and add 1 tablespoon chili powder.

Herb Sauce — follow basic recipe and add 2 cloves garlic, minced with onion and 1 teaspoon dried oregano leaves, 1 teaspoon dried basil leaves.

Mrs. Roger W. Gilbert (Ruthie)
Des Moines, Iowa

Roy Lee's Barbecue Sauce

3   (14 ounce) bottles catsup
3   (5 ounce) bottles A-1 Sauce
1   pound margarine
1   (5 ounce) bottle Worchestershire sauce
1   cup vinegar
1   (6 ounce) bottle Louisiana Red Hot Sauce (or to taste)
1   teaspoon garlic salt
1   cup sugar
1   tablespoon salt
4   medium onions, chopped
6   lemons, juiced
1   sweet pepper, chopped

Combine all ingredients in stainless cookwear. Heat to simmer for one hour, but DO NOT BOIL.

Mrs. James C. Ragan (Joyce)
Round Rock

245

Chicken Barbecue Sauce

For 4 to 6 chickens

½	pound margarine
¼	cup lemon juice
1	tablespoon A-1 sauce
½	teaspoon Tabasco sauce
½	teaspoon cayenne powder
2	teaspoons sugar
4	tablespoons flour
½	teaspoon salt
1½	cups water

Melt margarine in saucepan over low heat, add lemon juice, A-1 and Tabasco. In small bowl, combine cayenne, sugar, flour and salt. Gradually stir in small amount of water until flour mixture is smooth. Add flour mixture to margarine in saucepan and add remaining water. Cook over low heat, stirring constantly until sauce is thick. About midway through cooking time for chickens, start basting with sauce. This sauce is very good on turkey, dove or quail.

The absence of tomato sauce helps keep the meat from burning.

Zack Swenson
Austin

Barbecue Sauce for Pork

Serves 4 to 6

½	cup water
¼	cup vinegar
2	tablespoons sugar
1	tablespoon prepared mustard
½	teaspoon salt
½	teaspoon pepper
¼	teaspoon cayenne
1	lemon, thinly sliced
1	large onion, chunked
½	cup catsup
2	tablespoons Worcestershire sauce

Combine all ingredients except catsup and Worchestershire sauce and simmer 20 minutes, stirring a few times so it won't burn. Add catsup and Worchestershire sauce and bring to a boil. Remove from heat. Place pork chops or ribs in baking dish and cover with sauce. Bake till meat is tender. If sauce gets too thick, add a little water.

Mrs. Robert H. Block, Jr. (Debbie)
Austin

Texas Tomato Sauce

¼	cup oil
1	large onion, chopped
1	clove garlic, minced
1	(12 to 14 ounce) can tomato pureé
1	(6 ounce) can tomato paste
1	teaspoon salt
¼	teaspoon baking soda
1	teaspoon sugar
¼	teaspoon pepper
¼	teaspoon oregano
¼	teaspoon basil

Heat oil in saucepan, add garlic and onions. Sauté until light brown. Add pureé and paste and other seasonings. Simmer on low heat, uncovered, until thick. Good sauce for any pasta.

Mrs. David Biscomb (Lucretia)
Round Rock

Basic White Sauce

THIN WHITE SAUCE

1	tablespoon butter
1	tablespoon flour
1	cup milk

Salt and pepper to taste

MEDIUM WHITE SAUCE

2	tablespoons butter
2	tablespoons flour
1	cup milk

Salt and pepper to taste

THICK WHITE SAUCE

3	tablespoons butter
3	tablespoons flour
1	cup milk

Salt and pepper to taste

Melt butter in a heavy saucepan over low heat; add flour, stirring until smooth. Cook 1 minute, stirring constantly. Gradually add milk; cook over medium heat, stirring constantly, until mixture is thickened and bubbly. Stir in salt and pepper.

Cheddar Cheese Sauce

1	tablespoon butter
1	tablespoon flour
½	cup milk
2	tablespoons dry white wine
1	cup grated Cheddar cheese
Salt, pepper	
¼	teaspoon dry mustard

Melt the butter in a saucepan and slowly stir in the flour until a roux is formed. Mix the milk and wine together. Slowly pour the milk mixture into the roux, stirring with a wire whisk. When all the milk mixture has been used, begin to add the cheese, a little at a time. Continue to stir the mixture to keep the sauce smooth. Season with pepper, salt and mustard. Continue to stir until sauce is slightly thickened. Serve over vegetables.

Curry Sauce

2	medium onions, chopped
¼	cup butter
½	cup finely chopped ham
¼	teaspoon pepper
1	teaspoon celery salt
¼	teaspoon ground cloves
2 or more tablespoons curry powder	
⅛	teaspoon thyme
2	cups beef bouillon
2	beaten egg yolks
½	cup half and half cream

Slowly brown onions in butter over low heat. Add ham and seasonings, stir and add bouillon. Simmer 20 minutes. Add salt to taste. The seasonings blend and the sauce is more tasty if allowed to set 2 hours. Then reheat, adding egg yolks and cream gradually and simmering just till sauce thickens. DO NOT BOIL. Use this sauce over sliced lamb or beef on top of cooked rice. Top with your choice of condiments such as grated coconut, raisins, chutney, pineapple, chopped hard-boiled egg, etc.

Mrs. Henry Smyth (Scotty)
Colleyville

Arline's Sweet White Sauce

Serves 6

½	cup sugar
⅛	teaspoon salt
¼	cup flour
1	teaspoon cinnamon
3	cups milk

Mix sugar, salt, flour and cinnamon and add ½ cup milk. Mix until smooth. Pour remaining milk (2½ cups) into heavy saucepan and add sugar-flour mixture. Stir and cook over low heat until it thickens. Stirring constantly is important. This sauce sticks and scorches easily. Remove from heat and cool. It will thicken more as it cools. More milk may be added if desired. Delicious served over cobblers, or add sliced fresh fruit and serve over cake.

Mrs. Jimmie F. Johnson (Judy)
Corpus Christi

Heavenly Hot Fudge Sauce

½	cup margarine
4	ounces unsweetened chocolate
3	cups sugar
¼	teaspoon salt
1	(13 ounce) can evaporated milk
2	tablespoons white syrup

Melt margarine and chocolate in top of double boiler over boiling water. Turn heat to low and add sugar, salt, milk and syrup a little at a time beating thoroughly after each addition. Beating well and slowly is important to be sure the sugar is dissolved. It is well worth the extra time. Pour into container for storage and refrigerate when cool. This will keep for weeks in refrigerator and is great served hot or cold on your favorite dessert.

Mrs. Leonard Tallas (Jean)
Austin

Lemon Hard Sauce

½   cup butter, softened
1½   cups powdered sugar
2   teaspoons grated fresh
       lemon rind
1   tablespoon fresh lemon
       juice

Cream butter; beat in sugar. Blend in lemon rind and lemon juice and mix thoroughly. Chill in refrigerator.

Great on pound cake, gingerbread or angel food cake.

Kentucky Sauce

1   cup brown sugar
1   cup water
1   cup sugar
1   cup strawberry preserves
1   cup chopped pecans
1   cup bourbon whiskey
1   orange, pulp, juice and
       grated rind
1   lemon, pulp, juice and
       grated rind

Cook sugar with water until syrup spins a thread. Add remaining ingredients. Let stand in refrigerator for 24 hours to ripen. The longer it ripens the better it gets. Especially good over ice cream or plain cake.

Mrs. Warren D. Hodges (Kathleen)
Churchville, Maryland

Raisin and Cider Sauce

2   tablespoons butter
2   tablespoons flour
¾   cup apple cider
¾   cup light rum
¾   cup seedless raisins
1   teaspoon grated lemon
       rind
1   teaspoon dry mustard

Melt butter in a saucepan over low heat and slowly stir in flour. Continue to stir until roux is smooth and bubbly. Mix the cider and rum together and slowly add the mixture a little at a time to the roux. Continue to stir until the sauce is smooth. Add the raisins, lemon rind and dry mustard, stirring sauce until all is blended. Serve warm over ham slices or very good served over carrots or sweet potatoes.

Hot Mustard

Makes 1 pint

1	cup cider vinegar
1	(12 ounce) can Colman's dry mustard
4	egg yolks
1	cup sugar

Mix vinegar and dry mustard together and let stand overnight. Mix yolks and sugar and add to mustard mix the next day. Cook in double boiler over boiling water until mixture thickens. Stir occasionally. Cooking time about 15 minutes. This mustard keeps indefinitely in refrigerator.

Mrs. Charles M. Kiefner (Marilyn)
Perryville, Missouri

Peanut Butter

Bake at 300° for 1 hour

2	pounds raw shelled peanuts
1	cup peanut oil
Salt and honey to taste	

Spread peanuts in shallow baking pan. Roast for approximately 1 hour, stirring occasionally. Remove from oven and let cool. Grind peanuts into fine meal (food grinder or processor). Mix in peanut oil a *little* at a time to get consistency you desire. Add salt and honey to taste.

Hot Garlic Pickles

1	gallon hamburger dill pickles
½	bottle garlic chips
1	bottle Tabasco sauce
5	pounds sugar, less 6 cups

Drain pickles and leave overnight in an inverted position. Drain again and discard liquid. Layer pickles, garlic chips, Tabasco and sugar. Turn jar over every day for a week. After one week, the pickles are ready to serve.

Mrs. Jack Fisher (Alyne)
Austin

Watermelon Rind Pickles

**White portion of watermelon for
   cutting into strips
    for 2 quarts**
2   tablespoons lime powder
2   quarts water

Cut white part of watermelon rind in strips about 3 inches long and ¼-inch thick. Make a solution of lime powder and water, using 1 tablespoon of lime to 1 quart of water. Soak 2 quarts of rind in 2 quarts of lime water solution for 8 hours; then drain well and cover with clear water; boil slowly for 1 hour.

While rinds are boiling, make syrup:

Syrup:

2   cups sugar
1   quart water
1   cup vinegar
1   tablespoon whole cloves
1   tablespoon whole allspice
**1   tablespoon ginger root,
       crushed**
1   stick cinnamon

Boil syrup for 5 minutes; add rinds which have been cooked and drained. Simmer rinds in syrup for 30 minutes. Let stand overnight in syrup.

Add:

4   cups sugar
2   cups vinegar

After rinds have set overnight, add 4 cups sugar and 2 cups vinegar to rinds and syrup; boil gently until syrup is thick as honey and rinds are clear. Pour into jars and seal.

This recipe is over 100 years old and was handed down to my mother.

Mrs. Richard E. Harrison (Nancy)
Austin

Green Tomato Celery Relish

10	large green tomatoes, chopped
6	onions, chopped
2	celery stalks, chopped
1	Bell pepper, chopped
2	cups vinegar
1	cup sugar
2½	tablespoons salt

Mix all ingredients and boil 1 hour in large saucepan. Pour into hot sterilized pint jars. Seal and when cool store in refrigerator.

Great for scrambled eggs and to accompany meats.

Mrs. James E. Gravier (Donnie)
Austin

Quick Corn Relish

Yields 1½ pints

1	(15 ounce) can whole kernel corn
½	cup chopped celery
2	tablespoons chopped onion
2	tablespoons chopped Bell pepper
1	tablespoon diced pimiento
½	teaspoon salt
¼	cup French dressing
¼	cup pickle relish

Drain corn. Mix all ingredients. Toss with a fork. Chill. Toss before serving. Corn relish keeps well for several days in the refrigerator.

This dish tastes great with turkey or ham and is so colorful to serve at special occasions.

Mrs. Robert Owen (Jodie)
Elgin

Cranberry Apple Relish

4	cups fresh cranberries
2	apples, pared and cored
2	oranges
1	lemon
4	cups sugar

Put apples and berries through food chopper. Quarter oranges and lemon, remove seeds and put through chopper. Add sugar and blend. Chill in refrigerator. Should stand overnight before serving — keeps for weeks in refrigerator. Very good with turkey and dressing. Delicious on Ritz crackers.

Mrs. Guy C. Jackson (Linda)
Anahuac

Pickled Okra

1½   cups water
½   cup vinegar
Small fresh okra pods, washed
    and cut off stems
    close but do not
    cut pod
Salt
Dried dill weed

Sterilize jars, lids and rings. Bring water and vinegar to boil. In each hot sterilized quart jar, pack small okra very tight. In each jar, spoon ½ teaspoon salt and 1 teaspoon dried dill weed on top of okra. Pour boiling water/vinegar mix over okra to ½ inch of jar rim and seal. Refrigerate and let set a few days before serving. (If you want to keep jars longer than a few weeks, you should process jars for five minutes in cold water pack canner — count minutes when water starts boiling.)

Mrs. Jack D. Anderson (Mary Emma)
Fruitvale

Nina's Pickled Dill Beans

Yields 4 pints

2   pounds fresh green
    beans, clean and
    unblemished
1   cup white vinegar
3   cups water
2   tablespoons pickling salt
2   teaspoons dillweed
¼   teaspoon cayenne
2   cloves garlic, crushed

Wash beans, trim ends and cut beans to fit jars. Place beans in large Dutch oven pan. Cover beans with boiling water and cook 3 minutes. Drain and pack into hot sterilized jars, leaving ½ inch headspace. In a saucepan, combine vinegar with water, salt, dillweed, cayenne and garlic and bring to a boil. Pour over hot beans. Seal. Process in boiling water bath 10 minutes.

Apple Butter

8 to 10 large apples, wash, core
    and quarter
⅛   teaspoon sea salt
Lemon slice
2   cups apple juice
½   cup raw honey
1   teaspoon cloves
2   teaspoons cinnamon
½   teaspoon allspice
1   medium lemon, juice and
    grated rind

Place apples in saucepan and partially cover with water. Add salt and lemon slice. Cook over medium heat until tender; remove lemon slice and then pureé. Return applesauce to burner. Add juice, honey, cloves, cinnamon, allspice, lemon juice and rind and cook until the sauce turns brown, stirring often. Adjust seasonings to suit your taste. Pour into sterilized ½-pint jars and seal.

Mustang Grape Preserves

Yields 2 pints

1   pound green mustang
    grapes
1   pound sugar

Pick the grapes in late June or early July before the seed has formed. Wash thoroughly and put grapes in large kettle, pour sugar over grapes and cook, stirring occasionally until the skins pop. Pour into hot sterilized jars. Seal. The preserves will turn black and be tart. Very good served on butter cakes (see index).

This is an old pioneer recipe.

Mrs. Watson Arnold (Mary Beck)
Austin

In the Mexican War of 1846, food supply for the American forces was the responsibility of a "Subsistence Department" within the Army. Contracts were let to furnish beef, pork, bacon, flour and bread. The official ration had been established in 1832 when coffee was substituted for the grog allowance. In 1838, the coffee allowance was increased from four to six pounds per hundred, sugar was increased from eight to twelve pounds and whiskey was dropped permanently.
    —James A. Huston, The Sinews of War:
Army Logistics 1775-1953, *United States Army,*
Washington, D.C., 1966

Fried Apples

Serves 6 to 8

6	cooking apples
1	stick margarine
½	cup sugar

Wash apples, core, but do not peel. Cut into ¼-inch round slices. Melt margarine in a heavy skillet over low heat. Place apples in skillet, sprinkle with sugar. Cook until juice cooks down but apples still hold their shape.

Good at breakfast with sausage, ham or bacon.

Mrs. Johnny Cates (Bonnie)
Quitman

Texas Caviar

4	cans fresh black-eyed peas, rinsed and drained
1	medium red Bell pepper, diced
1	medium green Bell pepper, diced
½	cup finely diced celery
3 to 4	green onions with tops, diced
1	package Italian dressing mix

Cider vinegar
⅛	teaspoon garlic powder
¼	teaspoon red pepper flakes

Salt and pepper to taste

Mix peas with other vegetables. Make Italian dressing according to directions on package, except use cider vinegar and add 2 more tablespoons vinegar than called for in recipe. Add seasonings and dressing to peas and toss to mix. Refrigerate overnight. Will keep for weeks in refrigerator. Serve with corn chips as dip or as accompaniment to a meal.

Broiled Spiced Peaches

Bake at 350° for 10 minutes
400° for 10 minutes

1	(29 ounce) can peach halves, drained
¼	cup brown sugar
½	teaspoon ground cinnamon
¼	teaspoon ground nutmeg
¼	cup margarine, melted and divided
½	cup crushed raisin bran flakes
¼	cup chopped pecans

Drain peaches reserving ¼ cup juice. Place peaches, cut side up in long shallow casserole dish. Combine peach juice, sugar, cinnamon, nutmeg and 2 tablespoons margarine. Spoon over peaches. Bake at 350° for 10 minutes. Combine 2 tablespoons margarine, raisin bran flakes and nuts. Sprinkle on each peach and bake at 400° for 10 minutes. Spoon more juice from bottom of casserole over peaches. Serve warm.

Short-cut: Combine all ingredients, except peach halves, and spoon on peaches and broil till thoroughly heated.

Mrs. John Adams (Eleanor)
Austin

Hawaiian Delight

Bake at 350° for 30 minutes
Serves 4 to 6

1	(16 ounce) can pineapple chunks, drained
½	cup sugar
1	cup grated, sharp Cheddar cheese
2	tablespoons flour
8-12	Ritz crackers, crumbled
1	stick butter or margarine, melted

Mix pineapple, sugar, cheese and flour together well. Place in greased baking dish. Cover with crumbled cracker crumbs. Pour melted butter over top. Bake until bubbly.

Better double this one! It is good as a side dish with chicken, ham or pork.

Mrs. Allen Black (Wanda)
Austin

Baked Fruit Compote

Bake at 325° for 1½ hours
Serves 6 to 8

1	(12 ounce) package pitted dried prunes
1	(8 ounce) package dried apricots
1	(16 ounce) can pineapple chunks
1	(21 ounce) can cherry pie filling
½	cup dry sherry
1¼	cups water

Mix all ingredients together in a 9x13x2-inch baking dish. Bake at 325° for 1½ hours, stirring thoroughly every 15 minutes or so. Serve warm. It is an excellent accompaniment to ham, baked chicken, or pork roast.

Mrs. Alec Rhodes (Charlotte)
Dripping Springs

Hot Fruit Casserole

Bake at 350° for 1 hour
Serves 8 to 10

1	(20 ounce) can sliced pineapple
1	(16 ounce) can pear halves
1	(17 ounce) can apricot halves
1	(16 ounce) can peach halves
1	(16 ounce) can Bing cherries
1	(15 ounce) can applesauce
½	cup brown sugar
1	stick margarine

Drain all fruits (save juices for beverages, etc.); arrange fruit except applesauce in a large baking dish. Melt margarine slowly in a small saucepan. Add brown sugar and applesauce. Stir until blended and pour over fruit in baking dish. Bake uncovered for 1 hour at 350°.

Delightful accompaniment to baked ham or chicken.

Mrs. Cohen E. Robertson (Elizabeth)
Clinton, Mississippi

Anniversary Pound Cake

Bake at 325° for 1½ hours
Serves 18 to 20

2 sticks margarine
1 cup shortening
3 cups sugar
5 eggs
3 cups sifted flour
½ teaspoon salt
½ teaspoon baking powder
5 teaspoons cocoa
1 cup milk
1 teaspoon vanilla

In large mixing bowl, cream together butter, shortening and sugar. Add eggs, one at a time, beating after each. Sift together flour, salt, baking powder and cocoa. Add to creamed mixture alternately with milk and vanilla, beating after each addition. Pour into a greased and floured 8-inch layer cake pan, filling 1, then pour remainder of batter into greased and floured 10-inch tube pan. (Recipe makes too much batter for the tube pan alone.) Bake at 325° for 1½ hours.

This cake stays moist for several weeks.

Mrs. J. Travis Blakeslee (Gladys)
Austin

Coconut Pound Cake

Bake at 325° for 1 hour 25 minutes

1 pound (6 sticks) whipped margarine (no substitutes)
3 cups sugar
9 eggs
3 cups flour
1 teaspoon coconut extract
1 cup Angel Flake coconut

In large mixing bowl, cream margarine and sugar. Add eggs, 3 at a time and beat vigorously after each trio of eggs. Add flour and coconut extract and mix well. Fold in coconut. Pour in greased and floured tube pan. Bake at 325° for 1 hour and 25 minutes.

Word of caution - follow this recipe to the letter!

Mrs. Crawford Martin (Margaret)
Austin

Butter Cake Supreme

Bake at 325° for 1 hour 10 minutes

½ pound butter
3 cups sugar
4 eggs
¼ teaspoon soda
1 cup buttermilk
3 cups flour
2 teaspoons extract (I use 1
   teaspoon vanilla and 1
   teaspoon almond
   extract)

Cream butter and sugar well. Add eggs one at a time, creaming well after each addition. Add soda and extract to buttermilk. Add sifted flour and buttermilk alternately to creamed mixture, starting and ending with flour. Bake in greased and floured 10-inch tube pan.

I won first place in a dairy products recipe contest 30 years ago with this recipe. It is very moist and a good keeper; it is so rich that you really don't need to ice it but seven minute frosting with coconut on top makes it extra special!

Mrs. David Gannaway (Elda)
Austin

Man's Favorite Cake

Bake at 350° for 1 hour and 15 minutes
Serves 8 to 12

½ cup shortening
1 cup sugar
1 egg
1 cup sweetened
   applesauce
1 teaspoon cinnamon
½ teaspoon allspice
½ teaspoon nutmeg
½ teaspoon salt
2 cups flour
1 teaspoon soda
2 tablespoons hot water
1 cup raisins

In large mixing bowl, blend shortening, sugar and egg thoroughly. Add applesauce. Sift the spices and salt with flour and add a little at a time, mixing well after each addition. Before the last addition of flour, stir in soda dissolved in hot water and then the remainder of flour, mixing well. Fold in raisins. Mix well and pour into greased and floured loaf pan. Bake 1 hour and 15 minutes in 350° oven.

Mrs. Don Gregg (Jayme)
Seymour

Poppy Seed Pound Cake

Bake at 325° for 1 hour and 15 minutes
Serves 20 to 24

1   **tablespoon poppy seeds**
½   **cup hot water**
1   **cup shortening**
3   **cups sugar**
6   **eggs**
3   **cups flour**
¼   **teaspoon soda**
⅛   **teaspoon salt**
1   **cup buttermilk**
1   **teaspoon vanilla**
1   **teaspoon butter flavor**
1   **teaspoon almond extract**

GLAZE
⅓   **cup lemon juice (scant)**
1   **teaspoon vanilla**
1   **teaspoon almond extract**
1½   **cups powdered sugar, sifted**

Soak poppy seeds in hot water while mixing cake. Cream shortening and sugar together. Add eggs, one at a time, mixing after each addition. Add flour, soda and salt alternately with buttermilk. Add vanilla, butter flavor, almond extract and drained poppy seeds. Pour into greased and floured tube pan and bake at 325° for 1 hour and 15 minutes. To make glaze, combine all ingredients and spoon over warm cake.

Mrs. Jerry Duffey (Valerie Starr)
College Station

Pound Cake

Bake at 350° for 1 hour

1   **cup butter**
2   **cups sugar**
2   **teaspoons vanilla**
4   **eggs**
3   **cups flour**
1   **teaspoon soda**
1   **teaspoon baking powder**
1   **teaspoon salt**
1   **cup buttermilk**

Cream together butter and sugar and beat 3 minutes. Add vanilla and eggs and beat 1 minute. Sift together flour, soda, baking powder and salt and add to butter and sugar mixture alternately with buttermilk. Mix till thoroughly blended. Pour into greased and floured Bundt pan and bake at 350° for 1 hour.

Mrs. James H. Duran (Luella)
Red Rock

Diabetic Cake

Bake at 350° for 25 minutes

2	cups water
2	cups raisins
1	cup unsweetened applesauce
2	eggs
2	tablespoons liquid artificial sweetener
¾	cup cooking oil
1	teaspoon baking soda
2	cups flour
1½	teaspoons cinnamon
½	teaspoon nutmeg
1	teaspoon vanilla

Cook raisins in water until water evaporates. Add applesauce, eggs, sweetener, and cooking oil and mix well. Blend in baking soda and flour. Add cinnamon, nutmeg and vanilla and mix. Pour into greased 8x8-inch cake pan. Bake at 350° for 25 minutes or until done. For diabetics: 1 serving = ½ fruit, 1 bread and 2 fat exchanges. Calories: 1 serving = 177 calories.

Mrs. Robert Vass (Glenda)
Burleson

Suebian Apple Cake

Bake at 450° for 20 to 30 minutes
Serves 6

	Puff pastry, pie crust or any good kneaded dough
6	medium apples
2	eggs
1	egg yolk
½	cup sugar
½	pint whipping cream, unwhipped
	Powdered sugar

Roll out dough and fit into well buttered 10-inch spring form pan. Put in refrigerator. Peel apples, halve and cut round side up in six parts, removing seeds. Place on dough. Bake in preheated 450° oven until crust and apples begin to brown. Meanwhile, in a bowl beat together 2 eggs, one egg yolk, ½ cup sugar and ½ pint whipping cream. Pour over apples and bake another 15 to 20 minutes, until custard is done. Powder while still warm with powdered sugar.

Good warm or cold.

Mrs. Joseph M. Lank (Virginia)
Springfield, Virginia

Apricot Cream Cake

Bake at 350° for 50 to 55 minutes

¼ cup soft butter or
   margarine
1 butter recipe yellow cake
   mix
3 eggs
¾ cup apricot nectar

FILLING

2 (8 ounce) packages cream
   cheese
½ cup coconut
½ cup sugar
2 tablespoons lemon juice

GLAZE

2 cups powdered sugar
2 tablespoons lemon juice
2 tablespoons apricot nectar

Combine butter, cake mix, eggs and apricot nectar. Mix well and spoon into greased and floured Bundt pan. Prepare filling by combining cream cheese, coconut, sugar and lemon juice. Spoon over cake batter in pan, being careful not to let it touch the sides of pan. Bake at 350° for 50 to 55 minutes or until top springs back. Cool in pan 1 hour. Mix powdered sugar, lemon juice and apricot nectar and spoon over top of cake.

Mrs. Glenn Meadows (Martha)
Houston

English Lemon Pound Cake

Bake at 325°

2 cups sugar
1 cup shortening
4 eggs
1 tablespoon lemon extract
½ teaspoon vanilla
3 cups double sifted flour
½ teaspoon salt
¾ cup buttermilk
1 teaspoon soda
1 teaspoon vinegar

Cream sugar and shortening. Add eggs, one at a time. Stir in extracts. Sift flour and salt together, then add alternately with buttermilk. Mix soda and vinegar and stir in. Bake in 325° oven in Bundt or tube pan. Cake will crack around top when done.

This cake may be glazed, but is equally good without. May be served warm with ice cream.

Mrs. Don Fiero (Pat)
Leander

Almond Legend Cake

Bake at 300° for 1 hour

½	cup finely chopped whole almonds (reserve 1 whole almond)
2½	cups flour
2	teaspoons baking powder
¾	teaspoon salt
¼	teaspoon soda
⅓	cup shortening
⅓	cup butter
1½	cups sugar
1	teaspoon vanilla extract
1	teaspoon almond extract
3	large eggs, separated
¾	cup milk
2	tablespoons lemon juice
1	teaspoon grated lemon peel
½	teaspoon cream of tartar
½	cup thick apricot jam
2	teaspoons rum or orange juice

Grease Bundt pan heavily with shortening. Sprinkle with chopped almonds. Sift flour, baking powder, salt and soda; set aside. In large mixing bowl, cream shortening and butter well with 1¼ cup sugar and flavorings. Beat in egg yolks. Blend in sifted dry ingredients alternately with milk, lemon juice and peel. In separate bowl beat egg whites with cream of tartar. Gradually beat in remaining ¼ cup sugar, beating until stiff peaks form. Fold into batter gradually. Pour into prepared pan. Press whole almond just below surface of batter. Bake on lower rack at 300° for 1½ hours. Let stand after baking for 10 minutes, then turn out onto plate to cool. Brush with glaze. To make glaze, combine ½ cup thick apricot jam and rum or orange juice and pour over cake.

This legendary almond cake ... with one whole almond baked inside ... is fun to bake for friends or family. You slice and serve the cake in the usual way. The lucky person who receives the slice which contains the hidden almond is said to enjoy good fortune all year!

Cookbook Committee

Banana Cream Cheese Cake

Bake at 300° for 45 to 55 minutes

1	package Duncan Hines Banana Supreme Deluxe Cake Mix
4	eggs
3	tablespoons oil
1	cup brown sugar, divided
1	medium banana, sliced
2	(8 ounce) packages cream cheese, softened
1½	cups milk
2	tablespoons lemon juice
2	cups whipped topping

Reserve 1 cup dry cake mix. In large mixing bowl, combine remaining cake mix, 1 egg, oil and ½ cup brown sugar (mixture will be crumbly). Press crust mixture evenly into bottom and ¾ way up the sides of a greased 9x13x2-inch pan. Arrange banana slices on crust. In same bowl, blend cream cheese and remaining ½ cup brown sugar. Add remaining 3 eggs and reserved cake mix. Beat 1 minute at medium speed. At low speed, slowly add milk and lemon juice. Mix until smooth. Pour into crust. Bake at 300° for 45 to 55 minutes or until center is firm. When cool, spread with topping. Chill before serving. Store in refrigerator.

Mrs. Glenn Meadows (Martha)
Houston

Banana Nut Cake

Bake at 350°

1½	cups sugar
½	cup margarine
2	eggs, separated
3	ripe bananas
½	cup nuts
1	tablespoon soda dissolved in milk
4	tablespoons milk
1½	cups flour
⅛	teaspoon salt
1	teaspoon vanilla

Cream sugar, margarine, egg yolks, crushed bananas, nuts, milk and soda. Add flour and salt. Stir in egg whites and vanilla. Bake in loaf pan at 350° until toothpick comes out clean. Sprinkle with powdered sugar, or may be frosted with a butter frosting.

The unique cake texture will occur only if egg yolks and whites are separated and mixed as indicated.

Mrs. Louis Howard (Evelyn)
Garland

265

Lemon Chiffon Cake

Bake at 325° for 65 to 70 minutes
Serves 16 to 18

2 cups sifted flour
1½ cups sugar
3 teaspoons baking powder
1 teaspoon salt
½ cup oil
7 egg yolks, unbeaten
¾ cup water
2 teaspoons grated lemon rind
1 teaspoon lemon extract
1 teaspoon vanilla
1 cup egg whites (7 or 8)
½ teaspoon cream of tartar

Measure and sift flour, sugar, baking powder and salt. Pour into mixing bowl, make a well and add in order - oil, egg yolks, water, lemon rind, lemon extract and vanilla. Beat until smooth. In large mixing bowl beat egg whites and cream of tartar until very stiff peaks are formed. Gradually pour batter over whipped egg whites, folding gently with rubber scraper just until blended. DO NOT BEAT. Pour into ungreased 10-inch tube pan and bake for 65 to 70 minutes.

LEMON FILLING

1½ cups sugar
3 whole eggs, unbeaten
Juice and grated rind of 3 lemons
¾ cup water

Mix all ingredients in a medium saucepan and stir constantly until thick and transparent. Remove from heat, let cool and spread between layers of cake.

WHITE WONDER ICING

2 egg whites
2 tablespoons light syrup
½ cup sugar
1/16 teaspoon cream of tartar

Mix all ingredients in top of double boiler. Cook over medium heat, stirring with your *fingers* until too hot for your fingers. Remove from heat and beat with electric mixer until stiff and foamy and stands in peaks. (It is important to stir this with your fingers to reach right temperature.) This icing stays moist but if the cake is not eaten within a two day period, the cake will absorb most of the icing.

This cake is good eaten plain, but especially good sliced into 3 layers with the Lemon Filling spread between layers and iced with White Wonder Icing.

Mrs. J. Travis Blakeslee (Gladys)
Austin

Lemonade Cake

Bake at 325° for 1 hour

1	box white cake mix
4	eggs
¾	cup oil
1	small package lemon-flavored gelatin
½	cup boiling water
¼	cup Chenin Blanc wine
1	small can frozen lemonade concentrate
¾	cup sugar

In large bowl mix together cake mix, eggs and oil. Dissolve gelatin in boiling water and wine; cool and add to the cake mixture. Beat about 3 to 4 minutes. Pour mixture into greased and floured tube pan and bake 1 hour at 325°. While cake is baking, add sugar to lemonade concentrate (no water). As soon as cake is out of the oven, spread some of the lemonade mixture on top a little at a time. When cool, turn cake out on plate and spread remaining lemonade mixture over cake, spooning it over to let cake soak it up.

Mrs. John Adams (Eleanor)
Austin

Flower Garden Cake

6	eggs, separated
¾	cup sugar
¾	cup lemon juice
1½	teaspoons lemon peel, grated
1	envelope Knox gelatin, softened in
¼	cup water
¾	cup sugar
1	large angel food cake

Make a custard of beaten egg yolks, ¾ cup sugar, lemon juice and lemon peel. Cook until mixture coats spoon. Remove from fire; add gelatin. Beat egg whites with remaining ¾ cup sugar. Fold into custard mixture. Tear angel food cake in bite sized pieces. Place pieces in tube cake pan which has been oiled with salad oil. Pour custard over, making sure it goes to the bottom and cake is covered. Chill. When firm, ice with whipped cream. Keep refrigerated until ready to serve.

Mrs. Walter J. Dingler (Gayle)
Austin

Graham Cracker Fruit Cakes

40	marshmallows
1	cup sweetened condensed milk
1	pound graham crackers, crushed
½	cup chopped candied cherries
½	cup chopped candied pineapple
½	cup chopped nuts
2	(8 ounce) packages dates, chopped

In top of double boiler, melt marshmallows in milk. In mixing bowl combine crumbs, cherries, pineapple, nuts and dates. Pour marshmallow mixture over fruit mixture and mix well, using hands, if necessary. Divide dough into 2 equal parts and roll each in buttered foil to form 2 fat logs. Refrigerate and slice to serve.

Very attractive when ½-inch slice is topped with whipped cream and half a cherry.

Mrs. W. David Counts (Mary)
Knox City

Mexican Fruitcake

Bake at 350° for 1 hour

2	cups flour
2	cups sugar
2	teaspoons baking soda
1	(20 ounce) can unsweetened crushed pineapple, undrained
2	beaten eggs
1	cup chopped pecans
1	(8 ounce) package cream cheese, softened
2 to 2½	cups powdered sugar
1	teaspoon vanilla

In large mixing bowl, combine flour, sugar and soda. Pour in pineapple with juice, add eggs and pecans. Blend thoroughly. Pour into greased and floured 9x13-inch baking pan. Bake in 350° oven for 1 hour. During last few minutes cake is baking, prepare frosting. In small mixing bowl, beat softened cream cheese, adding powdered sugar gradually. Beat in vanilla and ice cake while still hot.

Mrs. Larry Yandell (Gayle)
Austin

Easy Pineapple Cake

Bake at 350° for 30 minutes

1½ cups sugar
1 teaspoon soda
2 cups flour
1 teaspoon salt
1 stick margarine (optional)
2 eggs
1 (8 ounce) can crushed
pineapple, undrained

ICING

½ cup sugar
1 (5.33 ounce) can
evaporated milk
1 stick margarine
1 (7 ounce) can coconut
1 teaspoon vanilla
1 cup chopped nuts

Sift sugar, soda, flour and salt together and set aside, if margarine is not used. If margarine is used, cream with sugar and combine with dry ingredients. Combine eggs and pineapple with juice. Add to dry ingredients and mix well. Pour into greased and floured sheet cake pan. Bake 30 minutes at 350° or until golden brown. To make icing combine sugar, evaporated milk and margarine. Cook to a boil and boil 2 minutes. Add coconut, vanilla and nuts and frost cake as soon as it comes from oven.

Mrs. Robert W. Anderson (Bertie)
Texarkana

Honey Applesauce Cake

Bake at 350° for 40 to 45 minutes

2¼ cups flour
1 (15 ounce) jar
unsweetened
applesauce
1 cup honey
⅔ cup oil
⅓ cup milk
2 eggs
2 teaspoons soda
1 teaspoon cinnamon
½ teaspoon salt
½ teaspoon nutmeg
½ teaspoon cloves
1 cup raisins

In large bowl of mixer, mix all ingredients in order listed, except raisins, on low speed until well blended. Then beat on high speed for 3 minutes. Stir in raisins. Pour batter into greased and lightly floured 13x9-inch baking pan and bake at 350° for 40 to 45 minutes or until toothpick inserted into center comes out clean.

Vermont is apple country and this cake is a big hit with our 5 teenagers.

Mrs. Donald E. Edwards (Wibs)
Middlebury, Vermont

Piña Colada Cake

Bake at 350° for 30 to 35 minutes

1   box white cake mix
1   small package coconut
      instant pudding mix
1   cup pineapple juice
½   cup oil
4   eggs
1   teaspoon rum flavoring

FROSTING

1   (16 ounce) box powdered
      sugar
¼   cup margarine, softened
½   cup pineapple juice
1   cup flaked coconut
2   teaspoons rum flavoring

Combine cake mix, pudding mix, pineapple juice, oil, eggs and rum flavoring in large mixing bowl and mix at low speed for 1 minute. Mix at high speed for 3 to 5 minutes. Pour into 2 greased and floured 8 or 9-inch layer cake pans or 1 9x12 baking pan. Bake at 350° for 30 to 35 minutes. Cool in pans 10 minutes, then remove from pans and finish cooling. To prepare frosting: Mix powdered sugar, margarine, pineapple juice, and rum flavoring at medium speed of mixer until fluffy. Add rum flavoring and blend. Spread on cake.

Mrs. Don Daniel (Gerry)
Portland

Vanilla Wafer Cake

Bake at 300° for 1½ hours
Serves 10 to 12

2   cups sugar
2   sticks margarine
6   eggs
1   cup milk
1   (11 ounce) box vanilla
      wafers, crushed
1   (14 ounce) package
      coconut
1   cup pecans
1   teaspoon vanilla

Cream sugar and margarine. Add eggs and milk. Stir in vanilla wafer crumbs, coconut, pecans and vanilla. Mix well. Pour batter into greased and floured tube or Bundt cake pan and bake at 300° for 1½ hours.

Mrs. W. L. Winkleblack (Linda)
Pampa

Hummingbird Cake

Bake at 350° for 25 to 30 minutes
Serves 15

3	cups flour
2	cups sugar
1	teaspoon salt
1	teaspoon soda
1	teaspoon cinnamon
3	eggs, beaten
1	cup oil
1½	teaspoons vanilla extract
1	(8 ounce) can crushed pineapple, undrained
1	cup pecans, chopped
2	cups bananas, chopped

FROSTING

2	(8 ounce) packages cream cheese, softened
1	cup butter or margarine, softened
2	(16 ounce) boxes powdered sugar
1	teaspoon vanilla
Chopped pecans	

In large bowl mix flour, sugar, salt, soda and cinnamon; add eggs and oil stirring just until moistened. DO NOT BEAT. Stir in vanilla, pineapple, pecans and bananas, again just until blended. Divide into 3 9-inch well greased and floured cake pans or 1 9x15-inch baking pan. Bake for 25 to 30 minutes for cake pans and bake for 40 to 45 minutes for long baking pan or until toothpick inserted in center of cake comes out clean. Cool in pans for 10 minutes. Remove cakes from pans and cool completely. Leave cake in long pan for frosting in pan. Prepare frosting. In mixing bowl combine softened cream cheese and butter, gradually add sugar and beat until light and fluffy. Add vanilla and mix well. If you bake the cake in a long baking pan, you only need to make ½ of the frosting recipe. Sprinkle top of frosted cake with chopped pecans.

When you are through Charleston, South Carolina, stop at Dianne's Restaurant. This is one of the delicious cakes they serve.

Mrs. Samuel P. White, Jr. (Sally)
Pampa

Mrs. Kenneth Green (Paula)
Crowley

Mrs. Douglas O. V. Rives (Jo)
Shamrock

271

Orange Delight Cake

Bake at 350° for 45 to 50 minutes
Serves 12 to 16

1¼	cups water
½	cup orange juice
1½	cups rolled oats, uncooked
¾	cup butter or margarine, melted
1½	cups sugar
1	cup brown sugar
3	eggs
1½	teaspoons vanilla
2¼	cups sifted flour
1	teaspoon soda
¼	teaspoon baking powder
1	teaspoon salt
1	teaspoon cinnamon
2	tablespoons grated orange rind

TOPPING

¼	cup butter or margarine
⅔	cup brown sugar
3	tablespoons orange juice
¾	cup pecans, chopped

In saucepan, combine water and orange juice and bring to a boil. Stir in oats, cover and let stand 20 minutes. In large mixing bowl beat butter, sugars and add eggs 1 at a time mixing well after each. Blend in vanilla and oat mixture. Sift dry ingredients and beat into creamed mixture, mixing thoroughly. Stir in grated orange rind. Pour into greased and floured 13x9-inch baking pan and bake at 350° for 45 to 50 minutes. Let cool 30 minutes and spread with topping. To prepare topping, in saucepan, mix all ingredients and cook till slightly thickened. After cake has cooled 30 minutes, spread topping over cake and place under broiler until brown and bubbly. Let set 15 minutes or more until topping hardens.

This cake is very rich . . . great for special occasions.

Mrs. Frank Keele (Mary)
Brownwood

During the years 1838-1840 Comanche Indian raids were frequent in the vicinity of San Antonio. To deal with the problem the legendary Texas Ranger Jack Hays organized volunteers into a unit of "Minute Men" to pursue the Indians and discourage their raids. The volunteers were called to action by a flag waved on the plaza in front of the Court House or by the ringing of the cathedral bell. As described by Mrs. Samuel Maverick, ". . . Each volunteer kept a good horse, saddle, bridle and arms, and a supply of coffee, salt, sugar and other provisions ready at any time to start on fifteen minutes warning, in pursuit of marauding Indians."
—Mildred P. Mayhall, Indian Wars of Texas, Texian Press, Waco, 1965, quoting from the Texas Sentinel, Austin, November 14, 1840.

Orange Butter Cake

Bake at 350° for 15 to 18 minutes

1 box butter recipe yellow
cake mix
1 cup Wesson buttery oil
4 eggs
2 (11 ounce) cans Mandarin
oranges, undrained

ICING

1 (8 ounce) can crushed
pineapple, drained but
reserve juice
1 large vanilla instant
pudding mix
1 (3 ounce) can coconut
1 (9 ounce) carton whipped
topping

In mixing bowl, blend cake mix, oil and add eggs one at a time, mixing well after each. Pour in Mandarin oranges and mix gently but thoroughly. Bake in 4 greased and floured cake pans to make 4 thin layers. Bake for 15 to 18 minutes at 350 °. Cool and ice with icing prepared as follows: Mix crushed pineapple and pudding mix. Add coconut. If mixture is too thick, add a little of the reserved pineapple juice. Fold in whipped topping and mix just until blended. Spread between and on top of layers. Refrigerate.

Mrs. Robert L. Herring, Jr. (Mary)
Dallas

Orange Galliano Cake

Bake at 350° for 55 minutes

1 box orange cake mix
1 small package vanilla
instant pudding
¾ cup orange juice
½ cup oil
¼ cup vodka
¼ cup Galliano
4 eggs, room temperature

GLAZE:

1 cup powdered sugar
1½ tablespoons orange juice
1½ tablespoons vodka
(optional)
1½ tablespoons Galliano

Combine cake and pudding mixes in large bowl. Add orange juice, oil, vodka and Galliano and mix well. Add eggs, one at a time, beating well after each addition. Pour into a greased and floured Bundt pan. Bake at 350° for 55 minutes. Cool 10 minutes before turning upside down on rack. Combine last four ingredients for glazed icing. Icing will be very liquid, requiring much patient spooning for a good glaze. Vodka may be omitted if a thicker glaze is desired.

Mrs. Bill W. O'Brien (Helen)
Winnsboro

Fruit Cocktail Cake

Bake at 350° for 40 minutes

1½	cups sugar
2	cups flour
2	teaspoons baking soda
¼	teaspoon salt
2	eggs
1	(16 ounce) can fruit cocktail
¼	cup brown sugar
½	cup nuts, chopped *or*
½	cup coconut
¾	cup sugar
½	cup milk
1	stick margarine
1	teaspoon vanilla

In large mixing bowl combine sugar, flour, baking soda and salt. Mix well. Add eggs and fruit cocktail and mix thoroughly. Pour into greased and floured 9x13-inch pan. Sprinkle top of cake with a mixture of ¼ cup brown sugar and ½ cup nuts or ½ cup coconut. Bake in 350° oven for 40 minutes. (Cake will still seem moist.) Remove from oven and pour on topping which has been prepared by combining ¾ cup sugar, ½ cup milk and 1 stick margarine. Bring to a boil and cook 1 minute; add 1 teaspoon vanilla. Pour over cake.

Mrs. James E. Parks, Jr. (Terry)
Austin

Big Red Strawberry Cake

Bake at 350° for 40 minutes

1	box white cake mix
1	large package strawberry flavored gelatin
1½	cups hot water
1	(12 ounce) can Big Red soda pop

TOPPING

1	large package instant vanilla pudding mix
⅔	cup milk
⅓	cup sugar
1	(8 ounce) carton whipped topping
1	box frozen strawberries, thawed

Beat cake mix according to package directions and bake in 9x13-inch baking pan. Cool 20 minutes. Mix strawberry gelatin, hot water and Big Red, punch holes in cake and pour mixture over the cake. Prepare pudding mix with milk and sugar; fold in whipped topping. Set aside. Spread thawed strawberries over cake then spread pudding mixture over strawberries. Chill.

Mrs. Arthur Allen (Billie)
Marlin

Fresh Apple Cake

Bake at 350° for 1 hour

3	cups flour
1	teaspoon soda
1	teaspoon cinnamon
½	teaspoon nutmeg
½	teaspoon salt
2	eggs
2	cups sugar
1½	cups Crisco oil
2	teaspoons vanilla
3	cups chopped apples, peeled
1	cup chopped pecans or walnuts

Sift dry ingredients. Set aside. Beat eggs, sugar and oil for three minutes and add dry ingredients. Mix thoroughly; add apples and nuts. Pour into greased and floured tube or Bundt pan and bake for 1 hour. Or pour into a greased and floured 9x13 baking pan and bake for 30 to 45 minutes.

GLAZE

1	cup powdered sugar
2	tablespoons milk
1	teaspoon vanilla

Beat all ingredients and pour over warm cake.

You can use apple juice for liquid in glaze . . . tastes terriffic!!

Mrs. John C. L. Scribner (Edna)
Austin

Groom's Chocolate Cake

Bake at 375° for 30 minutes

1	stick margarine or ½ cup Crisco
2	scant cups sugar
2	eggs
1	cup sweet milk, sour milk or buttermilk
2½	cups flour
9	teaspoons cocoa
⅛	teaspoon salt
2	teaspoons soda
1	cup warm coffee (not hot)

Cream margarine and sugar. Add eggs and beat. Sift flour, cocoa, and salt and add alternately with milk. Mix well. Add soda to warm coffee and add. Batter will be thin. Pour into 3 8 or 9-inch layer cake pans or 1 9x13-inch baking pan and bake at 375° for 30 minutes.

Mrs. Raymond J. Ooley (Birdie)
Borger

275

CAKES

Red Velvet Cake

Bake at 350° for 30 to 35 minutes

2	eggs
1	cup cooking oil
1½	cups sugar
1	teaspoon vinegar
2½	cups flour
1	tablespoon cocoa
½	teaspoon salt
1	teaspoon soda
1	cup buttermilk
1	teaspoon vanilla
4	tablespoons (2 ounces) red food coloring

ICING

1	(8 ounce) package cream cheese, softened
1	(16 ounce) package powdered sugar, sifted
1	stick margarine, room temperature

In large mixing bowl, combine eggs, cooking oil, sugar and vinegar and beat well. Sift flour, cocoa and salt together. Stir soda into buttermilk and add alternately with dry ingredients, ending with buttermilk. Add vanilla and food coloring. Bake in 2 9-inch cake pans which have been sprayed with Pam. Bake at 350° for 30 to 35 minutes. Remove cake, cool slightly, then cool on rack and frost. To prepare frosting, mix all ingredients and beat well. Spread on cake.

Makes a beautiful cake for birthdays, Valentine or Christmas.

Mrs. R. C. White (Elna)
El Paso

Mrs. Theophil Krienke (Sharon)
Round Rock

Dump Cake

Bake at 375° for 45 minutes

1	(8 ounce) can crushed pineapple, drained
1	(21 ounce) can cherry pie filling
1	cup butter or margarine, melted
1	yellow or white cake mix
	Nuts, chopped

In a 9x13-inch baking pan put crushed pineapple on bottom. Spread cherry pie filling over pineapple. Spread cake mix over cherry filling. Melt butter and pour over cake mix. Sprinkle with nuts and bake in 375° oven for 45 minutes.

Judy Whitley
Austin

7-Up Cake

Bake at 350° for 25 to 30 minutes

1   box yellow cake mix
1   (3¼ ounce) box instant
      pineapple pudding mix
⅔   cup vegetable oil
4   eggs
1   (10 ounce) bottle 7-Up

FILLING

1½ cups sugar
1   tablespoon flour
2   eggs
1   flat can crushed
      pineapple, undrained
1   stick margarine
1   teaspoon vanilla
1   small can flaked coconut
½   cup chopped pecans

In large mixing bowl combine cake and pudding mixes. Add oil and beat in eggs one at a time. Add 7-Up and mix thoroughly. Pour into greased and floured 9x13-inch pan and bake at 350° for 25 to 30 minutes. Remove from oven and cool cake. While cake is cooling, prepare filling. In saucepan combine sugar and flour. Add eggs and mix well. Add pineapple, margarine and vanilla. Bring to a boil and cook about 5 minutes, stirring constantly. Let cool, then add coconut and pecans. Spread over cooled cake.

Mrs. Herschel Kelley (Mary Jean)
Austin

Italian Cream Cake

Bake at 325° for 25 minutes

1   cup buttermilk
1   teaspoon soda
5   eggs, separated
2   cups sugar
1   stick margarine
½   cup shortening
2   cups flour, sifted
1   teaspoon vanilla
1   cup chopped pecans
1   (3 ounce) can Angel Flake
      coconut

ICING

1   (8 ounce) cream cheese,
      softened
1   stick margarine, softened
1   (16 ounce) box powdered
      sugar
1   teaspoon vanilla

Combine soda and buttermilk and let stand. Cream margarine, shortening and sugar. Add egg yolks and beat until fluffy. Add vanilla then add buttermilk mixture and flour alternately. Fold in coconut and pecans. Fold in stiffly beaten egg whites. Bake in 3 9-inch greased and floured cake pans. Cool before icing.

Blend the cream cheese and oleo. Add vanilla. Add sugar a little at a time and beat until fluffy.

Mrs. J. Robert (Bob) Pickle (Melanie)
Poynor

Oatmeal Cake and Topping

Bake at 350° for 30 to 40 minutes

1½	cups boiling water
1	cup quick cooking oats
1½	cups flour
1	teaspoon cinnamon
1	teaspoon soda
½	teaspoon salt
1	cup brown sugar
1	cup sugar
2	eggs
½	cup oil

Pour boiling water over oats and let stand while preparing the following: sift together flour, cinnamon, soda and salt. In large mixing bowl, cream sugar and oil and add sifted dry ingredients. Add oatmeal mixture and mix thoroughly. Pour into greased and floured 13x9-inch baking pan and bake for 30 to 40 minutes.

TOPPING

1	cup brown sugar
1	cup evaporated milk
1	stick butter or oleo
1	teaspoon vanilla
1	cup chopped nuts
1	(3 ounce) can coconut

In saucepan, mix sugar and milk until sugar is dissolved. Add butter and cook. Stir almost constantly until mixture boils and becomes thick. Remove from heat and add vanilla, nuts and coconut. Pour on cake while hot.

If this cake lasts — it gets better and better.

Mrs. Jerry Garlington (Melvia)
Plano

Stir Crazy Chocolate Cake

Bake at 350°

3	cups sifted flour
½	teaspoon salt
2	teaspoons soda
⅓	cup cocoa
2	cups sugar
¾	cup salad oil
1	teaspoon vanilla
2	tablespoons vinegar
2	cups water *or* cold coffee

In large mixing bowl, sift together flour, salt, soda, cocoa and sugar. Make three wells in dry ingredients and pour in salad oil, vanilla and vinegar and water. Stir with a fork only until dry ingredients are moistened. Pour into greased and floured loaf pan and bake until center springs back when touched.

Mrs. George M. Griffin (Gladys)
Austin

Chocolate Sheath Cake

Bake at 400° for 20 minutes

2 cups flour
2 cups sugar
2 sticks margarine
4 tablespoons cocoa
1 cup water
½ cup buttermilk
2 eggs, slightly beaten
1 teaspoon soda
1 teaspoon cinnamon
1 teaspoon vanilla

ICING

1 stick margarine
4 tablespoons cocoa
6 tablespoons milk
1 (16 ounce) box powdered
  sugar
1 cup pecans, chopped

Sift flour and sugar together into large mixing bowl. In saucepan mix 2 sticks margarine, 4 tablespoons cocoa and water. Bring to rapid boil and pour over flour and sugar mixture, stirring well. Add buttermilk, eggs, soda, cinnamon and vanilla. Mix all ingredients thoroughly and pour into greased 16x11-inch pan. Bake at 400° for 20 minutes. Start making icing 5 minutes before cake is done. In a saucepan combine 1 stick margarine, 4 tablespoons cocoa, and milk and bring to a boil. Remove from heat and add powdered sugar and pecans. Beat well. Spread on cake while both cake and icing are still hot.

Mrs. R. Bruce Harris (Georgia)
Austin

Bohemian Cake

Bake at 350° for 1 hour and 15 minutes

1 cup shortening
2 cups sugar
½ cup brown sugar
4 eggs, separated
1 cup milk (¾ cup
  evaporated milk, ¼ cup
  homogenized milk)
2 teaspoons vanilla
2½ cups flour
¼ teaspoon salt
2 teaspoons baking powder
½ cup pecans, chopped
1 cup flaked coconut

Cream together shortening, sugar and brown sugar; add egg yolks, one at a time. Add milk and vanilla. Sift together flour, salt and baking powder; add to creamed mixture. Add pecans, coconut. Beat egg whites until stiff and add last. Pour into greased and floured tube pan and bake at 350° for 1 hour and 15 minutes.

This cake is better if eaten the day after it's baked.

Mrs. Bennie Adair (Carol)
Austin

Better Than Sex Cake

Bake at 350° for 50 minutes

1   box yellow butter cake
     mix (without pudding)
1   (6 ounce) package
     chocolate chips
¾   cup pecans, chopped
4   eggs
½   cup oil
¼   cup water
1   teaspoon vanilla
1   small box instant vanilla
     pudding
1   (8 ounce) carton sour
     cream

CHOCOLATE FROSTING:

1   (16 ounce) box powdered
     sugar
3   squares baking chocolate,
     melted
¾   stick margarine, softened
Milk

Coat chocolate chips and pecans with a little of the dry cake mix. Mix remainder of cake mix, eggs, oil, water, vanilla, vanillla pudding and sour cream thoroughly. Fold in chocolate chips and pecans. Pour into a greased and floured tube pan and bake for about 50 minutes at 350°. Cool before frosting. Prepare chocolate frosting by combining all ingredients except milk. Add enough milk to make the frosting of a spreading consistency. Frost and serve — then *judge for yourself!!*

Mrs. Harold Loftis (Billie)
Austin

Cherry Nut Cake

Bake at 250° for 2 hours

4   cups pecans
1   pound dates
½   pound candied cherries
2   slices candied green
     pineapple
2   slices candied red
     pineapple
1   cup flour
¼   teaspoon salt
1   teaspoon baking powder
4   eggs
1   cup sugar
1   teaspoon vanilla

Mix pecans, dates, cherries, pineapple slices, flour, salt and baking powder by hand. Do not cut up nuts and cherries. Mix eggs, sugar and vanilla. Add to first mixture. Line bottom of pan with heavy brown paper (paper sack will do). Grease and flour pan and paper. Cook at 250° for about 2 hours or until done.

Mrs. David Biscomb (Lucretia)
Round Rock

Turtle Cake

Bake at 350° 10 minutes; then 25 to 30 minutes

1   (14 ounce) package
    caramel candies (Kraft
    individually-wrapped
    squares)
½   cup evaporated milk
1   (2-layer size) box German
    chocolate pudding-
    included cake mix
1⅓ cups water
¾   cup butter, softened
3   eggs
1   cup pecans, chopped
1   cup semi-sweet chocolate
    chips

Melt caramels with milk in top of double boiler. (Do this before mixing cake as it will take a while to unwrap and melt caramels.) Combine cake mix with water, butter and eggs in large mixer bowl and blend on low speed 30 seconds, then beat at medium speed 2 minutes. Pour half the batter in greased 13x9-inch pan and bake at 350° 10 minutes or until cake puffs up and is gooey. Pour caramel-milk mixture over partially baked layer to within ½ inch of edge. Sprinkle nuts and chocolate chips evenly over caramel. Pour remaining batter over all and bake at 350° 25 to 30 minutes, until top springs back when touched lightly. Cool in pan and cut into squares. Top with ice cream or whipped topping.

Mrs. T. F. Hahn (LaVelle)
Austin

Blackberry Wine Cake

Bake at 350° for 50 to 60 minutes

1   yellow cake mix
1   small package instant
    vanilla pudding mix
4   eggs
½   cup oil
1   cup blackberry wine

GLAZE:

1   cup sugar
1   stick margarine
½   cup blackberry wine

In large mixing bowl, combine cake mix, pudding mix, eggs, oil and blackberry wine. Beat together for 3 minutes and pour into greased Bundt pan. Bake in 350° oven for 50 to 60 minutes. Prepare glaze by mixing sugar, margarine and blackberry wine and boiling 2 to 3 minutes. Pour over cake while both cake and glaze are still hot. Leave cake in pan for about 30 minutes. Turn out.

Mrs. Stephen B. McElroy (Eleta)
Houston

281

Fig Preserve Cake

Bake at 350° for 1 hour and 15 minutes
Yields 1 10-inch cake

1½ cups sugar
2 cups flour
1 teaspoon soda
1 teaspoon salt
1 teaspoon nutmeg
1 teaspoon cinnamon
½ teaspoon allspice
½ teaspoon cloves
1 cup oil
3 eggs
1 cup buttermilk
1 tablespoon vanilla extract
1 cup fig preserves,
    chopped
1 cup pecans, chopped

BUTTERMILK GLAZE

¼ cup buttermilk
½ cup sugar
¼ teaspoon soda
1½ teaspoons cornstarch
¼ cup margarine
1½ teaspoons vanilla extract

In large mixing bowl combine dry ingredients; add oil, beating well. Add eggs and beat well. Add buttermilk and vanilla, mixing thoroughly. Stir in preserves and pecans. Pour batter into a greased and floured 10-inch tube pan and bake for 1 hour and 15 minutes at 350°. Let cool 10 minutes; remove from pan. Pour warm Buttermilk Glaze over warm cake. To prepare glaze, in saucepan combine all ingredients except vanilla. Bring to a boil, stirring constantly. Remove from heat, cool slightly and stir in vanilla. Spoon over cake.

Rum Cake

Bake at 350° for 45 minutes

1¾ cups sugar
1 teaspoon vanilla
2 sticks butter
5 eggs
2 cups flour

ICING:

1 cup sugar
½ cup water
1 teaspoon rum flavoring

Cream sugar, vanilla and butter together. Add eggs one at a time, beating well after each. Add flour and mix thoroughly. Pour into greased and floured tube pan and bake at 350° for 45 minutes. To make icing, in saucepan mix all ingredients and bring to a boil, stirring constantly. When cake is still warm in pan, pour part of icing on cake. After cake cools, turn out on plate and pour remainder of icing over cake.

Mrs. John L. Waldrip (Gayle)
Austin

"Rave Reviews" Almond Cake

Bake at 350° for 35 to 40 minutes

1   box white cake mix
2   eggs
1   stick butter, softened (not margarine)
1   teaspoon almond extract
1   (8 ounce) package cream cheese, softened
1   (16 ounce) box powdered sugar
2   eggs
2   teaspoons almond extract

In large mixing bowl beat together the cake mix, eggs, softened butter and almond extract. When thoroughly blended pour into greased and floured 9x13 baking pan. This batter will be stiff. In small mixing bowl beat together softened cream cheese, eggs, powdered sugar and almond extract until blended. Pour over batter and bake for 35 to 40 minutes. Cool before cutting into squares.

Rich and sensational!!

Mrs. James B. McGoodwin (Jane)
Fort Worth

Vesta's Gingerbread

Bake at 325° for 15 to 20 minutes
Yields 12 regular cupcakes

2   eggs
¾   cup brown sugar
¾   cup dark molasses
¾   cup melted shortening
2½   cups flour
2   teaspoons ginger
2   teaspoons soda
½   teaspoon nutmeg
1½   teaspoons cinnamon
½   teaspoon allspice
½   teaspoon baking powder
1   cup boiling water

In mixing bowl, beat eggs and then blend in brown sugar, molasses and melted shortening. Next add sifted dry ingredients and boiling water. Mix well. Bake in greased muffin pans at 325°. This batter may be stored in the refrigerator and used as needed.

Mrs. Delmer Nichols (Mary Ann)
Taylor

CAKES

Coconut Fruit Cake

Bake at 250° for 2 hours

4 to 5 gumdrops (different
    colors, no *black*)
    (large size)
2   cups pecans
1   cup candied cherries
4   slices candied pineapple
    (different colors)
1   (8 ounce) package dates
1   pound coconut
1   (14 ounce) can sweetened
    condensed milk

Chop all fruit, nuts and gumdrops, then mix all ingredients. Line pan with brown paper that has been well greased with shortening. You may use either a tube pan or loaf pan. Bake approximately 2 hours. Test with a toothpick.

The different colored fruits and gumdrops make this a beautiful Christmas cake. My mother has baked this cake every year since I was a child and now I am carrying on the tradition.

Edris Whitehall
Seabrook

Date Nut Cake

Bake at 300° for 45 to 50 minutes

1   cup flour
1   cup sugar
½   teaspoon salt
2   teaspoons baking powder
2   cups dates, chopped
2   cups pecan halves
4   eggs, separated
1   teaspoon vanilla

In large mixing bowl sift dry ingredients 2 or 3 times. Add dates and pecans and coat evenly. Blend in beaten egg yolks and vanilla. Beat well. In small mixing bowl beat egg whites till stiff peaks form. Fold egg whites in batter. Line a 10-inch tube pan with heavy duty foil and pour batter in. Bake 45 to 50 minutes at 300° or until toothpick inserted in center comes out clean. Remove from oven and let set a few minutes. Lift foil and cake out and let cool.

Orange Slice Cake

Bake at 250° for 2½ to 3 hours

1	(16 ounce) package orange slice candy
1	(8 ounce) package chopped dates
1	cup nuts, chopped
3½	cups flour
1	cup margarine
2	cups sugar
4	eggs
½	cup buttermilk
1	teaspoon soda
1	(7 ounce) can coconut

GLAZE

1	(16 ounce) box powdered sugar
1	cup orange juice

Cut candy into small pieces. Coat dates, candy and nuts in ½ cup flour. In large mixing bowl cream margarine and sugar well, add eggs and mix well after addition of each one. Add buttermilk. Stir in remaining flour and soda, mixing well. Fold in candy, dates and nuts; add coconut and mix well. Pour into greased and floured tube pan. Bake at 250° for 2½ to 3 hours, or until toothpick inserted into center comes out clean. Let cool 30 minutes, then turn out onto plate and cover with glaze. To prepare glaze, mix powdered sugar and orange juice and pour over cake.

Old Witch's Magic Nut Cake

Bake at 350° for 1 hour and 15 minutes

3	eggs
1	(16 ounce) can pumpkin
¾	cup oil
½	cup water
2½	cups flour
2¼	cups sugar
1½	teaspoons soda
1¼	teaspoons salt
¾	teaspoon nutmeg
¾	teaspoon cinnamon
1	cup raisins
½	cup walnuts, chopped

In large mixing bowl beat eggs and add pumpkin, oil and water and mix well. Add flour, sugar, soda, salt, nutmeg and cinnamon and mix well. Fold in raisins and walnuts. Pour into 3 well greased 1 pound coffee cans and place cans upright in oven. Bake for 1 hour and 15 minutes at 350°, or until a straw from the old witch's broom, inserted in the cake, comes out clean. Slide cakes out and cool on wire rack.

Mrs. John Ross (Dianne)
Alvin

Whiskey Cake

Bake at 300° for 3½ hours

1	**pound candied cherries, cut in pieces**
½	**pound raisins, cut in half**
1	**pint Kentucky bourbon whiskey**
¾	**pound butter (not margarine)**
2¼	**cups white sugar**
1	**cup brown sugar**
6	**eggs, separated**
5	**cups sifted flour**
2	**teaspoons nutmeg**
1	**teaspoon baking powder**
1	**pound shelled pecans**

Soak cherries and raisins for several days in bourbon. Cream butter until fluffy; add sugar and beat. Add egg yolks and beat well. Add soaked fruit and remaining bourbon and mix. Reserve a small amount of flour for nuts and add remainder to egg mixture. Add nutmeg and baking powder. Fold in egg whites which have been well beaten. Add lightly floured pecans last. Pour in a large tube pan which has been greased and lined with greased brown paper. Bake at 350° for approximately 3½ hours. WATCH BAKING TIME — this cake is dry if overbaked. Let set a few minutes and remove from pan while still warm. Cool on rack. When cool, wrap in cheesecloth soaked in bourbon and seal in foil. Renew moisture with bourbon as needed. Keeps several months in refrigerator. Warm to room temperature before serving — it improves the flavor.

Mrs. Clay Kruckemeyer (Rosie)
Arlington

Sock-It-To-Me Cake

Bake at 350° for 1 hour

1	**box butter recipe cake mix**
½	**cup sugar**
¾	**cup oil**
4	**eggs**
½	**pint sour cream**
⅓	**cup chopped pecans**
4	**tablespoons brown sugar**
2	**tablespoons cinnamon**

Mix cake mix, sugar and oil. Add eggs one at a time, beating after each addition. Add sour cream, pecans and mix well. Pour ½ batter into greased and floured tube pan. Sprinkle brown sugar and cinnamon over batter. Add remaining batter. Bake in tube or Bundt pan, 1 hour at 350°.

Mrs. Don Woolsey (Vicky)
Arlington

Pie Crust

Bake at 425° for 20 minutes
Yields 2 9-inch crusts

2   cups flour
⅛   teaspoon salt
½   cup Wesson oil
¼   cup milk
Wax paper

Combine all four ingredients and mix well. Divide dough in half and roll out each half between two sheets of wax paper. Place in 9-inch pie pans and bake.

Mrs. Vernon Scofield (Audrey)
Austin

Never Fail Pie Crust

Bake at 425° for 20 minutes
Yields 1 double pie crust
1 single pie crust

2½   cups flour
¼   teaspoon salt
1   cup Crisco shortening
6   tablespoons cold tap water
½   cup flour

Place 2½ cups of flour in a large mixing bowl. Add salt. Cut in 1 cup Crisco until it is pea-size. Mix the water and ½ cup of flour in a measuring cup to form a paste. Pour this paste into Crisco and flour mixture and stir with a fork to form a ball. Cover and let set for 30 minutes. Roll out into pie crust. Bake at 425° for 20 minutes for a single crust. This crust should be rolled out thin. It may be baked and frozen for future use and may also be halved with good results.

Mrs. Jimmie F. Johnson (Judy)
Corpus Christi

Perfect Pie Crust

Bake at 425° for 15 minutes
Yields 2 9-inch pie shells
or 3 8-inch pie shells

3   cups flour
1   teaspoon salt
1¼ cups shortening
5   tablespoons water
1   egg
1   teaspoon vinegar

Sift flour and salt into bowl and cut in shortening until coarse. Beat water, egg and vinegar together. Stir into flour mixture and shape into ball. Chill. Roll out into pie crust and bake at 425° for 15 minutes or until done.

Mrs. Roger R. Toon (Vonda)
Longview

Aunt Lillie's Lemon Meringue Pie

Serves 6

3   egg yolks
¾   cup sugar
2   tablespoons flour
1   cup water
⅛   teaspoon salt
Juice of 1 medium to
      large lemon
1   tablespoon butter or
      margarine
1   (9-inch) pie shell, baked

In a stainless steel saucepan, stir egg yolks, sugar and flour. Place on medium high burner and stir in 1 cup water, salt and lemon juice. Stir constantly on medium high heat until bubbles form. Continue to stir vigorously about 2 minutes until pudding is of thick consistency. Remove from burner and stir in butter. Pour into glass bowl and refrigerate. When completely cool, pour into 9-inch baked pie shell. Top with your favorite meringue recipe and brown.

Make sure to stir this recipe while cooking. It is important to let the mixture cook at least 2 minutes past the bubbling stage.

Mrs. Wilkes J. Kothmann (Lillian)
San Antonio

288

The Flag of the San Felipe Volunteers

Travis' appeal for Texans to rally to the support of the garrison of the Alamo did not fall on deaf ears. The colonists of San Felipe began immediately to raise a company under the leadership of Moseley Baker. The ladies of San Felipe prepared a battle ensign for the company. The flag, a composite of the U.S. flag, the British Union Jack, and a lone white star upon a green field, was taken from a design which had been proposed by Stephen F. Austin for the Flag of Texas. Presentation was made through Gail Borden, Jr., on March 2, 1836. Although the San Felipe Company was too late to participate in any action to relieve the Alamo garrison, it joined the army Houston assembled and participated in the San Jacinto campaign.

FLAG OF THE SAN FELIPE COMPANY

Moseley Baker's Company Flag

THE NAVAL FLAG OF THE REVOLUTION
The Hawkins Flag

Hawkins' Flag of the Texas Navy

In 1836, the Texas Provisional Government began issuing letters of marque to authorize the small Texas Navy to operate legitimately as vessels of war on the high seas. Since such ships represent nations and constitute governments, they must, in accordance with international custom, fly an identifying ensign. The Commodore of the Texas Navy designed such an ensign, adapting the national flag of the United States by replacing the field of stars with a single white star which had already become the symbol of Texas. Hawkin's naval ensign was used until it was replaced by another design during the period of the Republic.

Coconut Cream Pie

Bake at 400° for 10 minutes
Serves 6 to 8

1	cup sugar
½	cup flour
¼	teaspoon salt
3	cups milk
4	egg yolks, beaten
3	tablespoons butter
1½	teaspoons vanilla
1½	cups coconut
4	egg whites
¼	teaspoon cream of tartar
½	cup sugar
1	(9-inch) pie shell, baked

In medium saucepan combine sugar, flour, salt and egg yolks. Gradually add milk and cook over medium heat, stirring constantly. Cook until bubbly and cook 2 minutes longer, stirring constantly. Remove from heat. Stir in butter and vanilla. Stir in coconut, saving a little for top of pie. Pour coconut mixture into baked pie shell. Beat egg whites with cream of tartar until foamy. Add sugar, 1 tablespoon at a time, beating until stiff peaks form. Top pie with meringue and sprinkle additional coconut over it. Bake at 400° for 10 minutes or until brown.

Mrs. Roger R. Toon (Vonda)
Longview

Quick and Easy Pie

Bake at 325° for 25 to 30 minutes
Serves 8

16 to 20 Ritz crackers	
3	egg whites
1	cup sugar
½	teaspoon baking powder
¼	teaspoon salt
½	teaspoon vanilla
¾	cup chopped pecans
1	small carton Cool Whip

Crush crackers and set aside. Beat egg whites until stiff. Add sugar, baking powder, salt and vanilla to egg whites. Add crackers and nuts. Pour into a 9-inch greased pie plate. Bake at 325° for 25 to 30 minutes. Cool. Spread Cool Whip on top and chill for 1 hour before serving. Use a 9x13x2 inch pan for a double recipe.

Mrs. Clarence Koehn (Mildred)
Houston

Cocoa Meringue Pie

Bake at 400° for 10 minutes

¼	cup flour, heaping
¼	cup cocoa
1	cup sugar
1	cup milk
1	cup half and half cream
3	eggs, separated
3	tablespoons margarine
1	teaspoon vanilla
1	(9-inch) pie shell, baked
¼	teaspoon cream of tartar
6	tablespoons sugar

In large saucepan combine flour, cocoa and sugar. Add milk and cream. Cook until mixture thickens. Remove from heat. Beat egg yolks. Mix a little cocoa mixture with egg yolks so as not to cook eggs when added to hot mixture. Slowly add to cocoa mixture. Continue to cook, stirring constantly. When thick remove from heat and add margarine and vanilla and mix well. Cool. When thoroughly cool, pour into baked pie shell. Beat egg whites with cream of tartar until foamy. Add sugar, 1 tablespoon at a time, beating until stiff peaks form. Top pie with meringue and bake at 400° for 10 minutes or until brown. If you desire to use whole eggs in the filling, whipped cream may be used as a topping.

This was handed down from my great-grandmother.

Mrs. Scott Bennett (Charlene)
Austin

Memaw's Date Nut Pie

Bake at 300° for 45 to 50 minutes
Serves 6 to 8, each pie

6	eggs, separated
1	cup butter
2	cups sugar
1	cup chopped dates
1	cup chopped pecans
2	slightly pre-baked pie crusts

Blend beaten egg yolks, softened butter, sugar, dates and pecans. Fold in beaten egg whites. Pour into 2 slightly pre-baked pie crusts. Bake at 300° for 45 to 50 minutes.

Mrs. Walter J. Dingler (Gayle)
Austin

Ma's Banana Cream Pie

1½ cups sugar
½ cup flour
⅛ teaspoon salt
2 eggs
2 cups milk
1 tablespoon butter
1 teaspoon vanilla
2-3 medium bananas
1 (9-inch) pie crust, baked
1 (8 ounce) carton whipping
    cream, whipped
1 tablespoon sugar
1 teaspoon vanilla

In medium saucepan, mix sugar, flour, salt and eggs with hand mixer. Gradually add milk and beat until smooth. Cook over medium heat, stirring constantly, till mixture thickens. Remove and add butter and vanilla and blend well. Refrigerate.
Slice bananas into baked pie crust. Spoon pudding over bananas. Whip cream and gradually add sugar and vanilla. Beat until stiff. Spread over pudding and refrigerate.

Delicious!!

Mrs. Michael Small (Lisa)
Austin

Angel Chocolate Chiffon Pie

Bake at 300° for 1½ hours

2 egg whites
⅛ teaspoon salt
⅛ teaspoon cream of tartar
½ cup powdered sugar,
    sifted
½ cup chopped pecans
½ teaspoon vanilla

Beat egg whites, salt and cream of tartar until soft peaks form; add sugar and beat until stiff. Fold in chopped pecans and vanilla. Spread meringue mixture in and around the rim ½ inch of a greased 9-inch pan to form the crust. Bake at 300° for 1½ hours. Cool.

2 tablespoons sugar
1 (6 ounce) package semi-
    sweet chocolate chips
3 tablespoons milk
4 eggs, separated
Whipped cream

Melt sugar, chocolate chips and milk. Stir and cool. Add yolks one at a time, and beat well after each addition. Fold into stiffly beaten egg whites. Pour into meringue shell and chill. Top with whipped cream, slightly sweetened with powdered sugar.

Mrs. George Bowers (Jonnie)
Austin

Paper Bag Apple Pie

Bake at 425° for 1 hour
Serves 6 to 8

5   large cooking apples or 10
        small apples
2 to 3 tablespoons lemon juice
½   cup sugar
2   tablespoons flour
½   teaspoon nutmeg
½   cup margarine
½   cup sugar
½   cup flour
1   (9-inch) pie shell, unbaked

Peel apples and cut quarters into halves and place in bowl with lemon juice. Mix sugar, flour and nutmeg and pour over apples, stirring to mix well. Place apples in pie shell. Cream together margarine, sugar and flour. Sprinkle over top of apples to cover well. Slide pie into a heavy brown paper bag, fold edges of bag over and fasten with a paper clip. Do not fold bag down tight over pie. Place bag with pie on a cookie sheet and bake at 425° for 1 hour. Make sure bag is not touching top of oven.

Kathy Eastwold
San Antonio

Streusel Apple Pie

Bake at 425° for 10 minutes
375° for 30 minutes
Serves 6 to 8

6   apples, pared and sliced
        thin
2   tablespoons sugar
½   teaspoon cinnamon
2   tablespoons lemon juice
½   cup brown sugar, firmly
        packed
½   cup sifted flour
2   tablespoons shortening
2   tablespoons butter
½   cup chopped nuts
1   (9-inch) pie shell, unbaked

Fill unbaked 9-inch pie shell with sliced apples. Mix sugar, cinnamon and lemon juice. Sprinkle over apples. Mix brown sugar and flour together. Cut in butter and shortening until mixture is like meal. Add nuts and sprinkle over apples. Bake at 425° for 10 minutes, reduce heat to 375° and bake for 30 minutes or until set.

Mrs. Paul M. Carroll (Cathy)
Fredericksburg

Red, White and Blue Berry Pie

Serves 6

1	(3 ounce) package lemon flavored gelatin
⅔	cup boiling water
2	cups ice cubes
1	(8 ounce) container frozen whipped topping, thawed
1	cup sliced strawberries
1	cup whole fresh or frozen blueberries
1	9-inch graham cracker crust

Dissolve gelatin in boiling water, stirring about 3 minutes. Add cubes and stir constantly until gelatin is thickened — about 2 to 3 minutes. Remove any unmelted ice. Using a wire whip, blend in whipped topping and whip until smooth. Fold in sliced strawberries and blueberries. Chill, if necessary, until mixture will mound. Spoon mixture into prepared pie shell. Refrigerate until firm. Garnish with strawberries.

Cookbook Committee

Pineapple Millionaire Pie

Serves 6 to 8 per pie
Yields 2 pies

2	cups sifted powdered sugar
½	cup butter or margarine, softened
2	eggs
⅛	teaspoon salt
¼	teaspoon vanilla
1	cup whipping cream, whipped
½	cup sifted powdered sugar
1	cup crushed pineapple, well drained
½	cup chopped pecans
2	(9-inch) pie shells, baked

Cream together powdered sugar and butter. Beat in eggs, salt and vanilla until light and fluffy. Spread mixture evenly into baked pie crusts, then chill. DO NOT COOK THE MIXTURE. Whip cream until stiff. Add powdered sugar. Fold in pineapple and pecans. Spread this mixture on top of base mixture and chill thoroughly.

Mrs. Eugene A. Mees (Norma Blotter)
Austin

Banana-Blueberry Pie

Bake at 400° for 20 minutes
Serves 6 to 8

CRUST

1½	cups flour
1	teaspoon salt
1	tablespoon sugar
½	cup Mazola corn oil
2	tablespoons sweet milk

Combine all ingredients as listed and mix thoroughly. Press into 10-inch pie plate. Bake at 400° until slightly brown around edges. Cool.

FILLING

2	bananas
1	package Dream Whip topping mix
1	(8 ounce) package cream cheese, softened
1	cup sugar
1	can blueberry pie filling

Slice bananas and place in cooled crust. In medium bowl, prepare Dream Whip topping mix as directed on package. Add softened cream cheese and sugar. Blend thoroughly. Pour mixture over bananas in crust. Spread blueberry pie filling over the top of pie. Chill for 3 to 4 hours before serving.

Mrs. Michael H. Harris (Nancy)
Forney

Peanut Butter Pie

Serves 8 to 10

1	(8 ounce) package cream cheese, softened
½	cup peanut butter
1	cup powdered sugar
½	cup milk
1	(6 ounce) carton whipped topping
¼	cup finely chopped toasted peanuts
1	(9-inch) graham cracker crumb crust

In mixing bowl, beat cream cheese until soft and fluffy. Beat in peanut butter and sugar. Slowly add milk, beating until well blended. Fold topping into mixture. Ladle into pie crust, sprinkle top with peanuts. Place in freezer until ready to serve and slice as needed. Let slices thaw slightly before eating.

Very rich, but very good.

Mrs. James C. Vercher (Elaine)
Deer Park

Cherry-O-Cream Cheese Pie

Serves 6 to 8

1	(8 ounce) package cream cheese, softened
1	(14 ounce) can sweetened condensed milk
⅓	cup lemon juice
1	teaspoon vanilla
1	(1 pound, 15 ounce) can cherry pie filling or cherry glaze (see below)
1	(9-inch) graham cracker crumb crust

In medium bowl beat cream cheese until light and fluffy. Gradually add condensed milk and stir until well mixed. Blend in lemon juice and vanilla extract. Pour filling into pie crust and refrigerate 2 to 3 hours. Cover with cherry pie filling or glaze.

PIE GLAZE:

1	(1 pound) can sour pitted cherries, drained, reserving juice
¼	cup sugar
1	tablespoon cornstarch
2	drops red food coloring, if desired

Drain cherries, reserving juice. In small saucepan combine sugar with cornstarch and cherry juice. Stir over low heat constantly until thickened. Mix in food coloring and cherries. Refrigerate.

Mrs. Allan Shivers (Marialice)
Austin

Joy Choy Pie

Bake at 275° for 1 hour and 15 minutes

3	egg whites
¼	teaspoon cream of tartar
1	cup sugar
⅛	teaspoon salt
1	teaspoon vanilla
1	cup nuts, chopped fine
½	cup chow mein noodles, crushed
1	pint fresh strawberries
	Vanilla ice cream

Combine egg whites and cream of tartar and beat until stiff. Slowly add sugar and salt while beating. Fold in vanilla, nuts and crushed noodles. Pour mixture into a pie pan and bake at 275° for 1 hour and 15 minutes. Serve with strawberries and ice cream.

Mrs. Samuel H. Wilds (Betty)
Temple

Raisin Pie

Bake at 375° for 30 minutes
Yields 2 pies

3   cups raisins
2   cups milk
2   tablespoons flour
¼   cup butter or margarine
1   tablespoon vinegar
1   tablespoon vanilla
⅛   teaspoon soda
2   double pie shells,
       unbaked

Mix all ingredients together in pan and cook until raisins are tender. Pour in unbaked pie shell and cover with top crust. Bake at 375° for 30 minutes or until golden brown. This filling is enough for two pies.

Mrs. Herbert G. Purtle (Jan)
Manor

Raisin Cream Pie

Bake at 400° for 10 minutes
Serves 6 to 8

1   cup milk
¾   cup sugar
2   eggs, separated
2   tablespoons flour
1   teaspoon vanilla
1   teaspoon butter
1   cup cooked raisins
⅛   teaspoon cream of tartar
¼   cup sugar
1   (9-inch) pie shell, baked

In medium saucepan, scald milk. In mixing bowl, beat sugar, egg yolks, flour, vanilla and butter. Add a little hot milk to mixture before adding all of it to milk. After adding to hot milk, cook until thick, stirring constantly. Add raisins and pour into baked pie shell. Beat egg whites with ⅛ teaspoon cream of tartar until foamy. Add sugar, 1 tablespoon at a time, beating until stiff peaks form. Spread meringue over pie and bake at 400° for 10 minutes to brown.

Mrs. Clark Ginter (Lorraine)
Everman

Ginger Orange Pie

Bake at 425° for 5 minutes
Serves 6 to 8

CRUST

1⅛	cups crushed ginger snaps (reserve ⅛ cup)
1	tablespoon sugar
⅓	cup margarine, melted

Mix in bowl. Press into a 9-inch pie pan. Bake at 425° for 5 minutes. Cool.

FILLING

¾	cup sugar
3	tablespoons cornstarch
⅛	teaspoon salt
1	egg
2	cups milk, scalded
1	tablespoon margarine
1	teaspoon vanilla
1	can Mandarin oranges, drained

In medium saucepan, combine sugar, cornstarch, salt, egg and milk and cook over low heat until thickened. Add margarine and vanilla and stir well. Place Mandarin oranges in cooled crust. Pour filling over oranges. Refrigerate.

TOPPING

1	(8 ounce) carton whipping cream, whipped
1	tablespoon sugar
¼	teaspoon vanilla

Whip cream adding sugar gradually and beat to soft peaks. Add vanilla and beat well. Spread over filling and sprinkle reserved crumbs over top.

Mrs. Michael H. Harris (Nancy)
Forney

Candied Lemon Pie

Bake at 350° for 50 minutes

3	eggs, beaten
1½	cups sugar
2	tablespoons flour
½	cup lemon juice
½	cup milk
1	(9-inch) pie shell, unbaked

Mix all ingredients just until thoroughly mixed. Pour into unbaked pie shell. Bake at 350° for 50 minutes or until set.

This is a very old "country" recipe.

Buttermilk Pie

Bake at 350° for 40 to 45 minutes
Serves 6 to 8

2	cups sugar
½	cup butter, softened
3	tablespoons flour
3	eggs, beaten
1	cup buttermilk
1	teaspoon vanilla
1	(9-inch) pie shell, unbaked

Cream together sugar and softened butter. Add flour and eggs; beat well. Stir in buttermilk and vanilla. Pour into unbaked pie shell and bake at 350° for 40 to 45 minutes. Cool completely on wire rack before serving.

Mrs. Mike Beal (Sherilyn)
Plano

Southern Lemon Chess Pie

Bake at 375° for 35 to 45 minutes
Serves 6 to 8

1¾	cups sugar
1	tablespoon flour
1	tablespoon cornmeal
4	eggs, beaten
¼	cup butter, melted
¼	cup milk
4	tablespoons grated lemon rind
¼	cup lemon juice
1	(9-inch) pie shell, unbaked

Combine sugar, flour and cornmeal. Mix together lightly with fork. Add the remaining ingredients and beat until smooth. Pour into pie shell. Bake at 375° for 35 to 45 minutes.

Mrs. Samuel H. Wilds (Betty)
Temple

Black Bottom Pie

Serves 6 to 8

2	tablespoons flour
2	tablespoons cocoa
1	cup sugar
1½	cups milk
2	egg yolks
¼	cup butter
2	teaspoons vanilla
½	pint whipping cream, whipped
Vanilla and sugar to taste	
1	(9-inch) baked pie crust or vanilla wafer crust

Sift flour and cocoa and add to sugar. Mix dry ingredients well and add milk. Heat to lukewarm temperature and add beaten egg yolks. (Egg yolks dissolve better in warm, NOT HOT, liquids.) Cook slowly until mixture thickens. Add butter and vanilla. Pour into baked crust or vanilla wafer crust. Freeze. After frozen, top with whipped cream with sugar and vanilla added to taste. Freeze. Serve frozen.

Mrs. James Roden (Charley)
Denton

Maple Pie

Bake at 375° for 10 minutes
325° for 45 minutes

3	eggs
1	cup sugar
½	cup pure maple syrup
2	tablespoons butter, melted
⅛	teaspoon salt
1	teaspoon vanilla
1	(9-inch) pie shell, unbaked

Beat eggs until fluffy. Add sugar, syrup, butter and salt beating well after each addition. Add vanilla and mix just until blended. Pour into unbaked pie shell. Place pie on lowest rack in oven and bake at 375° for 10 minutes. Lower temperature to 325° and bake for 40-45 minutes.

Mrs. Douglas Nichols (Dorothy)
Austin

299

Ice Box Pie

Serves 6 to 8

1	large package instant pudding mix (any flavor)
1	envelope Dream Whip Topping Mix
1¾	cups cold milk
1	(8 ounce) carton whipped topping
1	(9-inch) graham cracker crust

In large mixing bowl pour pudding mix and Dream Whip Mix. Add cold milk gradually, mixing on low speed of electric mixer. After pudding is dissolved, beat 4 minutes at high speed. Pour into graham cracker crust and cool. Before serving, spread Cool Whip on top.

Our family favorite is chocolate!

Mrs. Les Gallatin (Kathy)
Austin

Lemon Sponge Cake Pie

Bake at 300° for 30 to 40 minutes
Serves 6 to 8

1	cup sugar
1	tablespoon butter
2½	tablespoons flour
2	eggs, separated
Juice of 1 lemon	
1	cup milk
1	(9-inch) pie shell, unbaked

Cream sugar and butter. Add flour and well beaten egg yolks. Also add lemon juice and milk. Mix well. Beat egg whites and fold into pie mixture. Pour into unbaked pie shell. Bake until knife blade inserted in center comes out clean.

Fran Arnold
Cedar Park

Maple Nut Pie

Serves 6

1	(14 ounce) can sweetened condensed milk
¾	cup Vermont maple syrup
2	eggs, beaten
1	cup chopped pecans
1	9-inch baked pie crust
1	(8 ounce) carton whipping cream whipped
2	tablespoons sugar
1	cup toasted coconut

In heavy saucepan, combine condensed milk, syrup and eggs. Beat and cook until thickened. Stir in ¾ cup chopped pecans; cool. Pour into baked crust. Whip cream gradually stirring in 2 tablespoons sugar. Whip to stiff peaks. Spread over pie filling and top with coconut and remainder of chopped pecans. Refrigerate until ready to serve.

Delicious ... serve for special occasions.

Mrs. Roy Hamor (Laverne)
Austin

Kahlúa Pecan Pie

Bake at 400° for 10 minutes
325° for 40 minutes

¼	cup butter, softened
¾	cup sugar
1	teaspoon vanilla
2	tablespoons flour
3	eggs
½	cup Kahlúa
½	cup dark corn syrup
¾	cup evaporated milk
1	cup chopped pecans

Cream together butter, sugar, vanilla and flour. Mix well. Beat in eggs one at a time. Stir in Kahlúa, corn syrup and milk and beat well. Fold in chopped pecans. Pour into unbaked pie crust. Bake at 400° for 10 minutes and then 325 ° for 40 minutes or until set.

Cookbook Committee

Condensed milk, still used extensively in cooking, was the product of a Texas revolutionary, Gail Borden, Jr. After founding a newspaper and serving the Republic of Texas as a public official, Borden patented the process of condensing milk in a vacuum. He also invented processes for condensing fruit juices, for extract of beef, and for coffee. The town of Borden, Fayette County, Texas is named for him as is Borden County, Texas.
—Walter Prescott Webb, ed., Handbook of Texas
Texas State Historical Association, Austin, 1952.

Holiday Pecan Pie

Bake at 400° for 15 minutes
350° for 35 minutes
Serves 6 to 8

3	eggs
1	cup sugar
1	cup light Karo syrup
⅛	teaspoon salt
2	tablespoons margarine, melted
1	teaspoon vanilla
2	cups pecans, chopped
1	(9-inch) pie shell, unbaked

Beat eggs slightly by hand. Add sugar, syrup, salt, margarine and vanilla and mix well. Fold in pecans and pour mixture into unbaked pie shell. Bake at 400° for 15 minutes, lower temperature to 350° and bake for 35 minutes longer or until firm.

Mrs. Buster Strickland (Shirley)
Hawley

Lorene Stein
Baytown

Creamy Pecan Pie

Bake at 225° for 1 hour
Serves 6

1	(3¾ ounce) package regular vanilla pudding mix
1	cup white Karo syrup
1	egg
¾	cup evaporated milk
⅛	teaspoon salt
2	teaspoons vanilla
1	cup pecans, chopped
1	(9-inch) pie shell, unbaked

Beat all ingredients together and pour into unbaked pie shell. Bake at 225° for 1 hour or until top is crusty.

Mrs. J. C. Kirschner (Judy)
Austin

Wickedly Rich Pie

Bake at 400° for 30 minutes

4	squares semi-sweet chocolate
¼	cup butter or margarine
1	(13 ounce) can evaporated milk
1⅓	cups flaked coconut
3	eggs, slightly beaten
½	cup sugar
1	9-inch pie shell, unbaked
Whipped topping (optional)	

Melt chocolate and butter over low heat in a medium saucepan. Add milk, coconut, eggs and sugar and stir until well blended. Pour into pie shell. Bake at 400° for 30 minutes. Cool. Serve with whipped topping if desired.

Pecos Cantaloupe Pie

Serves 6 to 8

1	cup sugar
2	tablespoons flour
3	eggs, beaten
1	cup pureed cantaloupe
1	teaspoon vanilla
2	tablespoons margarine or butter
1	cup whipping cream, whipped
1	(8-inch) pie shell, baked

Combine sugar and flour in saucepan. Add eggs, mixing well. Stir in cantaloupe puree and cook over medium heat 8 to 10 minutes, stirring constantly until mixture boils and thickens. Remove from heat, stir in vanilla and butter. Cool. Pour filling into baked pie shell, spread with whipped cream. Refrigerate.

Mrs. David A. Smith (Betty)
Pecos

Pink Lemonade Pie

Serves 6 to 8

1	(14 ounce) can sweetened condensed milk
1	(6 ounce) can frozen pink lemonade, undiluted
1	(9 ounce) carton whipped topping
1	graham cracker crumb crust

In medium bowl combine condensed milk and lemonade and mix well. Stir in whipped topping just until blended well. Pour into crust and chill thoroughly. You may want to add a few drops of red food coloring to make a little pinker.

Mrs. Bill Leon (Jeanette)
Austin

Sunrise Pie

Serves 6 to 8

1	(8¼ ounce) can crushed pineapple, drained
1	(8 ounce) package cream cheese, softened
½	teaspoon vanilla
1	(21 ounce) can cherry pie filling
1	cup whipping cream, whipped
¼	cup powdered sugar
1	(9-inch) graham cracker crumb pie crust

Drain pineapple well, reserving 2 tablespoons syrup. Combine softened cream cheese, vanilla and reserved syrup, mixing until well blended. Stir in ¼ cup pineapple and ½ cup pie filling. Gradually add sugar to whipping cream, beating until soft peaks form. Fold into cream cheese mixture. Pour into crust. Top with remaining pineapple and pie filling. Chill until firm.

Mrs. Gary Davis (Sharon)
Arlington

Cherry Almond Pie

Serves 6 to 8

¼	cup slivered almonds
1	(9-inch) pie shell, unbaked
1	(14 ounce) can sweetened condensed milk
⅓	cup lemon juice
½	cup whipping cream, whipped
1	teaspoon vanilla
½	teaspoon almond extract
1	can cherry pie filling

Add ¼ cup slivered almonds to your favorite pastry. Bake and cool pie shell. Combine condensed milk and lemon juice. Fold in whipped cream. Stir in flavorings and pour into cooled pie crust. Top with cherry pie filling. Refrigerate.

Mrs. Thomas D. Blackwell (Rosemary)
Austin

Pumpkin Pecan Pie

Bake at 350° for 40 minutes
Serves 6 to 8

3   eggs, beaten
1   cup canned pumpkin
1   cup sugar
½   cup dark corn syrup
1   teaspoon vanilla
1   teaspoon cinnamon
¼   teaspoon salt
1   cup pecans, chopped or
     halves
1   (9-inch) pie shell, unbaked

Combine all ingredients except pecans. Mix well and pour into unbaked pie shell. Put 1 cup pecans on top of filling. Bake at 350° for 40 minutes or until knife inserted comes out clean. Chill.

This pie is also great served with whipped cream or vanilla ice cream.

Mrs. O. W. McClure (Louise)
Friendswood

Peanut Pie

Bake at 350° for 45 minutes
Serves 8 to 10

3   eggs
1   cup sugar
3   tablespoons butter, melted
1   cup light corn syrup
1   teaspoon vanilla
⅛   teaspoon cloves
⅛   teaspoon nutmeg
⅛   teaspoon cinnamon
⅛   teaspoon salt (omit if
     using salted peanuts)
1½   cups peanuts (can use dry
     roasted peanuts)
1   9-inch pie shell, unbaked

Beat eggs lightly. Stir in sugar, butter and syrup. Add vanilla, spices and salt. Beat gently. Stir in peanuts. Pour into shell and bake for 45 minutes on lower rack of oven until filling is golden and set.

We had peanuts left over from the Signal Battalion Hospitality Room after NGAT Conference, so Jack and I shelled peanuts, and I baked 11 pies to serve the fellows for the weekend drill. They enjoyed it!!!

Mrs. Jack D. Anderson (Mary Emma)
Fruitvale

PIES

Renfro's Fresh Pumpkin Pie

Bake at 450° for 10 minutes
325° for 45 minutes
Serves 6 to 8

1¼   cup fresh pumpkin, cooked and mashed
1   cup brown sugar
1   tablespoon flour
1   teaspoon cinnamon
½   teaspoon ginger
½   teaspoon allspice
½   teaspoon salt
2   eggs
½   cup evaporated milk
¾   cup milk
1   teaspoon vanilla
1   cup pecans, optional
1   (9-inch) pie shell, unbaked

Combine brown sugar, flour, cinnamon, ginger, allspice and salt. Mix well. Beat eggs, add milk together with vanilla. Add dry ingredients to the egg mixture and beat well. Fold in pumpkin and stir just until blended. Pecans should be placed in bottom of pie shell, then pour pie mixture on top and bake at 450° for 10 minutes, lower oven to 325° and bake for 45 minutes.

Mrs. Jimmie F. Johnson (Judy)
Corpus Christi

Chocolate Microwave Pie

3   egg yolks
1¼   cups sugar
2   tablespoons cocoa
3   tablespoons cornstarch
2   cups milk
1   tablespoon butter
2   teaspoons vanilla
1   9-inch pie shell, baked

Blend all ingredients in blender or mixer. Pour into glass bowl and microwave on high for 4 minutes. Stir and return for 2 more minutes. Continue until desired consistency. Remove and add butter and vanilla and beat well. Pour into baked pie shell and refrigerate.

Variation - for coconut pie substitute 1 cup coconut for chocolate.

Mrs. William L. Byrd (Maxine)
Round Rock

Coconut Macaroon Pie

Bake at 375° for 50 minutes
Serves 6 to 8

¼	teaspoon salt
4	eggs, separated
1½	cups sugar
½	cup milk
3	tablespoons margarine
2	teaspoons lemon juice
½	teaspoon almond extract
1½	cups coconut
1	(9-inch) pie shell, unbaked

Add salt to egg yolks. Beat until thick and lemony colored. Add sugar, ½ cup at a time, beat well after each addition. Add milk, margarine, lemon juice and extract. Fold in coconut and stiffly beaten egg whites; pour into unbaked pie shell. Bake at 375° for 50 minutes or until knife comes out clean when tested. Cool and serve.

Mrs. Jim Key (Janiece)
Amarillo

All American Pie

Ingredients:

In equal amounts: life, liberty and the pursuit of happiness.

A heaping helping of American pride.

A bunch of truths we still hold to be self-evident.

208 years to look back on with honor.

A "fourth of" recalling on what beliefs we were founded.

13 broad stripes, and 50 bright stars.

Add to taste: old fashioned friendship, kindness and brotherly love.

Blend ingredients well. Fill to overflowing from sea to shining sea.

Bake to perfection in warm hearts.

Ask God's continued blessings and you are *ready to serve* with pride.

Coconut Macaroons

Bake at 325° for 12 to 15 minutes
Yields 2 dozen

3   egg whites
1½   cups sugar
1   teaspoon vanilla
2   cups corn flakes
1   cup chopped pecans
2   cups coconut

Beat egg whites until stiff; add sugar and vanilla and blend well. Fold in corn flakes, pecans and coconut. Drop by teaspoon on ungreased brown paper bag cut to fit in baking sheet. Bake 12 to 15 minutes.

Mrs. James C. Ragan (Joyce)
Austin

Sugar Cookies and Icing

Bake at 350° for 6 to 7 minutes
Yields 2½ to 3 dozen

COOKIE

1½   cups sugar
1   cup shortening
2   eggs
3   tablespoons milk
½   teaspoon lemon flavoring
1   teaspoon vanilla
½   teaspoon soda
3   cups flour

Cream sugar, shortening, eggs, milk and flavorings. Slowly mix in dry ingredients thoroughly. Roll out and cut into desired shapes. Bake for 6 to 7 minutes.

ICING

1   cup shortening
1   teaspoon vanilla
1   teaspoon butter flavoring
¼   teaspoon almond flavoring
⅛   teaspoon salt
5   tablespoons milk
4   cups powdered sugar

Mix shortening, flavorings, milk and salt. Add powdered sugar 2 cups at a time, mixing until smooth. Tint with food coloring, if desired. Frost cooled cookies.

Mrs. Harold "Snake Eyes" Reid (Gwen)
Skellytown

Butter Cakes

Bake at 400° until brown
Yields 4 dozen

1   pound flour
1   pound butter (do not
       substitute)

Mix ingredients thoroughly. Roll out to ¼-inch thickness on floured board. Cut three inches in diameter and place on cookie sheet. Do not let touch. Bake at 400° just until brown.

These very rich cakes are delicious with a tablespoon of mustang grape preserves. This is an old family recipe.

Mrs. Watson Arnold (Mary Beck)
Austin

See index for Mustang Grape Preserves.

Easy Cheesy Lemon Bars

Bake at 350° for 30 to 40 minutes
Yields 24 bars

1   package lemon cake mix
½   cup butter or margarine,
       melted
1   egg, slightly beaten
1   (16 ounce) container
       lemon frosting mix
1   (8 ounce) package cream
       cheese, softened
2   eggs, beaten

Combine cake mix, butter and 1 beaten egg. Blend with fork and pour into 9x13-inch pan, greased on bottom only. Blend frosting mix into softened cream cheese, reserving ½ cup of this mixture. Combine 2 beaten eggs into blended frosting and cream cheese, spread over mixture in pan. Bake for 30 to 40 minutes. Cool slightly. Spread with reserved frosting mix while cake is warm.

Barbara O'Connell
Austin

Forgotten Cookies

Yields 2½ dozen

2 egg whites
⅔ cup sugar
1 (6 ounce) package chocolate chips
1 cup chopped nuts

Beat egg whites until stiff. Add sugar gradually to beaten egg whites and continue beating until stiff peaks are formed. Fold in chocolate chips and nuts. Drop by teaspoonful on a large greased cookie sheet. Preheat oven to 350°, place cookies in oven. Turn off heat as soon as cookies are in. Keep oven closed overnight or at least 3 hours.

Mrs. Jerry Garlington (Melvia)
Plano

Mrs. Danny L. Golden (Evelyn)
Irving

Almond Macaroons

Bake at 325° for 20 to 25 minutes
Yields 24

2 (8 ounce) cans almond paste (Reese's or Blue Diamond)
6 egg whites, unbeaten
2 cups sugar
2 cups powdered sugar

In a large bowl, work almond paste with 2 egg whites and 1 cup granulated sugar until blended. Gradually add 2 more egg whites and remaining sugar, beating until smooth. Blend in powdered sugar and last 2 egg whites, beating until smooth. Grease and flour cookie sheets. Drop by teaspoon onto cookie sheet and bake for 20 to 25 minutes, or until light brown. Remove to rack and cool. Store in airtight container.

Mrs. Louis E. Holder, Jr. (Louise)
Many, Louisiana (Toledo Bend Lake)

Morning Tea Cakes

Bake at 350° for 15 minutes
Yields 4 to 5 dozen

4	cups flour
3	teaspoons baking powder
2	cups sugar
2	eggs, beaten
1	teaspoon vanilla
²/₃	cup milk
1	cup melted butter

Sift flour, baking powder and sugar into large bowl. Make hole in center of dry ingredients. Beat eggs, melt butter and pour into hole. Add milk and vanilla, stir until stiff. Add more flour, if needed. Roll out on floured board or pastry cloth and cut as desired. Bake for 15 minutes. Serve with jelly and coffee.

Mrs. Jimmy Leggett (Judy)
Katy

Jelly Cookies

Bake at 325° for 15 to 18 minutes

½	cup margarine
¼	cup brown sugar
1	egg yolk
1	cup flour
1	egg white, slightly beaten
1	cup finely chopped pecans

Cream margarine and brown sugar. Add egg yolk and flour gradually, beating well. Form into small balls and dip into slightly beaten egg white and roll in chopped pecans. Place on lightly greased cookie sheet. Press in centers slightly and bake 8 minutes. Press centers in again and bake an additional 10 minutes or until done. Fill with jelly of your choice while still warm. Cool on rack.

Mrs. John Adams (Eleanor)
Austin

COOKIES

Refrigerator Cookies

Bake at 325° for 10 to 12 minutes
Yields 12 dozen

1	pound margarine,
	softened
1	cup sugar
4	cups flour
1	teaspoon vanilla
Powdered sugar

Cream margarine and sugar. Add flour and vanilla. Pat into 4 rolls about 12 inches long, wrap in wax paper and chill thoroughly. Slice and place on ungreased cookie sheet. Bake for 10 to 12 minutes. Top with sifted powdered sugar.

I took these cookies to school for the teachers' coffee break. I am sure it helped get Tommy through elementary school!

Mrs. Thomas D. Blackwell (Rosemary)
Austin

Sand Tarts

Bake at 250° for 40 to 50 minutes
Yields 2 dozen

1	cup margarine or butter
5	tablespoons powdered
	sugar
1	tablespoon hot water
1	teaspoon vanilla
2	cups flour
1½	cups finely chopped
	pecans
Powdered sugar

Cream margarine and sugar. Add hot water and vanilla. Add flour and nuts, kneading well. Shape into crescents. Place on ungreased cookie sheets and bake for 40 to 50 minutes. When cool, roll in powdered sugar.

Mrs. Charles Hodde (Mary)
Austin

Snickerdoodles

Bake at 400° for 8 to 10 minutes
Yields 5 dozen

1	cup shortening
2	eggs
1½	cups sugar
2¾	cups flour
2	tablespoons cream of tartar
¼	teaspoon salt
1	teaspoon soda
2	tablespoons sugar
2	teaspoons cinnamon

Cream shortening, eggs and sugar thoroughly. Blend in flour, cream of tartar, salt and soda and mix well. Roll into 1-inch balls and roll balls in mixture of cinnamon and sugar. Place on ungreased cookie sheet. Bake for 8 to 10 minutes.

Mrs. Bobby King (Judy)
Pearland

Sour Cream Cookies

Bake at 350° for 10 to 12 minutes
Yields 5 to 6 dozen

2	cups sugar
1	cup butter
1	cup sour cream
2	eggs, slightly beaten
1½	teaspoons nutmeg
1	teaspoon mace
1½	teaspoons vanilla
1	teaspoon soda
3½	cups flour

Cream sugar, butter and sour cream. Add remaining ingredients and blend. Drop on cookie sheet and bake 10 to 12 minutes.

A pecan half placed on top before baking adds a special touch.

Mrs. Robert H. Block, Jr. (Debbie)
Austin

Potato Chip Cookies

Bake at 400° for 8 minutes
Yields 4 dozen

1	cup margarine or butter, softened
½	cup sugar
1½	cups flour
1	teaspoon vanilla
30	crushed Pringle's potato chips
½	cup chopped pecans
Powdered sugar	

Cream margarine and sugar. Blend in flour, vanilla, potato chips and pecans; mix well. Line baking sheet with foil, shiny side up. Drop by teaspoon and flatten each cookie with fork. Bake for 8 minutes or until light brown. Leave on foil until cool, dust with powdered sugar.

These are good, but very rich.

Mrs. Robert W. Anderson (Bertie)
Texarkana

Peanut Butter Cookies

Bake at 350° for 10 to 12 minutes
Yields 4 dozen

½	cup shortening
½	cup margarine, softened
1	cup peanut butter
1	cup brown sugar
1	cup sugar
2	teaspoons vanilla
2	eggs
3	cups sifted flour
2	teaspoons soda
¼	teaspoon salt

Cream shortening, margarine, peanut butter, sugars and vanilla. Add eggs and beat well. Sift dry ingredients and blend with creamed mixture. Roll into 1-inch balls and place on ungreased cookie sheet. Press each ball with fork to make criss cross pattern. Bake 10 to 12 minutes.

This recipe came from Grandma Hairrell.

Mrs. James C. Hairrell (Frances)
Houston

Praline Cookies

Yields 40

½   cup margarine
½   cup evaporated milk
1   cup sugar
10   large marshmallows
1   cup graham cracker
      crumbs
1   cup chopped nuts
1   teaspoon vanilla

Over medium heat bring margarine, milk and sugar to a rolling boil. Boil for 6 minutes. Remove from heat and add marshmallows, stir until melted. Add graham cracker crumbs, nuts and vanilla. Stir 1 minute and drop onto waxed paper.

Mrs. Dean Hayley (Lucille)
Austin

Oatmeal Crispies

Bake at 375° for 10 minutes
Yields 3 dozen

1   cup shortening
1   cup brown sugar
1   cup sugar
2   eggs, beaten
1½   cups flour, sifted
1   teaspoon salt
1   teaspoon soda
3   cups quick cooking oats
½   cups broken walnuts

Cream shortening and sugars. Add beaten eggs and vanilla; beat well. Sift dry ingredients and blend into creamed mixture. Stir in oats and nuts. Shape into rolls (logs), wrap in foil and freeze. To bake, slice ¼-inch thick. Place on ungreased cookie sheet and bake 10 minutes. Cool slightly and remove from cookie sheet.

Mrs. Gerald T. Garlington (Melvia)
Plano

Cousin Emmie Lou's Butter Cookies

Bake at 300° for 12 minutes
Yields 3 to 4 dozen

1   pound butter (do not
      substitute)
2   cups sugar
1   egg
4   cups flour
Pecan halves

Cream butter, sugar and egg. Add flour gradually. Divide into 3 rolls about the size of a half dollar. Chill several hours and slice as needed. Top slices with a pecan half and bake 12 minutes in a preheated oven.

These are very rich and delicious cookies.

Mrs. Jay Matthews (Babs)
Austin

Zucchini Bars

Bake at 350° for 1 hour

**6 to 8 cups zucchini, peeled
and sliced**
⅔   cup bottled lemon juice
1   cup sugar
¼   teaspoon nutmeg
½   teaspoon cinnamon
4   cups flour
3   sticks margarine
2   cups sugar
½   teaspoon salt

Simmer zucchini and lemon juice until tender and add sugar, nutmeg and cinnamon. Set aside. Cut flour, margarine, sugar and salt together thoroughly and press half of mixture into a 9x13-inch baking dish, reserving ½ cup. Bake for 10 minutes. Mix ½ cup reserved crumbs into zucchini mixture and pour over crumb crust. Sprinkle remaining half of crumb mixture over zucchini mixture and bake for 1 hour. Cool and cut into bars.

Another use for all those extra zucchinis at harvest time.

Mrs. Vernon Andrews (Grace)
Lansing, Michigan

Texas farms of the old Austin Colony by the mid-nineteenth century were supplied with vegetables from kitchen gardens. Orchards of figs and peaches were common. Chickens, turkeys, and ducks provided poultry products. Milk cows supplied milk, cream, butter and cheeses. Swine were the source of bacon, ham, and sausage which were smoked. Cracklings and other by-products of swine were used in cooking. Corn, white potatoes and sweet potatoes were principle crops as well as staples of the diet.
—Terry G. Jordan, German Seed in Texas Soil

Black Forest Cookies

Bake at 350° for 10 minutes
Yields 4 dozen

½	cup butter or margarine, softened
1	cup sugar
1	egg
1	teaspoon vanilla
1½	cups flour
½	cup cocoa
¼	teaspoon salt
¼	teaspoon baking powder
¼	teaspoon soda
1	(10 ounce) jar maraschino cherries

In a large bowl, cream butter, sugar, egg and vanilla until light and fluffy. Add remaining ingredients, except cherries, and blend at low speed until a stiff dough forms, about 1 minute. Shape dough into 1-inch balls, using a heaping teaspoon of dough for each. Place 2 inches apart on ungreased cookie sheet. Push one whole cherry halfway into each ball. When all cookies are molded and cherries are pushed in, prepare frosting and use immediately.

FROSTING

1	(6 ounce) package semi-sweet chocolate chips (not milk chocolate)
½	cup sweetened condensed milk
¼	teaspoon salt
1 to 1½ teaspoons maraschino cherry juice	

In small, heavy saucepan, melt chocolate and condensed milk over low heat, stirring constantly. Remove from heat. Add remaining ingredients and stir until smooth. Frost each cherry by spreading ½ teaspoon of frosting over each cookie. Bake frosted cookies for 8 to 10 minutes until puffy. Store tightly covered.

Mrs. Joe Montgomery (Norma)
Austin

Mrs. Paul E. Tressa, Jr. (Nancy)
Lewisville

Brownies

Bake at 350° for 20 to 30 minutes
Yields 30

1	cup margarine, softened
2	cups sugar
4	eggs
1	teaspoon vanilla
1	cup flour
½	cup cocoa
1	cup chopped pecans

Cream margarine and sugar, blend in eggs and vanilla. Add flour and cocoa, mix well. Stir in pecans. Pour into greased 9x13-inch pan and bake at 350° for 20 to 30 minutes. DO NOT OVERBAKE.

Mrs. Arthur Allen (Billie)
Marlin

Carmelitas

Bake at 375° for 20 to 25 minutes
Yields 36 squares

32	light candy caramel squares
¼	cup half and half cream or evaporated milk
1	(16 ounce) roll chocolate chip refrigerator cookies
1	(6 ounce) package milk or semi-sweet chocolate pieces
½	cup chopped pecans

Melt caramels and cream in top of double boiler. Slice cookie dough ¼-inch thick and place in greased 8 or 9-inch square pan. Bake for 20 to 25 minutes. They will be puffy when removed from oven. Cool slightly. Sprinkle chocolate pieces over warm cookies. Carefully spread caramel mixture over top of chocolate, then sprinkle with chopped pecans. Refrigerate 1 to 2 hours.

Mrs. Willie L. Scott (Billie)
Austin

Chocolate Crinkle Cookies

Bake at 350° 10 minutes
Yields 3 dozen

2   cups sugar
¾   cup cocoa
¾   cup vegetable oil
4   eggs
2   teaspoons vanilla
2¼   cups flour
2   teaspoons baking powder
½   teaspoon salt
Powdered sugar

Mix thoroughly sugar, cocoa and oil. Add eggs one at a time, stirring after each. Add vanilla and mix well. Add flour, baking powder and salt and mix well. Chill several hours or overnight. Shape into balls and roll in powdered sugar. Place on ungreased cookie sheet and bake at 350° for 10 minutes. DO NOT OVERCOOK. Cookies will be soft and puffy when cool.

Mrs. Immel Ooley (Mary K.)
San Angelo

No-Bake Chocolate Cookies

Yields 3 dozen

2   cups sugar
½   cup cocoa
½   cup milk
½   cup butter
3   cups quick oats
½   cup peanut butter
½   cup coconut (optional)
½   teaspoon vanilla

Combine sugar, cocoa, milk and butter in saucepan. Place over medium heat, bring to a boil and boil for 1 minute. Stir well, because it can burn easily. Remove from heat and add remaining ingredients. Drop from teaspoon onto waxed paper. Let cool.

Fantastic oatmeal recipe!

Mrs. Mickey Francis (Jo Ann)
Austin

Fudge Nut Bars

Bake at 350° for 25 to 30 minutes
Yields 24 to 36

FIRST LAYER

1	**cup butter or margarine**
2	**cups light brown sugar**
2	**eggs**
2	**teaspoons vanilla**
2½	**cups flour**
1	**teaspoon soda**
1	**teaspoon salt**
3	**cups quick rolled oats, uncooked**

In a large bowl, cream margarine and sugar; beat in eggs and vanilla. Sift flour, soda and salt then stir in oats. Stir dry ingredients into creamed mixture. Blend. Put ⅔ of mixture into 10x5-inch pan.

SECOND LAYER

1	**cup sweetened condensed milk**
1	**(12 ounce) package chocolate chips**
2	**tablespoons margarine**
½	**teaspoon salt**
2	**teaspoons vanilla**
1	**cup chopped nuts (optional)**

In a heavy saucepan, blend milk, chocolate chips, margarine and salt. Stir until smooth and melted. Stir in vanilla and nuts. Spread chocolate mixture over dough. Dot with remaining dough mixture and bake for 25 to 30 minutes. Cool. Cut into bars.

Mrs. Johnny Cates (Bonnie)
Quitman

Indian Nut Cakes

Bake at 350° for 20 minutes
Yields 4 dozen

½	**cup butter, melted**
1	**cup sugar**
½	**cup flour**
2	**eggs, beaten**
¼	**cup cocoa**
1	**teaspoon vanilla**
½	**cup chopped walnuts**
	Powdered sugar for coating

Pour melted butter into sugar and stir well. Sift flour and stir into mixture. Add beaten eggs, cocoa and vanilla. Stir in chopped nuts. Pour mixture into a greased 10x10-inch pan. Bake for about 20 minutes. Cut into squares or rectangles. Cool, then roll in powdered sugar.

These little cakes are attractive and a bit different from the usual brownie.

Mrs. Francis X. Bostick (Helen Timpson)
Austin

Vienna Chocolate Bars

Bake at 350°

1	cup butter
1¼	cups sugar
2	egg yolks
2½	cups flour
1	(10 ounce) jar jelly (raspberry or apricot)
1	cup semi-sweet chocolate chips
¼	teaspoon salt
4	egg whites
2	cups finely chopped pecans

Cream butter, ½ cup sugar and egg yolks. Add flour and knead with fingers. Pat butter out on a greased cookie sheet to ⅜-inch thickness. Bake 15 to 20 minutes. Remove from oven and spread with jelly and top with chocolate chips. Beat egg whites and salt until stiff. Fold in remaining cup of sugar and nuts. Gently spread on top of jelly and chocolate. Bake for about 20 to 25 minutes. Cut into squares or rectangles.

In 1903 Congress enacted the National Militia Act, also known as the Dick Law. This Act brought the states' militia into a federal status. In this manner the Texas Volunteer Guard was succeeded by the Texas National Guard.
     —Walter Prescott Webb, ed., Handbook of Texas
          Texas State Historical Association, Austin, 1952.

Date-Nut Pinwheels

Bake at 350° for 10 to 12 minutes
Yields 6 dozen

1 pound chopped dates
1 cup sugar
1 cup water
1 cup chopped nuts
1 cup margarine
2 cups brown sugar
3 eggs, well beaten
4 cups flour, sifted
½ teaspoon salt
½ teaspoon soda

Combine dates, sugar and water in saucepan and cook slowly until thick. Add nuts and cool. Cream shortening and brown sugar. Add well beaten eggs, then combined dry ingredients. Chill thoroughly, then divide into four parts. Roll out about ¼-inch thick, spread with the date mixture and make into rolls. Chill for 24 hours, then slice ¼-inch thick and place on cookie sheet. Bake for 10 to 12 minutes.

Mrs. James C. Ragan (Joyce)
Austin

Honey Spice Bars

Bake at 350° for 20 minutes
Yields 24 bars

¾ cup oil
¼ cup honey
1 cup sugar
2 cups flour
¼ teaspoon salt
1 teaspoon soda
1 teaspoon cinnamon
1 egg, beaten
½ cup chopped nuts

In mixing bowl, blend oil, honey and sugar. Add dry ingredients and mix well. Add beaten egg and nuts. Press mixture into slightly greased 9x13-inch pan. Bake for 20 minutes. Cool, glaze and cut into bars.

This is a family favorite.

Mrs. Marvin Brown (Shirley)
Wake Village

GLAZE

1 cup powdered sugar
½ teaspoon vanilla
1 tablespoon Miracle Whip
   Salad Dressing
1 tablespoon water

322

Fran's Christmas Cookies

Bake at 375° for 12 minutes
Yields 5 dozen

½ cup butter, softened
½ cup shortening
2 cups brown sugar
2 eggs
4 cups flour
1 teaspoon salt
1 teaspoon vinegar
1 cup evaporated milk
1½ cups chopped pecans
1 cup chopped dates
1 cup raisins
1 cup chopped candied
  cherries

Cream butter, shortening, sugar and eggs thoroughly. Add flour and salt alternately with milk mixed with vinegar. Beat well. Fold in pecans, dates, raisins and cherries. Drop on ungreased cookie sheet. Bake for 12 minutes.

Mrs. Hugh Hall (Fran)
Austin

Texas Lizzies

Bake at 350° for 10 minutes

1 cup margarine
1 (16 ounce) package dark
  brown sugar
4 eggs, well beaten
1 cup bourbon
3 cups flour (mix 1 cup with
  pecans and fruit)
3 teaspoons soda
½ teaspoon salt
1 teaspoon cinnamon
2 cups chopped pecans
1½ cups raisins
1½ cups white raisins
1 cup chopped red and
  green candied cherries

Cream margarine and sugar; add eggs and beat well. Add bourbon alternately with the 2 cups of flour and other dry ingredients and mix well. Stir in flour-coated pecans and fruits. Spoon into large container with cover and chill overnight. Drop by teaspoon onto cookie sheet and bake approximately 10 minutes. Dough will keep in refrigerator up to a month and the flavor gets better and better.

Butter Creme Mints

Yields 100 small mints

2   tablespoons butter
2   teaspoons flavoring
3   tablespoons sweetened
       condensed milk
Paste color desired
1   (16 ounce) box powdered
       sugar

Blend butter, flavoring and condensed milk. Add coloring and blend well before sugar is added. After adding sugar, continue to mix until mixture becomes like a stiff pie dough. Roll into small balls, press ball into a rubber candy mold. Unmold at once. (Wilton's color pastes work well.)

Mrs. Clarence Koehn (Mildred)
Houston

Microwave Peanut Brittle

High 8 to 11 minutes
Yields 1 pound

1   cup sugar
½   cup white corn syrup
1   cup roasted, salted
       peanuts
1   teaspoon butter
1   teaspoon vanilla
1   teaspoon soda

In 1½-quart casserole or glass dish, stir sugar and syrup together. Microwave on high for 4 minutes. Stir in peanuts, microwave on high 3 to 5 minutes, until light brown. Add butter and vanilla, blending well. Microwave on high 1 to 2 minutes, add soda. Gently stir until light and foamy. Pour onto greased cookie sheet. Let cool 30 minutes to 1 hour. When cool, break into pieces and store in airtight container.

Suzanne Ragan Crawford
Paige

No-Cook Fondant for Party Mints

Yields 180 roses

1 (8 ounce) package cream
cheese
½ teaspoon peppermint oil
or
1½ teaspoon peppermint
extract
Choice of food coloring
2 (16 ounce) boxes
powdered sugar

Mix cream cheese and extract. Add coloring (darker color than you want finished mints). If more than one color is desired, separate batch at this time. Mix in sugar, kneading with hands until consistency of stiff pie dough. More sugar may be needed. Wrap in plastic to prevent drying. Work with a small amount. Pinch off and roll into ball and place one side in sugar, brush off excess and push sugar side into mold. Unmold at once onto waxed paper. (Use color and extract of your choice.)

Peanut Patties

3 cups sugar
½ cup water
3 cups raw peanuts
1 cup white corn syrup
½ cup margarine
1 tablespoon vanilla
⅛ teaspoon salt
Red food coloring (optional)

Combine in heavy saucepan sugar, water, peanuts and syrup. Bring to boil, stirring constantly. Remove from heat and stir in last four ingredients. Beat approximately 5 minutes. It will turn a creamy pink when ready. Drop onto foil lined pan.

Work quickly as it starts to harden fast!

Mrs. Maurice G. Lambert (Janis)
Fort Worth

Mrs. Thomas J. Abel, III (Laverne)
Bertram

Brodnax Divinity

Yields 2 pounds

2   egg whites, stiffly beaten
3   cups sugar
1   cup water
3   tablespoons white corn
       syrup
¼   teaspoon vanilla
Amount of nuts desired

Boil sugar, water and corn syrup to soft ball stage (238°) and add one half of it to the stiffly beaten egg whites, beating constantly. Cook the other half of the syrup mixture until it spins a hard thread (300°) and add to candy very slowly while beating. Add vanilla and nuts. Rapidly drop by teaspoon onto waxed paper.

This recipe was my husband's Grandmother's. Throw away all other divinity recipes - this is the best!

Mrs. Cox R. Crider (Pam)
Mexia

Holiday Delight

3   cups sugar
1   cup white syrup
1½   cups half and half cream
2   cups chopped Brazil nuts
2   cups chopped walnuts
2   cups pecan halves
1   cup chopped candied
       green pineapple
2   cups chopped candied red
       cherries
½   teaspoon vanilla

In large, heavy saucepan, cook sugar, syrup and cream to very soft-ball stage. Remove and beat. When thick add vanilla. Beat again thoroughly and add nuts and fruit. Mix well. Pack in buttered loaf pan. Place in refrigerator 24 hours. Cut into squares.

Homemade Fire Sticks (Hard Candy)

Yields 20 to 30 sticks

2   cups sugar
1   cup water
¾   cup light corn syrup
Red food coloring
¾   teaspoon cinnamon *oil*
Powdered sugar

Mix sugar, water and corn syrup together in heavy pan. Cook to 300° on candy thermometer. Remove from heat, add flavoring and color and mix well. Pour onto buttered cookie sheet. When cool enough to handle, break into small pieces. Roll lightly in powdered sugar to coat.

Mrs. Bobby Ingram (Dorothy)
Smithville

Peppermint Bark

Yields 1 pound

1   pound white chocolate
½   cup peppermint candy,
         crushed fine
4 to 7 drops red food coloring

Melt chocolate in glass bowl in microwave 3 to 4 minutes, or until melted. Stir in candy and food coloring. Spread on cookie sheet which has been lined with foil (shiny side up). Place in freezer 5 to 10 minutes until firm. Store in airtight container.

Mrs. Morris Abercrombie (Barbara)
Sulphur Springs

Agricultural records from the mid-nineteenth century reveal that the populated areas of Galveston and Indianola on the Texas coast were well supplied with vegetables from "market garden" vendors. Poultry products and milk products were also available from vendors.
    —Terry G. Jordan, German Seed in Texas Soil

Hawaiian Fudge

2	cups sugar
½	cup half and half cream
1	(8 ounce) can crushed pineapple, well drained
1	tablespoon butter
3	drops green food coloring
½	cup chopped nuts

Boil sugar, cream, pineapple and butter to soft ball stage (238°). Remove from heat and add coloring and chopped nuts. Beat until creamy. Pour into buttered 8-inch square pan. The flavor is enhanced if aged a few days.

David Counts
Knox City

Magic Chocolate French Fudge

Yields 1¾ pounds

3	(6 ounce) packages semi-sweet chocolate morsels
1	(14 ounce) can sweetened condensed milk
⅛	teaspoon salt
1½	teaspoons vanilla
½	cup chopped nuts

In heavy saucepan, over low heat, melt chocolate morsels with sweetened condensed milk. Remove from heat, stir in remaining ingredients. Spread evenly onto waxed paper-lined 8-inch square pan. Chill 2 to 3 hours or until firm. Turn fudge onto cutting board, peel paper off and cut into squares. Store loosely covered at room temperature.

Mrs. Harold Loftis (Billie)
Austin

Microwave Fudge

Yields 36 pieces

1 (16 ounce) box powdered sugar
½ cup cocoa
¼ cup milk
¼ cup butter or margarine
1 tablespoon vanilla
½ cup chopped nuts

Blend powdered sugar and cocoa in microwave mixing bowl. Add milk and butter. Cook 2 minutes or longer in microwave. Remove bowl and stir. Add vanilla and nuts. Stir with spoon until blended. Pour into greased 9-inch square pan and set in freezer for 20 minutes or in refrigerator 1 hour. Slice and serve.

Mrs. Jon Pfennig (Glena)
Baytown

See-Saw Fudge

3 (6 ounce) packages chocolate chips
1 cup margarine, softened
2 teaspoons vanilla
2 teaspoons maple flavoring
2½ cups chopped nuts
1 (7 ounce) jar marshmallow whip
4½ cups sugar
1 (13 ounce) can evaporated milk

In large mixing bowl combine chocolate chips, margarine, vanilla, maple flavoring, nuts and marshmallow whip. In a large pan (I use my pressure cooker pan) mix sugar and milk, stirring constantly as this sticks very easily. Bring to a full rolling boil for 8 minutes. Remove from heat immediately and pour over ingredients in bowl. Do not beat; mix only until chocolate chips are melted. Pour into buttered 10x15-inch pyrex dish.

Prepare this recipe using mint-flavored chocolate chips . . . delicious!

Mrs. Stan Murrell (Sherry)
El Paso

Velveeta Cheese Fudge

Yields 6½ pounds

1   pound Velveeta cheese
1   pound butter or margarine
4   (16 ounce) packages
        powdered sugar
1   cup cocoa
2   tablespoons vanilla
2   cups chopped pecans

Cook cheese, butter and cocoa in double boiler, beating until smooth. Gradually add powdered sugar and beat well. Mix in vanilla and nuts and spread in buttered pan. Cut when cool.

Mrs. W. David Counts (Mary)
Knox City

Chocolate Peanut Butter Clusters

Yields 5 dozen

1   (6 ounce) package milk
        chocolate chips
1   (12 ounce) package
        peanut butter chips
1   tablespoon creamy peanut
        butter
¼   of 1 (4 ounce) block
        paraffin
3½   cups Spanish peanuts,
        salted

In double boiler, melt paraffin; add chips and peanut butter. Blend until very creamy. Remove from heat and add peanuts, stirring thoroughly. Drop from teaspoon onto waxed paper. Cool until firm.

Mrs. Morris Abercrombie (Barbara)
Sulphur Springs

Apricot Sticks

1   pound ground apricots
1   ground orange
1¾   cups sugar
½   cup chopped pecans
Powdered sugar

Cook apricots, orange and sugar in saucepan 10 minutes after it comes to a boil, stirring constantly. Add pecans and mix well. Spread on waxed paper. Cool. Roll into small rolls. Dip in powdered sugar and place on waxed paper to "dry".

Texas Millionaires

Yields 5 to 6 pounds

3   (4½ ounce) Hershey bars,
       or 13½ ounces milk
       chocolate
2   (6 ounce) packages
       chocolate chips
1   tablespoon margarine
4½ cups sugar
1   (13 ounce) can evaporated
       milk
1   pint marshmallow cream
1   teaspoon vanilla
4   cups chopped nuts

Melt chocolate and margarine in saucepan. Remove from heat and set aside. Boil sugar and milk for 6 minutes. While this is cooking, place marshmallow cream and vanilla in large bowl. Pour in cooked sugar, milk mixture and chocolate and blend. Fold in nuts and drop on waxed paper or greased pan. Keep bowl in warm water when dropping to keep it soft enough.

Mrs. James Hamilton ('Cille)
Austin

Glazed Chocolate Dates

½   cup ground nuts
½   cup powdered sugar
2   tablespoons rum
1   (7 ounce) package pitted
       dates
1   small package semi-sweet
       chocolate pieces
1   tablespoon shortening
3   tablespoons light corn
       syrup
4   tablespoons milk

Mix ground nuts, sugar and rum together and stuff dates; set aside. In top of double boiler melt chocolate pieces over hot water. Stir in shortening, syrup and milk and stir until smooth. Remove chocolate glaze from heat and dip in both ends of the stuffed dates. Place on cooling rack to dry. May be necessary to dry for 1 to 2 days.

Mrs. John A. (Jack) Farrand (Phyllis)
Austin

Toffee

8	(1.45 ounce) Hershey bars
1	cup butter (not margarine)
1	cup sugar
3	tablespoons water
1	cup finely chopped almonds
Nut meal	

Lightly butter 9x9-inch pan. Arrange 4 Hershey bars in pan. Cook butter, sugar and water together over high heat until it begins to turn color, stirring constantly. Add 1 cup finely chopped almonds and continue cooking to 295° on candy thermometer. Quickly pour over chocolate bars in pan. Place additional Hershey bars on top. Let candy melt slightly and spread to cover. Sprinkle with nut meal. Break into pieces when cool.

Mrs. Harold Prichard (Ruth)
San Antonio

Microwave Pecan Pralines

Yields 3 dozen

1	cup brown sugar
1	cup sugar
⅓	cup light corn syrup
¼	cup water
1½	cups broken pecans
1	tablespoon margarine
1	teaspoon vanilla

In medium glass bowl mix together first four ingredients. Cook on high 7 to 9 minutes (238° - soft ball stage). Stir in last three ingredients. Let stand 2 minutes. Drop by tablespoon onto well-greased wax paper.

Mrs. Bill Abernathy (Mary Helen)
Fort Worth

Pralines

Yields 2 pounds

1	(16 ounce) box brown sugar
1	cup sugar
¼	cup butter
2	cups broken pecans
¼	cup white corn syrup
⅔	cup water
⅛	teaspoon salt
1	teaspoon vanilla

Combine all ingredients except vanilla in heavy saucepan. Cook until syrup reaches soft ball stage (238°). Remove from heat and cool slightly. Add vanilla and beat until it begins to thicken. Drop by spoonful onto wax paper.

Mrs. Stan Murrell (Sherry)
El Paso

Caramel Pecan Turtles

3	cups roasted pecan halves
1	pound caramels
2	tablespoons cream or evaporated milk
½	block paraffin
2	(8 ounce) bars chocolate

Arrange nuts on buttered waxed paper-lined baking sheets to resemble turtles. Combine caramels with cream in double boiler and melt. Pour caramel mixture over pecans; let cool in refrigerator. Place paraffin in top of double boiler and melt, adding broken pieces of chocolate and stirring until creamy. Dip turtles into mixture using tongs or fork and place on waxed paper. Place each turtle in candy liner to serve or in a box to store or share.

Mrs. James C. Ragan (Joyce)
Austin

Caramel Corn

Yields 3 quarts

3	quarts popcorn, popped
1	cup nuts
½	cup butter
1	cup brown sugar
¼	cup light corn syrup
½	teaspoon salt
½	teaspoon vanilla
¼	teaspoon baking soda

Spread popcorn and nuts in jellyroll pan. Melt butter and stir in brown sugar, corn syrup and salt. Bring to a boil and cook for 5 minutes without stirring. Remove from heat and stir in vanilla and baking soda. Pour over the popcorn and nuts and place in a 300° oven for 15 minutes. Remove from oven and stir well; return to oven and bake 15 minutes more. Remove from pan. Break apart and cool.

I usually double the recipe, as this is a favorite of our grandchildren.

Mrs. John Sockwell (Billie)
Arlington

Mom's Ice Cream

Yields 1 gallon

5	eggs
2½	cups sugar
3	tablespoons flour
1	quart milk
1	(13 ounce) can evaporated milk
2	tablespoons vanilla
1	quart milk

In large saucepan, beat eggs with a wire whisk, add sugar and flour. Add the milk a little at a time, stirring with whisk. Cook until mixture comes to a boil. Strain and chill. When ready to freeze, pour custard into freezer container. Add vanilla, evaporated milk and the second quart of milk. Freeze well.

Variations: Add two small packages of frozen (thawed) strawberries, before final milk. (six to eight peaches sugared; four to five ripe mashed bananas)

BLUE BELL, eat your heart out!!

Walter J. Dingler
Austin

334

Homemade Ice Cream

Yields 1 gallon

4 eggs
1 (8 ounce) carton whipping cream
1 cup sugar
¼ teaspoon salt
1 tablespoon vanilla
¼ teaspoon lemon extract
2 (14 ounce) cans sweetened condensed milk
Milk (approximately 1½ quarts)

Combine eggs, whipping cream, sugar, salt, vanilla and lemon extract in bowl. Mix thoroughly with mixer. Pour into freezer container, add condensed milk and stir well. Add milk to fill-line of freezer can. Stir well and freeze.

Mrs. Robert F. Mann (Louella)
Leander

Lemon Ice Cream

1½ pints whipping cream
Milk
1 cup fresh lemon juice
3 cups sugar
2 teaspoons lemon extract

Pour whipping cream into freezer container and add enough milk to fill ⅔ full. Add lemon juice, sugar and lemon extract. Mix well and freeze.

Mrs. Edgar Perry (Linda)
Austin

Fresh Peach Ice Cream

Yields 1½ gallons

6 eggs
1 (14 ounce) can sweetened condensed milk
1 cup sugar
2 cups mashed fresh peaches
2 teaspoons vanilla
Milk to fill freezer 2 inches from top

Mix all ingredients together except milk. Pour into freezer; add milk, stir and freeze.

Mrs. John B. Connally (Nellie)
Austin and Houston

Good News Apricot Squares

Bake at 375° for 20 to 25 minutes
Serves 10

1	(6 ounce) package dried apricots
⅔	cup orange juice
1	tablespoon margarine
½	cup applesauce
2	teaspoons vanilla
½	cup margarine
½	cup brown sugar, packed
1	cup whole wheat flour
1	cup uncooked oatmeal
½	cup wheat germ
1	teaspoon baking powder
¾	teaspoon cinnamon
½	teaspoon nutmeg
1	tablespoon sesame seeds
½	cup chopped nuts

Simmer apricots in orange juice until soft enough to mash with a fork. Add the tablespoon margarine, applesauce and vanilla. Mash it all together and set aside to cool slightly. Cream ½ cup margarine and sugar. Combine remaining ingredients and add to sugar-margarine mixture. Mix until crumbly. Cover bottom of 9x9-inch pan with half of the crumbly mixture. Spread with apricot filling and top with remaining crumbly mixture. Bake at 375° for 20 to 25 minutes.

Now the bad news ... 300 calories per serving if cut into 10 squares.

Cookbook Committee

Chocolate Ice Cream

Yields 1½ gallons

¼	cup cocoa
2½	cups sugar
⅛	teaspoon salt
¾	cup water
2	(14 ounce) cans sweetened condensed milk (stand in hot water before opening for easier pouring)
10	eggs
2	tablespoons vanilla
Milk (enough to fill freezer can to ¾ full)	

Sift together cocoa, sugar and salt. Mix water with dry ingredients in saucepan and bring to boil. Remove from heat and stir in canned milk. Set aside to cool. Beat eggs *well* and POUR THROUGH STRAINER. Add to chocolate mixture, then add vanilla. Pour into cold freezer can, fill can to ¾ full with homogenized milk and freeze.

This is a Weber family favorite handed down to me by LaVern's mother.

Mrs. LaVern E. Weber (Bette)
McLean, Virginia

Quick Chocolate Mousse

Serves 6

2 eggs
2 egg yolks
¼ teaspoon salt
6 ounces semi-sweet
chocolate chips, melted
and slightly cooled
1 (8 ounce) carton whipping
cream, *not* whipped
2 teaspoons vanilla *or*
4 teaspoons brandy *or* light
rum
Whipped cream for garnish

In mixing bowl beat eggs, yolks and salt with electric mixer until fluffy. Add cooled chocolate and beat till well blended. Add cream and vanilla and beat till mixture mounds and is smooth. Spoon into serving dishes and chill. Garnish with whipped cream.

This dessert is very rich.

Mrs. Harry Smith (Ginny)
Austin

Pineapple Cheesecake

Bake at 350° for 20 minutes

2 cups graham cracker
crumbs (or 26
crackers), crushed
¼ cup melted butter
2 tablespoons sugar
1 teaspoon vanilla
1 (20 ounce) can crushed
pineapple
2 tablespoons cornstarch
3 (8 ounce) packages cream
cheese, softened
1 cup sugar
4 eggs
Juice of 1 lemon
1 (8 ounce) carton sour
cream
1 tablespoon sugar
2 teaspoons vanilla

Mix crumbs, melted butter, 2 tablespoons sugar and vanilla. Pat in bottom of 9x13-inch baking dish. In saucepan, heat pineapple and cornstarch and spread over crust. In mixing bowl, combine cream cheese and sugar, then add eggs, one at a time. Add lemon juice. Pour over pineapple mixture. Bake at 350° for 20 minutes. Mix sour cream, 1 tablespoon sugar, and 2 teaspoons vanilla and pour over cake. Return to oven and bake 5 minutes at 400°.

This makes a large cheesecake and can easily be made the day before serving it.

Mrs. Thomas Stone (Claudette)
Temple

337

Tipsy Pudding

4   **eggs, separated**
½   **cup sugar**
2   **cups milk**
2   **envelopes unflavored gelatin**
¼   **cup water**
1   **teaspoon vanilla**
½   **cup whiskey**
1   **cup chopped dates**
1   **cup white raisins**
1   **cup chopped pecans**

Beat egg yolks with sugar. Add milk. Cook in double boiler until thick. Dissolve gelatin in water and add to milk mixture. Beat egg whites until stiff and fold into pudding. Gradually add 1 teaspoon vanilla and whiskey to the mixture. Fold in dates, raisins and nuts. Put into mold. Chill until firm. Serve with whipped cream.

Mary Shary
Mother of Mrs. Allan Shivers

Capirotada (Mexican Bread Pudding)

Bake at 350° for 30 minutes
Serves 6 to 8

4   **slices toasted white bread, cubed (Can use old bread, hamburger buns, hot dog buns, etc.)**
3   **cups milk, scalded (can use evaporated milk)**
1   **cup brown sugar**
1   **teaspoon nutmeg**
1½   **teaspoons cinnamon**
⅛   **teaspoon salt**
3   **eggs, well beaten**
¼   **cup butter, melted**
1   **teaspoon vanilla**
½   **cup pecans, chopped**
½   **cup seedless raisins**
1   **(3 ounce) package cream cheese, cubed**

Combine bread cubes and scalded milk in a buttered 2-quart baking dish; let soak for about 10 minutes. In a bowl, combine sugar with spices and salt, stir in beaten eggs and melted butter. Mix in rest of ingredients. Pour mixture over bread cubes and stir lightly until well blended. Bake for 30 minutes in a preheated 350° oven. Can be served warm or cold.

This is a traditional Lenten dish.

Mrs. Gilberto S. Pena (Teresa)
Weslaco

Bread Pudding With Rum Sauce

Bake at 350° for 30 minutes

4   cups broken pieces French bread (day-old preferably)
1   teaspoon cinnamon
½   cup raisins (more if desired)
2   tablespoons melted butter
4   eggs, slightly beaten
½   cup plus 2 tablespoons sugar
2   cups milk
1   teaspoon vanilla

Place pieces of bread in buttered 1½-quart deep baking dish. Sprinkle cinnamon, raisins and melted butter over bread and mix lightly. Mix beaten eggs, sugar, milk and vanilla. Pour over bread mixture. Bake at 350° for 30 minutes or until center is set.

RUM SAUCE

2   tablespoons flour and 1 tablespoon oil mixed to make a roux.
2   cups milk
½   stick margarine or butter
½   cup sugar
1   tablespoon nutmeg
1   tablespoon vanilla
1   tablespoon rum extract or to taste

In a medium saucepan, place milk, margarine and sugar and bring to a boil. Thicken with the roux stirring constantly. Remove from burner and add nutmeg, vanilla and rum. Mix thoroughly and serve warm over Bread Pudding.

Be careful . . . you won't believe you ate the whole thing!!!

Banana Nut Ice Cream

6   very ripe bananas
6   eggs
2   cups sugar
1   (13 ounce) can evaporated milk
2   tablespoons vanilla
1   cup chopped pecans
Milk

Mash bananas and set aside. Beat eggs until frothy, add sugar and continue beating until smooth. Add mashed bananas, evaporated milk and vanilla and continue beating until well blended. Add nuts. Pour into freezer container and fill with milk. Freeze.

Mrs. Joe Gartman (Vonnie)
Leander

DESSERTS

Strawberry Surprise

Bake at 400° for 7 minutes

1   large package strawberry
     flavored gelatin
1½   cups boiling water
2   (10 ounce) cartons frozen
     strawberries, do not
     thaw
1   (8 ounce) can crushed
     pineapple, undrained
2   cups crushed pretzels
¾   cup melted butter or
     margarine
3   tablespoons sugar
1   (9 ounce) carton whipped
     topping, thawed
1   (8 ounce) package cream
     cheese, softened
¾   cup sugar

Dissolve gelatin in boiling water and cool. Stir in strawberries and pineapple and refrigerate until slightly congealed. Mix crushed pretzels, butter and sugar and pat into a 9x13-inch glass dish. Bake at 400° for 7 minutes. Cool. Mix whipped topping, cream cheese and sugar until thoroughly blended. Spread over cooled crust. Spoon gelatin mixture over cream cheese mixture and refrigerate until completely congealed. Cut into squares to serve.

Mrs. David Bradford (Cindy)
Austin

Strawberry Thing

Serves a bunch!

1   angel food cake
4   (10 ounce) cartons frozen
     strawberries, thawed
1   large package instant
     vanilla pudding mix
3   cups milk
5 to 6 bananas
1   (8 ounce) carton whipped
     topping, thawed
1   punch bowl

Slice angel food cake in half and place one layer in bottom of punch bowl, cutting it if necessary. Spoon 2 of the cartons of strawberries over the cake. Mix instant pudding with milk and beat until thickened. Spread half of pudding over strawberries. Slice 2 or 3 bananas over the pudding. Repeat the above procedure by placing the other layer of cake on top, then 2 cartons strawberries, ½ of pudding, 2 or 3 sliced bananas and then cover this whole "thing" with whipped topping. Garnish as desired.

Mrs. Roy Hamor (Laverne)
Austin

Regal Cheesecake

Bake at 300° for 1 hour
Serves 10 to 12

1¼	cups fine sugar cookie crumbs
2	tablespoons butter or margarine
3	tablespoons sugar
2	(8 ounce) packages cream cheese, softened
1	cup sugar
5	eggs, separated
2	(8 ounce) cartons sour cream
1	teaspoon vanilla
1	teaspoon lemon juice
2	(10 ounce) boxes frozen whole strawberries (or fresh, if available)
1	(10 ounce) jar currant jelly (optional)

Blend crumbs, butter and sugar together; press in bottom of 9-inch springform pan. Cream together cream cheese, sugar, egg yolks, sour cream, vanilla and lemon juice. Beat thoroughly. Fold in stiffly beaten egg whites just until blended. Fill crumb-lined pan. Bake for 1 hour. Turn oven off and let cake set in oven 1 hour longer with door closed. Open oven door and let cake set 30 minutes longer. Refrigerate overnight. Arrange strawberries on top of cake, soften jelly over hot water and spoon over strawberries to glaze.

Mrs. Tip Lewis (Nita)
Raymond, Mississippi

Party Cheesecakes

Bake at 350° for 15 to 20 minutes
Yields 18 minature cheesecakes

18	vanilla wafers, whole
2	(8 ounce) packages cream cheese, softened
¾	cup sugar
2	eggs
1	tablespoon lemon juice
1	teaspoon vanilla extract
1	can cherry pie filling (or any flavor desired)
Whipped cream (optional)	

Place paper liners in 18 muffin cups. Put one whole vanilla wafer in bottom of each. Combine cream cheese, sugar, eggs, lemon juice and vanilla; beat until smooth and creamy. Fill each muffin cup ⅔ full. Bake at 350° for 15 to 20 minutes. Cool thoroughly. Place a teaspoonful of cherry pie filling on each or any other flavor desired. Place a dab of whipped cream on top, if desired.

Mrs. Kelly Cloud (Lisa)
Cedar Park

341

Cherry Cheesecake

Bake at 350° for 60 to 70 minutes
Serves 10

1¾   cup graham cracker
     crumbs
⅓   cup butter or margarine,
     softened
1¼   cup sugar
3   (8 ounce) packages cream
     cheese, softened
2   teaspoons vanilla extract
3   eggs
1   (8 ounce) carton sour
     cream
1   (21 ounce) can cherry pie
     filling

Thoroughly blend graham cracker crumbs, butter or margarine, and ¼ cup sugar. Press firmly against bottom and 2½ inches up sides of an 8-inch springform pan. Beat cream cheese until fluffy. Gradually add remaining 1 cup sugar and vanilla. Beat in eggs, one at a time. Fold in sour cream. Spread in prepared pan. Bake in preheated 350° oven for 60 to 70 minutes, or until firm. Turn off oven, leaving door slightly ajar. Allow cheesecake to remain in oven for 1 hour. Cool in pan and chill 4 hours, or overnight. Remove side of pan. Top with cherry pie filling.

Mrs. Harold A. Miller (Cheri)
Converse

Bavarian Cheesecake

2   (8 ounce) packages cream
     cheese, softened
2   packages unfilled lady
     fingers
1½ to 2 cups sugar (use 2 cups
     if not topping cake)
¼   cup fresh lemon juice
4   teaspoons vanilla
1   (8 ounce) carton whipping
     cream, whipped

Line a springform pan with lady fingers. Mix all other ingredients except cream. Stir in cream carefully. Fill pan and cover with plastic wrap. Refrigerate overnight. Before serving, decorate with fresh strawberries, cherry pie filling, or other fruit and optional whipped cream.

Mrs. John Muegge (Marjie)
Austin

Apricot Cheesecake

Bake at 350° for 40 to 45 minutes

CRUST

¾ cup walnuts, coarsely
  ground
¾ cup graham cracker
  crumbs
3 tablespoons melted oleo

Combine walnuts, graham cracker crumbs and butter. Press firmly into 10-inch springform pan.

FILLING

4 (8 ounce) packages cream
  cheese, softened
4 eggs
1 tablespoon lemon juice
1¼ cups sugar
2 teaspoons vanilla

In mixing bowl beat cream cheese until smooth. Add eggs, lemon juice, sugar and vanilla and mix thoroughly. Spoon over crumb crust. Set pan on baking sheet to catch any batter that may drip out. Bake for 40 to 45 minutes. Remove and let stand 15 minutes.

TOPPING

1 (16 ounce) carton sour
  cream
¼ cup sugar
1 teaspoon almond extract

Combine sour cream, sugar and almond extract, beating well. Spoon over cake; return to oven and bake 5 minutes. Let cool.

GLAZE

1 (12 ounce) jar apricot preserves
1 tablespoon cornstarch
¼ cup Amaretto
Water

In saucepan combine preserves, cornstarch and Amaretto. Stir over heat until cornstarch is dissolved. Let mixture cool and thicken. If too thick, add a little water. Spoon over cheesecake and refrigerate.

Delicious and well worth the extra effort. The flavor actually is better after it is refrigerated 2 to 3 days.

Mrs. Lewis King (Pat)
Austin

Heavenly Delight Dessert

Bake at 350° for 20 minutes
Serves 12 to 16

1   cup flour
½   cup margarine, softened
1   cup finely chopped
       pecans
1   (8 ounce) package cream
       cheese, softened
1   cup powdered sugar
1   (12 ounce) carton whipped
       topping
1   (4 ounce) package instant
       chocolate pudding mix
1   (4 ounce) package instant
       vanilla pudding mix
3   cups milk
1   teaspoon vanilla
Chopped pecans

In small mixing bowl combine flour, softened margarine and 1 cup pecans with pastry blender until crumbly. Pat into a 9x13-inch baking pan to form crust. Bake for 20 minutes and set out to cool. To mix first layer combine softened cream cheese, powdered sugar and ½ of the whipped topping. Mix well and spread over cooled crust. For second layer, mix pudding mixes, milk and vanilla. Beat until mixture thickens. Spread over cream cheese layer. Top with remainder of whipped topping. Sprinkle chopped pecans over top. Refrigerate, then cut in squares to serve.

Variations: May use butterscotch instant pudding mix or pistachio instant pudding mix or apricot pie filling.

Mrs. R.C. White (Elna)
El Paso

Mrs. Tip Lewis (Nita)
Raymond, Mississippi

The relatively mild climate of the Texas hill country allowed settlers to enjoy two growing seasons as long as water was available. Travellers of the time noted that the farmers and townspeople enjoyed a remarkable variety of vegetables and spices including mustard, parsley and leek. The dry climate was favorable to wheat which supplied white flour. Orchards were limited principally to figs and peaches but of such quality that the area is still well known for peaches.
—*Terry G. Jordan,* German Seed in Texas Soil

Frozen Chocolate Frango

Serves 18

18 cupcake liners
1 cup vanilla wafer crumbs
1 cup margarine
2 cups sifted powdered
sugar
4 ounces unsweetened
chocolate, melted
4 eggs
¾ teaspoon peppermint
flavoring
2 teaspoons vanilla
1 (8 ounce) carton whipping
cream whipped
Maraschino cherries for
decoration

Using an electric mixer, beat margarine and sugar. Add chocolate and beat thoroughly. Add eggs and beat until fluffy. Then add peppermint and vanilla. Sprinkle half of crumbs into 18 cupcake liners. Spoon chocolate mixture into liners and top with remaining crumbs. Freeze until firm. Top with whipped cream and decorate with cherries.

Mrs. Willard A. Shank (Elizabeth)
Sacramento, California

Easy Fruit Cobbler

Bake at 350° for 50 minutes

¾ cup flour
2 teaspoons baking powder
⅛ teaspoon salt
2 cups sugar
¾ cup milk
½ cup margarine
2 cups peaches or any fruit
desired

Sift flour, baking powder and salt together. Mix with 1 cup sugar; add milk and mix well. Melt margarine in 8-inch square baking dish. Pour batter into center of melted margarine, but do not stir. Mix 1 cup sugar with fruit and pour over batter. Bake at 350° for 50 minutes.

Variations: Any fresh or canned fruit can be used, or any of the fruit pie fillings can be used.

Mrs. John W. Daniel (Karen)
Houston

Mrs. Milton Herber (Peg)
Corpus Christi

Mrs. Bill Wagner (Cindy)
Grand Prairie

Blueberry Dessert

Bake at 350° for 20 minutes
Serves 12

2	cups graham cracker crumbs
½	cup powdered sugar
½	cup chopped pecans
½	cup margarine, melted
1	(8 ounce) package cream cheese, softened
1	cup sugar
2	tablespoons lemon juice
2	eggs
1	(21 ounce) can blueberry pie filling
1	(8 ounce) carton whipped topping

Combine crumbs, sugar, pecans and margarine. Mix all ingredients together and press into 9x13-inch pan. Mix cream cheese, sugar, lemon juice and eggs together and beat until smooth. Pour over crust and bake 20 minutes at 350°. Cool. Top with blueberry pie filling. Spread whipped topping over blueberry filling and cut into squares.

Mrs. Herbert G. Purtle (Jan)
Manor

Old Fashioned Fruit Cobbler

Bake at 350° for 45 minutes
Serves 8

1	cup sugar
⅛	teaspoon salt
1	cup flour
2	teaspoons baking powder
¾	cup milk
2	tablespoons butter
2	cups fruit
1	cup sugar
1	cup boiling water
1	teaspoon cinnamon

Combine first six ingredients; mix and beat until creamy. Pour into greased baking dish. Put the fruit on top and sprinkle with 1 cup of sugar. Pour 1 cup boiling water over mixture and sprinkle with cinnamon. Bake at 350° for 45 minutes.

This was my great-grandmother's recipe.

Mrs. John E. Mathis (Virginia)
Arlington

Chocolate Eclair Dessert

Serves 12 to 15

2   packets graham crackers
    (from 16 ounce box)
2   small boxes French vanilla
    instant pudding mix
3   cups milk
1   teaspoon vanilla (Mexican
    vanilla if available)
1   (9 ounce) carton whipped
    topping

Mix pudding, according to directions but only use 3 cups of milk. Add vanilla and beat to thicken. Fold in whipped topping thoroughly and refrigerate. Place whole double crackers in bottom of 9x13-inch casserole dish. This takes about 6 double crackers. Then pour ½ of pudding mixture over crackers and repeat with crackers and remainder of pudding, ending with a layer of crackers on top. Spread chocolate topping over graham crackers. Refrigerate several hours or overnight. Cut in squares when ready to serve.

CHOCOLATE TOPPING

3   tablespoons butter or
      margarine
1½   squares semi-sweet
      chocolate
2   teaspoons white Karo
1   teaspoon vanilla
1½   cups powdered sugar
3   tablespoons milk

Melt margarine and chocolate in saucepan. Add remaining ingredients and mix well with electric hand mixer. Add more or less milk to make it of spreading consistency.

You will love this dessert!!

Mrs. Lewis King (Pat)
Austin

Mousse au Chocolate

4	tablespoons water
1	package Sweet German chocolate
4	eggs, separated
¼	cup whipping cream, not whipped
2	tablespoons brandy *or* rum

In saucepan, melt chocolate in water over low heat. Remove from heat and stir well. Cool. Add egg yolks, one at a time, beating well after each addition. Add whipping cream and brandy and beat well. Beat egg whites to form stiff peaks and fold into chocolate mixture. Refrigerate several hours before serving.

Mrs. Arthur G. Coley (Susie)
San Antonio

Tartoni

Bake at 350° for 20 minutes
Serves 12

½	cup margarine, melted
1	cup finely chopped pecans
1	cup flour
¼	cup brown sugar
½	gallon vanilla ice cream, softened
1	(10 ounce) jar Smucker's apricot preserves

Melt margarine, add pecans, flour and sugar. Stir well. Spoon into a 9x13x2-inch dish. Bake at 350° for 20 minutes. Stir occasionally. Remove ½ of the crumb mixture and reserve for topping. Pat remaining mixture in bottom of pan. Spread half of the ½ gallon of ice cream on top. Spread preserves over ice cream and cover with the remaining ice cream. Top with reserved crumb topping, cover and freeze.

This dessert will keep indefinitely.

Mrs. John B. Garrett (June)
Arlington

Vinegar Roll

Bake at 400°

2	cups flour
1	teaspoon salt
⅔	cup shortening
6	tablespoons water
½	cup butter, softened
2½	cups water
⅔	cup vinegar
2	cups sugar

Combine first 4 ingredients as you do a pie crust. Roll out pie dough in thin oblong shape. Spread with ¼ cup butter. Sprinkle with 1 cup sugar. Roll as a jellyroll and slice in 1-inch slices. Place in baking dish and spread the remainder of the butter on top. Combine 2½ cups water, vinegar and 1 cup sugar in pan. Bring to boil. Remove from heat and pour over dough slices. Bake at 400° until golden brown.

This will be creamy. Tart and delicious!

Mrs. Henry Fouts (Gladis)
Austin

English Trifle

½	pound cake *or* 1 yellow cake layer
½	cup currant or strawberry jam
½	cup sherry
¼	cup blanched almonds
2	cups soft custard
1	(8 ounce) carton whipping cream, whipped

Spread jam over cut cake or layer cake. Pour ¼ cup sherry over mixture. Sprinkle almonds over and spoon custard and other ¼ cup sherry over trifle. Chill. Pile whipped cream over top just before serving.

CUSTARD

1¾	cups milk
3	tablespoons flour
2	egg yolks
¼	cup sugar
½	teaspoon salt
½	teaspoon vanilla

Mix all ingredients and cook until thickened. Cool before spooning over Trifle.

A favorite family dessert from my home in England.

Mrs. John A. (Jack) Farrand (Phyllis)
Austin

349

Banana Split Dessert

Bake at 350° for 15 to 20 minutes

1½   cups flour
¾   cup plus 2 tablespoons
      margarine, softened
2   tablespoons sugar
1   cup chopped pecans
1   (16 ounce) box powdered
      sugar
2   eggs
1   cup margarine, softened
1   (20 ounce) can crushed
      pineapple, *well* drained
3 to 4 medium bananas, sliced
1   (5½ ounce) can chocolate
      syrup
1   (9 ounce) container
      whipped topping
Chopped cherries and pecans
      (optional)

Mix flour, margarine, sugar and pecans. Press into a 9x13-inch baking dish and bake. Cool completely. Mix powdered sugar, eggs and margarine. Beat well and spread over cooled crust. Then layer the crushed pineapple, bananas and drizzle the chocolate syrup over. Spread whipped topping over all. Garnish with chopped cherries and pecans.

Crust Variation:

2   cups graham cracker
      crumbs
1   stick margarine, softened

Mix together and press into bottom and sides of 9x13-inch pan. Proceed with above filling.

Mrs. Leonard Tallas (Jean)
Austin

Mrs. Thomas R. Hyde (Edna)
San Juan

Sweet Cobbler Dough

Bake at 350° for 40 to 50 minutes

3 cups flour
5 teaspoons baking powder
1½ teaspoons salt
3 tablespoons sugar
1 teaspoon cream of tartar
¾ cup butter or margarine, melted
1 cup milk
1 egg, beaten

In mixing bowl combine all dry ingredients. Mix in melted butter, milk and beaten eggs and mix thoroughly. Roll out on floured board about ⅓-inch thick. Place in 12-inch square baking pan or 9x13-inch baking pan. Then add the fruit of your choice. Use about 3 cups sweetened fruit and juice for 12-inch pan and a little more for larger pan. 1 tablespoon cornstarch may be added to juice to thicken. Cut remaining dough into 1-inch wide strips and lay across fruit to form lattice top. Sprinkle top with cinnamon and sugar. Bake at 350° for 40 to 50 minutes.

Mrs. Martin Haskett (Gloria)
Aransas Pass

Macaroon Pudding

1 tablespoon unflavored gelatin
2 cups milk
3 eggs, separated
½ cup sugar
1 teaspoon vanilla
¼ cup maraschino cherries, chopped
¾ cup pecans, chopped
12 almond macaroons (see index)
1 (8 ounce) carton whipping cream, whipped
Whipped cream, for garnish

Soften gelatin in ¼ cup milk. Make custard of egg yolks, sugar and remaining milk in heavy saucepan. Stirring constantly, cook until mixture thickens or coats the spoon. Remove from heat, add softened gelatin and stir until blended. Chill until mixture begins to set. Blend in vanilla, maraschino cherries, chopped pecans and almond macaroons, broken into pieces. Beat egg whites until stiff and glossy, fold into pudding. Whip ½ pint of whipping cream and fold into pudding. Pour into individual molds. Chill until set and garnish with whipped cream.

This is a Christmas dessert in my family, and a Virginia recipe from my mother's people in Hampton, Virginia.

Mrs. Louis Holder (Louise)
Many, Louisiana

351

Grandma Koepsel's Rice Custard

Bake at 375° for 1 hour
Serves 6

1	cup cooked rice, drained
1	quart warm milk (not hot)
5	eggs, beaten
1	cup sugar
¼	teaspoon salt
¼	teaspoon cinnamon
¼	teaspoon nutmeg

Mix all ingredients together except cinnamon and nutmeg. Pour into a 1½ or 2-quart pyrex loaf pan. Sprinkle nutmeg and cinnamon on top, lightly. Begin baking at 375° for 1 hour. If mixture begins to bubble too much, turn down the heat to 350° and then to 325°. Knife inserted will come out clean when done.

Mrs. Jimmie F. Johnson (Judy)
Corpus Christi

Christmas Plum Pudding

Bake at 350° for 30 to 45 minutes

3	cups chopped suet (ask your butcher)
3	cups sugar
3	cups molasses
3	cups raisins and/or any other candied fruits i.e., pineapple, cherries, etc.
9	cups flour
6	eggs
2	teaspoons cinnamon
6	teaspoons soda
Enough apple cider to make a stiff batter	

Combine all ingredients and spoon into a jar; tie a cover over top and keep in a cool place. When ready to serve allow 1 tablespoon of batter per person and place in individual baking dishes. Set dishes into pan with water to half cover baking dishes. Steam until done, approximately 30 to 45 minutes.

This is good served with a hard sauce. This is a family recipe used for four generations at Christmas.

Mrs. William Green (Irene)
Houston

Preacher's Delight

½   pound vanilla wafers,
        crushed
1½   cups powdered sugar
½   cup butter, softened
2   eggs
1   (8 ounce) carton whipping
        cream, whipped
Small bottle maraschino
        cherries, drain and
        quarter
¾   cup finely chopped
        pecans
½   teaspoon vanilla

Crush vanilla wafers until very fine. Place ½ of crumbs in 8x8-inch glass dish. Cream 1 cup powdered sugar, butter and eggs and beat thoroughly. Spoon over wafer crumbs. Combine whipped cream, remainder of powdered sugar, cherries, pecans and vanilla. Spoon over egg mixture and sprinkle remaining crumbs over top. Refrigerate overnight before serving.

Mrs. Robert Preston (Judy)
Indian Mills, New Jersey

Ricotta Cheesecake

Bake at 300° for 1½ hours

2   (8 ounce) packages cream
        cheese, softened and
        whipped
1   (8 ounce) carton ricotta
        cheese
2   cups sugar
4   eggs, lightly beaten
1   teaspoon vanilla
1   stick butter, melted
3   tablespoons flour
3   tablespoons cornstarch
1½   tablespoons lemon juice
1   (8 ounce) carton sour
        cream

Mix together cheeses, sugar, eggs, vanilla and butter. Add flour and cornstarch and mix well. Add lemon juice and sour cream and mix well. Grease cheesecake pan, pour mixture in and cook at 300° for 1½ hours. Let cool in oven with door open for 1 hour. Remove and refrigerate until next day.

Mrs. P. Rowland Greenwade (Karen)
Austin

Artillery Punch

Yields 2½ gallons of punch base

1 (4 ounce) can gunpowder
green tea
2 quarts cold water
Juice of 9 oranges
Juice of 9 lemons
1 (1 pound) package light
brown sugar
½ cup light brown sugar
2 (10 ounce) jars maraschino
cherries, drained
2 (50.7 ounce) bottles rhine or
catawba wine
1 quart light rum
1 quart rye whisky
1 quart gin
1 (25.4 ounce) bottle brandy
½ cup benedictine
Champagne or club soda,
chilled

Combine tea and water; let stand overnight. Stir fruit juices into tea; strain. Combine tea and remaining ingredients except champagne in a 3 gallon crock or glass container. Cover lightly and let stock ferment 2 to 6 weeks. Strain stock; discard cherries and pour liquid into bottles. Chill as needed. At serving time, dilute each gallon of chilled stock with 1 quart champagne and pour over ice.

Paul N. Biediger, Jr.
Foy R. Spann
San Antonio

When Texas voted for the Articles of Secession, the dissent was not insubstantial. The most famous dissenter was Governor Sam Houston who resigned his office rather than oppose the Union. But once the decision was made to join the Confederacy, the Texas militia served with distinction. Terry's Texas Rangers were without equal. Hood's First Texas is remembered today by 1st Battalion, 1st Brigade, 49th Armored Division which carries the name "First Texas."

Texts-Style Chili Dip

Serves 100

6	pounds ground beef
2	tablespoons oil
1	cup flour
2	(10 ounce) cans beef consommé
6	large onions, chopped
2	tablespoons chili powder
2	tablespoons powdered comino
1	tablespoon oregano
2	tablespoons salt
6	pounds Cheddar cheese, cubed
12	(16 ounce) bags Doritos *or*
12	(16 ounce) packages of corn tortillas, quartered and fried

Sauté ground beef in a large pot. It will take several times to cook all the meat. When cooked, remove all meat, drain, and return 2 tablespoons fat to pot. Blend in flour, add 1 can heated consommé, stirring until mixture is smooth. Return beef to pot, add onions, remaining consommé, chili powder, comino, oregano and salt. Simmer for 30 minutes, stirring often. Turn up heat and stir continually until it becomes thick.

This can be frozen, or will keep in the refrigerator a couple of days. Reheat in 6 parts, so store either way in 6 equal containers.

When ready to serve, put one part in the top of a double boiler with 1 pound of Cheddar cheese cubes. In 15 to 20 minutes, the cheese will be melted. The second part can be heating while the first part is being eaten from a chafing dish. Serve with Doritos or fried quarters of corn tortillas.

Glenn Whatley
Waco
One of the delicious recipes from Glenn Whatley Catering Service.

Canned and dehydrated foods were introduced to the Army diet in 1857. However, the basic ration was salt beef or pork and hardtack. Potatoes were introduced to the ration in 1862. As a result of the meager fare, supplements were obtained by "foraging" or by local procurement.
—James A. Huston, The Sinews of War: Army Logistics 1775-1953, *United States Army, Washington, D.C., 1966*

Jalapeño Cornbread

Bake at 350° for 1 hour
Serves 25

6	cups yellow cornmeal
1	(16 ounce) can cream style corn
2	teaspoons sugar
3	teaspoons salt
2	cups chopped onion
2½	cups grated Cheddar cheese
3	teaspoons baking powder
2	cups vegetable oil
6	eggs
3	cups sweet milk
¾	cup chopped jalapeño peppers

Mix all ingredients as listed. Pour into 2 9x16-inch ungreased pans and bake in a preheated oven at 350° for one hour.

Glenn Whatley
Waco

Bonfire Chili

Serves 20 to 25

4	pounds coarsely ground meat (beef, pork, venison)
2	medium onions, chopped
2	Bell peppers, chopped
1	cup chili powder
4	tablespoons comino
2	tablespoons crushed red pepper (or cayenne)
4	(8 ounce) cans Rotel tomatoes
2	(12 ounce) cans stale beer
1	cup Masa (tortilla flour)

Combine ground meat with onions, Bell pepper and brown in a little hot oil. Drain. Add chili powder, comino, red pepper, Rotel tomatoes and beer. Simmer 2 to 4 hours over a campfire or on low heat. Before serving, mix masa flour and enough water to make a thin paste. Blend into chili mixture and cook for 30 more minutes.

This recipe evolved over 2 years of "cookin for the troops" (Texas A&M students) as they worked building the annual Bonfire. The authentic version includes ½ cup fresh Copenhagen Snuff and ½ teaspoon gunpowder!!!

L. James Starr, III
College Station

Chili Con Carne

Yields 6 quarts

2	cups pinto beans (pre-soak the night before in salt water)
½	cup olive oil
6	pounds chili meat (lean) (or 6 pounds rump roast cut into ½-inch squares)
2	cups very finely minced onion
2	tablespoons very finely minced garlic
2	large Bell peppers, minced
2	large bay leaves
2	teaspoons oregano
3	tablespoons chili powder
2	teaspoons ground cumin
½	teaspoon cayenne pepper
1	teaspoon freshly ground black pepper
2	tablespoons paprika
4	teaspoons crushed red pepper
9	tablespoons flour
2	(16 ounce) cans Campbell's double strength chicken broth
1	(16 ounce) can water
2	cans whole tomatoes, cut up
4	teaspoons sugar
½	cup cracker crumbs
Salt to taste	

Cook beans until tender, approximately 2½ hours. Meanwhile, heat olive oil over low fire in a large heavy saucepan (must hold minimum 6 quarts). Add meat, stirring frequently until it loses its red color. Add onions, garlic, Bell pepper, bay leaves, oregano, chili powder, cumin, cayenne pepper, black pepper, paprika, and crushed red peppers. Stir well. Cover pan and simmer for 10 minutes. Stir in flour, blending well. Add chicken broth, water, tomatoes, bean water (not to exceed 16 ounces), and bring to a boil. Reduce flame and simmer about 1 hour. Stir in sugar, cracker crumbs and beans and simmer approximately 1 hour more. Add salt if necessary.

To make hotter, add more crushed peppers and chili powder 1 teaspoon at a time until desired taste is achieved. This test must be done after cooking ½ hour, in order to allow the additional spices to cook in.

David Guettner
Freeport

Throughout the period of the Republic, the Mexican War, and the Civil War, the militia within Texas was composed of locally organized and commanded units. In 1870 the Militia Act provided for organization of the militia on a statewide basis as the Texas Volunteer Guard. By 1896, the Texas Volunteer Guard consisted of 48 companies of 2,461 officers and enlisted men.
    —*Walter Prescott Webb, ed.,* Handbook of Texas, *Texas State Historical Association, Austin, 1952.*

Hopkins County Chicken Stew

Yields 18 to 20 gallons
Serves 75 to 100

10 to 12 fryers or 5 hens, cut up
Water
5   gallons canned tomatoes
10   pounds potatoes, diced
5   pounds onions, diced
¾   gallon cream style corn
2   pounds butter
½   cup Morton's chili blend or
       chili powder
½   cup sugar
Salt and pepper to taste (and it
       takes a lot of testing)
Hot peppers may be added if
       you like it real hot

Put chickens in pot with water enough to be about 2 inches above chicken. Cook until chicken is tender enough to be boned. Remove chicken from pot, cool, bone and return to pot. Add tomatoes, potatoes and onions. Cook about an hour then add seasonings. Don't add corn until just before serving; it will stick if cooked too long. All this takes about 3 to 4 hours. If cooking over a wood fire, pull the wood away when you add the corn. The stew will stay hot about an hour in the black pot. This is cooked in a cauldron (in East Texas we call this a black wash pot) outside over wood fire or a butane burner.

In Sulphur Springs, we have a Hopkins County Stew Contest each fall during our Fall Festival. This is the recipe I use in the contest.

Mrs. Morris Abercrombie (Barbara)
Sulphur Springs

In 1858, the Militia Act directed that state militia be organized. In 1861, under direction of Governor Edward Clark, Adjutant General William Byrd directed the organization of companies of not less than thirty-two nor more than one hundred. These militia units were vital to the protection of the western frontier against Indians and federal forces and the protection of the border with Mexico where bandits ranged. Significant members and leaders of these units were the "Tejanos," Texans of Mexican ancestry who served with marked distinction.
—Jerry Don Thompson, Vaqueros in Blue and Gray, Presidial Press, Austin, 1976

Texas Union Beef Stew

Yields 100 (6 ounce) servings

15½	pounds beef stew meat, cubed
2¾	gallons water
2½	tablespoons liquid smoke
2½	tablespoons Kitchen Bouquet
⅓	cup salt
¼	cup pepper
2	tablespoons sugar
1	teaspoon Tabasco sauce
2¾	teaspoons garlic powder
½	cup seasoning salt
½	cup Worcestershire sauce
1	cup flour
½	cup water
2	cups catsup
3½	pounds yellow onions, chopped
4½	pounds carrots, sliced
3½	pounds Bell pepper, chopped
2	pounds celery, chopped
4½	pounds potatoes, quartered

Brown meat in kettle. Add water and all spices except catsup. Bring to a boil and let simmer until meat is tender. About 1½ hours. Mix flour and ½ cup water until smooth. Add to kettle to thicken. Add vegetables and catsup. Simmer until vegetables are tender.

Beans at Their Best

4	pounds pinto beans
2	large chopped onions
2	(6½ pound) cans Rotel tomatoes
1	pound bacon
Chili powder	
2	(12 ounce) cans Coca Cola
Salt	

Put beans in large pot and let soak overnight. Dice onion in small pieces and sauté until soft. Add onions to beans, along with tomatoes, bacon and chili powder. Simmer over medium heat for about 3 hours. Add Coca Cola and cook over low heat for 2 hours more. Salt to taste. Continue cooking until beans are tender. Serve with fried venison for a meal fit for a king!

The reason for the cans of Coca Cola is to remove the force behind the beans!

James R. Dickson
Bonham

Duck and Sausage Gumbo

3   cups flour
3½   cups cooking oil
A mixture of 6 cups of: onion,
Bell pepper and celery
2   gallons water
8   large ducks, cut into
       serving pieces and
       browned in oil
5   tablespoons salt
2   teaspoons black pepper
1   teaspoon red pepper
Tabasco sauce to taste
2   pounds smoked sausage
       (hot links)
½   cup chopped green onion
       tops
Canned shrimp or crab meat
       (optional)

Mix flour and oil; cook until dark brown, stirring constantly. (This is a roux.) Remove from fire and add 6 cups mixture of onion, Bell pepper and celery. Add water (a small amount at a time). When water is all added, return to fire. Add browned duck, salt, pepper and Tabasco. Cook slowly until duck meat is tender and falls off the bone. Remove ducks from liquid, bone and return to pot. Skim off fat, or refrigerate overnight and skim off congealed fat. Reheat and add sausage, cut into slices. Cook 1 hour more. Season to taste again, add chopped onion tops and canned shrimp or crab, if using, just before serving over rice. It freezes beautifully, and just gets better, the more it's warmed up!

A good Louisiana cook can make gumbo from almost anything, but in our family, duck and sausage gumbo and seafood gumbo are the very best.

Mrs. Louis E. Holder, Jr. (Louise)
Many, Louisiana (Toledo Bend Lake)

Established as a summer encampment for the Texas Volunteer Guard in 1890, Camp Mabry was named in 1892, by vote of the companies, to honor Adjutant General W. H. Mabry. The Camp served as headquarters for the Texas Volunteer Guard and for the Texas Rangers who were under the command of the Adjutant General until 1935. The Camp served as a training and supply facility during the punitive force activity against Francisco (Pancho) Villa in 1916. It later served as a mobilization point, training station and demobilization point for the 36th Division in World War I and World War II. The Camp now houses the Adjutant General's Department; the Headquarters, State Area Command for Texas (STARC); the Headquarters, 49th Armored Division; and several subordinate units including the Texas National Guard Academy.

—Walter Prescott Webb, ed., Handbook of Texas,
Texas State Historical Association, Austin, 1952,
Handbook of Texas – Supplement.

Golden Hominy

Bake at 350° for 1½ hours
Serves 40

10 (1 pound, 14 ounces each) cans golden hominy
20 green onions, diced
1 (4 ounce) can sliced pimientos
9 ounces seasoned bread crumbs
6 pounds sour cream
Salt and pepper to taste
Parmesan cheese

Mix together and put in baking dish. Sprinkle generously on top with Parmesan cheese, cover with foil and bake for 1½ hours.

Mrs. William F. Engel (Sharon)
Reno, Nevada

Hot Cha Cha

Serves 20

4 (16 ounce) bags Doritos or Fritos
2 pounds pinto beans, cooked
Meat sauce (recipe below)
1 pound Cheddar cheese, grated
2 heads lettuce, shredded
2 purple onions, thinly sliced
Guacamole (8 to 10 avocados, your favorite recipe)
2 (16 ounce) cartons sour cream

MEAT SAUCE
6 to 8 pounds ground meat
1 cup chopped onions
2 cloves garlic, chopped
2 (16 ounce) cans tomato sauce
2 (4 ounce) cans green chilies, chopped

Sauté meat, onion and garlic. Add remaining ingredients and simmer 30 minutes. Serve in chafing dish.

Build your own Hot Cha Cha salad from ingredients arranged on buffet or table in the order listed.

This is a great recipe for a large group (especially youth groups). Everyone loves to build their own!

Mrs. Thomas Stone (Claudette)
Temple

Picadillo

Serves 100

10 pounds ground beef
5 Bell peppers, chopped
25 large tomatoes, chopped (whole canned may be used)
6 (6 ounce) cans tomato paste
5 (8 ounce) cans tomato sauce
10 large onions, chopped
2 cups dark raisins
3 cups white raisins
4 packages onion soup mix
Salt and pepper to taste

In a Dutch oven, sauté ground beef and drain. Add remaining ingredients, mix well and simmer slowly for 2½ to 3 hours. If mixture becomes too thick, add water. Serve in a chafing dish as a dip.

Mrs. Jackie D. Stephenson (Mary)
San Marcos

Best Little Cookie In Texas (Circa 1954)

Bake at 275° for 20 minutes
Yields 20 dozen small cookies

4 eggs, beaten
2 cups sugar
1 teaspoon cinnamon
2 teaspoons cloves
8 cups chopped pecans
1 pound dates, chopped
1 pound raisins
3 cups flour
1¼ cups butter, melted
2 teaspoons soda
1 tablespoon water

Cream beaten eggs and sugar. Stir in cinnamon and cloves. Combine pecans, dates, raisins and flour and add to sugar mixture. Beat well and gradually beat in melted butter. Mix soda in water and add to dough. Mix thoroughly. This dough must be stiff. Drop by teaspoon on greased cookie sheet and bake for 20 minutes.

This is an original recipe from the cook at the La Grange "Chicken Ranch"!

Cookbook Committee

Dishpan Cookies

Bake at 325° for 12 minutes
Yields 12 dozen

2　cups sugar
2　cups brown sugar
2　cups salad oil
2　teaspoons vanilla
4　eggs
4　cups flour
2　teaspoons baking soda
1　teaspoon salt
1　cup coconut
1　cup chopped nuts
1½　cups oatmeal
4　cups cornflakes, crushed
1　cup chopped dates
　　(optional)

Use large bowl or dishpan for mixing the ingredients. Cream first four ingredients. Add eggs one at a time, mixing well. Add flour, soda and salt and mix well. Set aside. Mix remaining ingredients and add to flour mixture, using hands to mix. Drop by teaspoon or shape into balls and place on lightly greased cookie sheet. Bake for 12 minutes.

Mrs. Gayle Squyres (Patsy)
Clifton

New Orleans Pralines

Yields 200 small pralines

½　cup butter
3　(13 ounce) cans
　　evaporated milk
3　cups whipping cream
9　cups sugar
1　(16 ounce) box light brown
　　sugar
4　cups finely minced pecans
2　teaspoons vanilla
4　cups pecan halves

Melt butter, add evaporated milk, cream, sugars and minced pecans. Boil until mixture thickens (245°). Take from heat. Add vanilla and pecan halves. Beat until smooth. Drop from teaspoon onto a greased cookie sheet.

Nut Bon Bons

Yields 100 small bon bons

2 pounds powdered sugar
1 (14 ounce) can sweetened condensed milk
2 cups Angel Flake coconut
1 teaspoon vanilla
½ cup margarine
1 pound chopped pecans

DIPPING MIXTURE
2 (8 ounce) Hershey bars or chocolate chips
⅔ bar paraffin

Combine sugar, milk, coconut and vanilla. Blend well. Melt margarine and pour over pecans. Work this into sugar mixture. Roll into ¾-inch balls and chill or freeze before dipping in chocolate dipping mixture. Melt paraffin in double boiler over medium heat, add broken pieces of chocolate bars, or chocolate chips. Stir until thoroughly melted and blended. Using tongs or a dipping spoon or toothpicks, dip to cover with chocolate and place on wax paper to set.

Mrs. Jerry Duffy (Valerie Starr)
College Station

Mrs. James C. Ragan (Joyce)
Austin

Flying Saucers

Bake at 350° for 10 to 15 minutes
Yields 50 to 60 large

5½ sticks butter or margarine, softened
2 pounds brown sugar
4 eggs
10 ounces molasses
½ tablespoon salt
1 tablespoon allspice
1 tablespoon cinnamon
¾ tablespoon baking soda
6¼ cups flour
1 (1 pound, 2 ounce) box oatmeal
1 to 1½ cups raisins, optional

In a large bowl, cream the butter and sugar. Add eggs and molasses. Then add spices and baking soda. Add flour, then oatmeal. Stir in raisins, if desired. Let dough stand for 30 minutes. Scoop dough out with an ice cream dipper. Place 5 to 6 scoops on a greased cookie sheet and pat flat with wet hands. Bake for 10 to 15 minutes but *do not overbake*. Remove from pan while hot.

Dredge Yeast Rolls

Bake at 425° until brown
Serves 50

7   packages dry yeast
1   teaspoon sugar
2   cups warm water
2   (13 ounce) cans
      evaporated milk
2   milk cans hot tap water
6   tablespoons sugar
3   tablespoons salt
2   cups cooking oil
Flour

Mix yeast, sugar and warm water. Let rest for 15 minutes. Add milk, hot water, sugar and salt. Now start adding flour to make a light paste. Then add the oil, mix well, keep adding flour till the dough does not stick to the pot. It will still be tacky but not sticky.

Let rise for 1 to 1½ hours, then push down dough on a floured table, cut off 1/4 to 1/5 and knead dough, then roll out to about ½-inch to ⅝-inch thick, cut with a #3 can and put on a greased pan, touching. Repeat with the rest of the dough. Let rise 1 hour. Bake at 425° until golden brown.

Bobby Newman
Port Neches

This is the "famous" recipe from the cook with the 211th Engineer Detachment (Dredge).

Crispy Cornbread

Bake at 425° for 25 minutes
Serves 25

1½   cups sifted flour
3   cups yellow cornmeal
2   tablespoons baking
      powder
¼   cup sugar
2   teaspoons salt
⅓   cup eggs
2   cups milk
½   cup butter, melted

Sift together dry ingredients. Combine eggs, milk and melted butter. Add to dry ingredients and stir to blend. Pour into well greased 16½x10½-inch baking pan. Bake for 25 minutes at 425°.

I Am The Guard

ivilian in Peace, Soldier in War . . . of security and honor, for three centuries I have been the custodian, I am the Guard. ❧

I was with Washington in the dim forests, fought the wily warrior, and watched the dark night bow to the morning. ★ At Concord's bridge, I fired the fateful shot heard 'round the world. ★ I bled on Bunker Hill. ★ My footprints marked the snows at Valley Forge. ★ I pulled a muffled oar on the barge that bridged the icy Delaware. ★ I stood with Washington on the sun-drenched heights of Yorktown. ★ I saw the sword surrendered . . . I am the Guard. ★ I pulled the trigger that loosed the long rifle's havoc at New Orleans. ★ These things I knew – I was there! ★ I saw both sides of the War between the States – I was there! ★ The hill at San Juan felt the fury of my charge. ★ The far plains and mountains of the Philippines echoed to my shout . . . On the Mexican border I stood . . . I am the Guard. ★ The dark forest of the Argonne blazed with my barrage. ★ Chateau Thierry crumbled to my cannonade. ★ Under the arches of victory I marched in legion – I was there! ★ I am the Guard. I bowed briefly on the grim Corregidor, then saw the light of liberation shine on the faces of my comrades. ★ Through the jungle and on the beaches, I fought the enemy, beat, battered and broke him. ★ I raised our banner to the serene air on Okinawa – I scrambled over Normandy's beaches – I was there! . . . I am the Guard. ★ Across the 38th Parallel I made my stand. ★ I flew MIG Alley – I was there! . . . I am the Guard. ❧

Soldier in war, civilian in peace . . . I am the Guard. ❧

I was at Johnstown, where the raging waters boomed down the valley. ★ I cradled the crying child in my arms and saw the terror leave her eyes. ★ I moved through smoke and flame at Texas City. ★ The stricken knew the comfort of my skill. ★ I dropped the food that fed the starving beast on the frozen fields of the west and through the towering drifts I ploughed to rescue the marooned. ★ I have faced forward to the tornado, the typhoon, and the horror of the hurricane and flood – these things I know – I was there! . . . I am the Guard. ★ I have brought a more abundant, a fuller, a finer life to our youth. ★ Wherever a strong arm and valiant spirit must defend the Nation, in peace or war, wherever a child cries, or a woman weeps in time of disaster, there I stand . . . I am the Guard. ★ For three centuries a soldier in war, a civilian in peace – of security and honor, I am the custodian, now and forever . . . I am the Guard. ❧

Contributor's Index

A

Abel, Mrs. Thomas J., III (Laverne) 325
Abercrombie, Mrs. Morris (Barbara) 100, 327, 330, 358
Abernathy, Mrs. Bill (Mary Helen) 171, 332
Abrahamson, Mrs. Edward D. (Trisha) 228
Adair, Mrs. Bennie (Carol) 116, 279
Adams, Mrs. John (Eleanor) 257, 267, 311
Ahner, Mrs. Alfred F. (Betty) 41
Allen, Mrs. Arthur (Billie) 274, 318
Allen, Mrs. George (Frances) 192
Anderson, Mrs. Gene (Becky) 162
Anderson, Mrs. Jack D. (Mary Emma) 254, 305
Anderson, Mrs. Robert W. (Bertie) 269, 314
Andrews, Mrs. Vernon (Grace) 30, 145, 316
Arnold, Fran 300
Arnold, Mrs. Watson (Mary Beck) 219, 255, 309
Ayers, Ross 16

B

Bachle, Mrs. Cliff (Linda) 161, 194, 217
Baitz, Joe 175
Baker, Mrs. Darrel (Linda) 136, 191, 232
Balagia, Mrs. Ed (Billie) 122
Barmore, Mrs. Gaston (Camille) 154, 156, 160, 218
Barton, Kenneth P. 234
Beal, Mrs. Mike (Sherilyn) 48, 298
Bell, Roberta 62
Bennett, Mrs. Scott (Charlene) 99, 290
Berry, Mrs. Thomas (JoAnn) 227, 240
Biediger, Paul N., Jr. 354
Binder, Mrs. Edward C. (Roma) 18, 123
Birdwell, Mrs. Arthur (Becky) 120, 167
Biscomb, Mrs. David (Lucretia) 247, 280
Bishop, Mrs. Thomas S. (Bettymarie) 13
Black, Mrs. Allen (Wanda) 230, 257
Black, Mrs. Charles (Jo) 216, 221, 222
Blackshear, Mrs. Harold (Marilyn) 51
Blackwell, Mrs. Thomas D. (Rosemary) 304, 312
Blakeslee, Mrs. J. Travis (Gladys) 55, 56, 86, 104, 105, 109, 112, 147, 215, 259, 266
Blatsos, Mrs. John (Aphrodite) 11, 133
Block, Mrs. Robert H., Jr. (Debbie) 246, 313
Boehm, Mrs. E. Lewis (Marsha) 126
Bond, Mrs. Christopher S. (Carolyn) 14
Bostick, Mrs. Francis X. (Helen Timpson) 320
Bottoms, John 190, 201
Bottoms, Mrs. John (Diane) 57, 69, 120, 122, 143, 178, 223
Bowers, Mrs. George (Jonnie) 65, 119, 130, 228, 291
Bradford, Mrs. David (Cindy) 340
Briscoe, Mrs. Dolph (Janey) 30, 94
Brissette, Mrs. Ron (Kerin) 66, 81

Brito, Mrs. Richard (Joanne) 232
Brown, Marvin 93
Brown, Mrs. Marvin (Shirley) 118, 322
Buettner, Mrs. Ron (Cindy) 129
Butler, Mrs. Bernard (Bonnie) 197
Byrd, Mrs. Victor (Jean) 120, 146
Byrd, Mrs. William L. (Maxine) 143, 306
Byrns, Mrs. John (Helen) 149, 215, 225, 242

C

Cantu, Mrs. Sam (Sandra) 129
Carlson, Mrs. Wallace (Ellen) 122
Carroll, Mrs. Paul M. (Cathy) 292
Cartmell, Thom 173
Castellano, Mrs. Vito (Lynda) 42
Castles, Mrs. John G. (Towlesey) 39, 235
Cates, Mrs. Johnny (Bonnie) 256, 320
Cavett, Mrs. Robert M. (Dorothy) 150, 188
Cegelski, Mrs. Benedict (Dorothy) 120
Cheshire, Mrs. Douglass (Joanne) 73
Clements, Mrs. William P., Jr. (Rita) 37
Cloud, Mrs. Kelly (Lisa) 341
Coates, Mrs. George E. (Betty) 18, 121
Coley, Mrs. Arthur G. (Susie) 63, 163, 348
Connally, Mrs. John B. (Nellie) 14, 335
Cormier, Mrs. Horace (Marie) 164
Counts, David 328
Counts, Mrs. W. David (Mary) 44, 145, 229, 268, 330
Covert, Mrs. Gary (Susan) 123
Crawford, Suzanne Ragan 95, 324
Crider, Mrs. Cox R. (Pam) 112, 326

D

Daniel, Mrs. Don (Gerry) 149, 189, 270
Daniel, Mrs. Jim (Julia Ann) 77, 181, 189
Daniel, Mrs. John W. (Karen) 345
Daniel, Mrs. Manuel (Bertha) 131, 202
Daniel, Mrs. Price (Jean) 36
Davenport, Mrs. Jack (Linda) 125
Davis, Mrs. Gary (Sharon) 304
Day, Mrs. Paul R. (Mary) 28, 225
Dennis, Mrs. James T. (Mavis) 60, 87
Dickson, James R. 359
Dingler, Mrs. Walter J. (Gayle) 45, 78, 102, 106, 113, 142, 158, 235, 267, 290
Dingler, Walter J. 334
Dixon, John L. 103
Duffey, Mrs. Jerry (Valerie Starr) 261, 364
Duffy, Mrs. James W. (Barbara) 12
Duhe, Mrs. Lane A. (Lois) 237
Duncan, Judy 236
Duran, Mrs. James H. (Luella) 132, 261

E

Eastwold, Kathy 292
Edwards, Mrs. Donald E. (Wibs) 26, 269

L

Lagunas, Mrs. Jessie (Janie) 126
Lambert, Mrs. Maurice G. (Janis) 325
Lank, Mrs. Joseph M. (Virginia) 17, 262
Leggett, Mrs. Jimmy (Judy) 311
Leon, Mrs. Bill (Jeanette) 170, 179, 303
Lewis, Mrs. Tip (Nita) 341, 344
Llenza, Mrs. Orlando (Krystyna) 27
Loftis, Mrs. Harold (Billie) 45, 53, 140, 280, 328
Lucas, Mrs. Clarence (Thelma) 151
Luersen, Jewell D. 49, 50
Lum, Mrs. Alexis T. (Momi) 29

M

Mahaffey, John D. 49
Mann, Mrs. Robert F. (Louella) 335
Marchant, Mrs. T. Eston (Caroline) 35
Martin, Mrs. Crawford (Margaret) 65, 259
Martin, Mrs. Jack T. (Shirley) 48, 61
Martin, Mrs. Rufus G. (Dee) 67, 196
Martin, Mrs. Wilford A. (Cathy) 135
Mathews, Mrs. Terry (Candy) 180
Mathis, Mrs. John E. (Virginia) 346
Matthews, Mrs. Jay (Babs) 82, 182, 315
Matthews, Mrs. John L. (Darlene) 40
McClure, Mrs. O. W. (Louise) 148, 305
McCoy, Mrs. Gerald W. (Nancy) 111
McElroy, Mrs. Stephen B. (Eleta) 137, 172, 281
McGoodwin, Mrs. James B. (Jane) 80, 283
McGuire, Mrs. Cortis (Neta) 155
McKinney, Mrs. Mike (Judy) 210
McLain, Mrs. Don (Shirley) 127, 154
Meadows, Mrs. Glenn (Martha) 241, 263, 265
Mees, Mrs. Eugene A. (Norma Blotter) 133, 157, 180, 195, 293
Messina, Mrs. Jake F. (Dorothy) 165
Migl, Mrs. Dennis (Sandra) 172
Miller, Mrs. Harold A. (Cheri) 342
Miller, Mrs. R. V. (Dick) 47
Miller, Mrs. Richard A. (Maryann) 39, 72
Milne, Mrs. John R. (Beverley) 231
Miranda, Mrs. Louis (Lorna) 121
Montgomery, Mrs. Joe (Norma) 135, 190, 213, 317
Morgan, Mrs. Robert M. (Ladean) 34
Morrison, Mrs. W. R. (Mavis) 127, 185
Morrison, William Roy 208
Morriss, Mrs. Josh, Sr. (Mabel) 42
Muegge, Mrs. John (Marjie) 59, 342
Murrell, Mrs. Stan (Sherry) 329, 333
Murry, Mrs. C. Emerson (Donna) 32, 77

N

NGAT Office Staff 97
Nash, Mrs. Don (Blanche) 239
Neitz, Mrs. Robert H. (Laura) 41
Newman, Bobby 365

Nichols, Mrs. Delmer (Mary Ann) 216, 283
Nichols, Mrs. Douglas (Dorothy) 299

O

O'Brien, Mrs. Bill W. (Helen) 273
O'Connell, Barbara 91, 309
Ooley, Mrs. Immel (Mary K.) 319
Ooley, Mrs. Milton Ray 139
Ooley, Mrs. Raymond J. (Birdie) 275
Orman, Mary 244
Ottley, Mrs. Barry (Sandra) 187
Owen, Mrs. Robert (Jody) 193, 253

P

Paige, Mrs. Woody (Margaret) 71
Parks, Mrs. James E., Jr. (Terry) 274
Patterson, Mrs. Garry D. (Sharon) 234
Pena, Mrs. Gilbert S. (Teresa) 338
Pennington, Mrs. Stephen (Cathy) 70
Perry, Mrs. Edgar (Linda) 192, 335
Peterson, Mrs. George (Margie) 89
Pfennig, Mrs. Jon (Glena) 329
Phillips, Mrs. Clyde (Betty) 58, 64, 70
Phipps, Mrs. John (Pauline) 33
Pickle, Mrs. J. Robert (Melanie) 277
Pope, Mrs. Billy B. (Vanessa) 52, 81, 167
Preston, Mrs. Robert (Judy) 68, 353
Preston, Robert 196
Prichard, Mrs. Harold (Ruth) 332
Pruitt, Mrs. Kenneth R. (Nevellyn) 131, 231
Purtle, Mrs. Herbert G. (Jan) 70, 296, 346

R

Ragan, Mrs. James C. (Joyce) 58, 245, 308, 322, 333, 364
Reagan, Mrs. Ronald (Nancy) 20, 84
Redmond, Mrs. Jack (Sue) 67, 148
Reid, Mrs. Harold (Gwen) 308
Rhodes, Mrs. Alec (Charlotte) 177, 182, 258
Richardson, Mrs. Gerald (Sheila) 168
Riley, Mrs. Celeste Berry 15
Rives, Mrs. Douglas O. V. (Jo) 271
Robertson, Mrs. Cohen E. (Elizabeth) 21, 258
Roden, Mrs. James (Charley) 192, 299
Ross, Mrs. John (Dianne) 285

S

Scherz, Mrs. Otto (Gwen) 156
Scherz, Otto 169
Scofield, Mrs. Vernon (Audrey) 79, 130, 224, 287
Scott, Mrs. Richard M. (Flo) 23
Scott, Mrs. Willie L. (Billie) 10, 141, 152, 318
Scott, Willie L. 16
Scribner, Mrs. John C. L. (Edna) 197, 275
Seals, Mrs. William L. (Betty) 76, 117, 137, 226

Shank, Mrs. Willard A. (Elizabeth) 38, 345
Sharp, Mrs. Gary (Sandra) 179
Shary, Mary 338
Shaw, Mrs. Jackie (Marlene) 147
Shivers, Mrs. Allan (Marialice) 27, 60, 132, 295
Sieben, Mrs. James G. (Charlotte) 28
Slaughter, Mrs. Johnye L. (Tommie) 194, 213
Small, Mrs. J. W. (Polly) 153, 210
Small, Mrs. Michael (Lisa) 158, 291
Smith, Cindy 159
Smith, Mrs. David A. (Betty) 303
Smith, Mrs. Harry (Ginny) 69, 110, 233, 337
Smith, Mrs. Preston (Ima) 7
Smyth, Mrs. Henry (Scotty) 248
Sockwell, Mrs. John (Billie) 129, 334
Spann, Foy R. 354
Spence, Mrs. James L. (Esther) 19
Spraberry, Mrs. Rufus (Doris) 66, 133
Spray, Mrs. Leigh (Patsy) 155, 166
Squyres, Mrs. Gayle (Patsy) 363
Starr, L. James, III 356
Starr, Mrs. L. James, Jr. (JoAnn) 46, 59, 75, 115, 200
Starr, Mrs. Luther J. (Lucille) 90
Steel, Mrs. Harry (Louisa) 129, 236
Stegall, John (Cajun) 233
Stein, Lorene 302
Stephens, Mrs. Lewis (Nancy) 82, 236
Stephenson, Mrs. Jackie D. (Mary) 67, 362
Stockton, Mrs. Robert L. (Sylvia) 79, 175
Stone, Mrs. Thomas (Claudette) 150, 337, 361
Strickland, Mrs. Buster (Shirley) 302
Stroud, Mrs. Ansel M., Jr. (Barbara) 17
Stuart, Mrs. Sherwood (Vivian) 209, 222, 223
Swenson, Mrs. Zack (Carolyn) 174
Swenson, Zack 246

T

Tallas, Leonard T. 96
Tallas, Mrs. Leonard (Jean) 66, 134, 140, 141, 142, 183, 186, 249, 350
Taylor, Mrs. James E. (Estelle) 34
Temple, Mrs. Herbert R., Jr. (Pat) 22
Tice, Mrs. Ralph T. (Nadine) 29, 119

Tomac, Mrs. Stephen (Bonnie) 151
Toon, Mrs. Roger R. (Vonda) 288, 289
Torres, Mrs. Ruben (Olga) 87, 144, 214
Tressa, Mrs. Paul E., Jr. (Nancy) 217
Tumlinson, David L. 44
Tumlinson, Mrs. David L. (Juanita) 107

V

Van Cleave, Mrs. A. W., III (Virginia) 128
Vass, Mrs. Robert (Glenda) 262
Vercher, Mrs. James C. (Elaine) 120, 294
Vinson, Mrs. Darrell (Anita) 92, 226
Vinyard, Mrs. Sherman L. (Naomi) 211
Voelker, Mrs. Gary (Pat) 126, 176

W

Waggoner, Mrs. Curtiss R. (Sheila) 44, 128
Wagner, Mrs. Bill (Cindy) 345
Waldrip, Mrs. John L. (Gayle) 119, 124, 282
Walker, Mrs. E. H. "Mickey", Jr. (Tuta) 19, 219
Wallace, Mrs. Carl D. (Yvonne) 7, 152
Weber, Mrs. LaVern (Bette) 10, 336
Wellman, Mrs. Billy G. (Betty) 38, 239
Whatley, Glenn 68, 72, 355, 356
White, Mrs. Mark (Linda Gale) 25, 238
White, Mrs. R. C. (Elna) 276, 344
White, Mrs. Samuel P., Jr. (Sally) 271
Whitehall, Edris 109, 284
Whitehead, Mrs. C. D. (Ginny) 163
Whitley, Judy 276
Wilds, Mrs. Samuel H. (Betty) 170, 295, 298
Williams, Mrs. Thomas E. (Jody) 78
Williamson, Mrs. Ronald F. (Betsi) 43
Willis, Mrs. D. J. (Grace) 159
Wilson, Mrs. John A., III (Elizabeth) 9
Winkleblack, Mrs. W. L. (Linda) 270
Wood, Mrs. Doyle (Brenda) 163
Wooldridge, Mrs. John (Pally) 213
Woolsey, Mrs. Don (Vicky) 157, 286

Y

Yandell, Mrs. Larry (Gayle) 134, 268

Index

A

B

Ready to Serve

Texas National Guard Auxiliary of Austin
P.O. Box 5733
Austin, Texas 78763

Please send me _____ copies of **READY TO SERVE**

Retail Price $12.95 each
Postage & handling $2.00 each   Make checks payable to
 (Texas residents $ .65 each   "Ready to Serve"
 add tax)
                            $_____   Total Enclosed $_____

Name _____

Address _____

City _____ State _____ Zip _____

Ready to Serve

Texas National Guard Auxiliary of Austin
P.O. Box 5733
Austin, Texas 78763

Please send me _____ copies of **READY TO SERVE**

Retail Price $12.95 each
Postage & handling $2.00 each   Make checks payable to
 (Texas residents $ .65 each   "Ready to Serve"
 add tax)
                            $_____   Total Enclosed $_____

Name _____

Address _____

City _____ State _____ Zip _____

Ready to Serve

Texas National Guard Auxiliary of Austin
P.O. Box 5733
Austin, Texas 78763

Please send me _____ copies of **READY TO SERVE**

Retail Price $12.95 each
Postage & handling $2.00 each   Make checks payable to
 (Texas residents $ .65 each   "Ready to Serve"
 add tax)
                            $_____   Total Enclosed $_____

Name _____

Address _____

City _____ State _____ Zip _____
